English the Easy Way

Fifth Edition

NORMAN SCHACHTER • ALFRED T. CLARK, JR.

LOS ANGELES CITY UNIFIED SCHOOL DISTRICT
LOS ANGELES, CALIFORNIA

E88 *Published by*
SOUTH-WESTERN PUBLISHING CO.

CINCINNATI   WEST CHICAGO, IL   DALLAS   PELHAM MANOR, NY   PALO ALTO, CA

ISBN: 0-538-05880-3

Library of Congress Catalog Card Number: 83-51555

123456789 W 210987654

Printed in the United States of America

PREFACE

ENGLISH THE EASY WAY, Fifth Edition, is an easy-to-teach, easy-to-learn presentation of English grammar. This short yet intensive text-workbook provides students with practical, varied, and meaningful content and exercises.

ENGLISH THE EASY WAY, Fifth Edition, is designed to meet a wide range of student needs and expectations. ENGLISH THE EASY WAY can be used as a text for basic English, basic English review, remedial courses, or as a supplemental text for other courses in which only a limited time can be given to English fundamentals. This text-workbook employs a self-teaching, highly motivated, classroom-tested plan of instruction and instructional material.

The content is organized in an orderly, sequential manner. Each of the eleven units consists of the following:

1. *Student objectives* to direct students to the purposes of each unit.

2. *Sections* with short reading assignments which include instructive examples with analytical explanations.

3. *Cartoon drawings* which provide additional clarification and reinforcement of the reading material.

4. *Tryout exercises* designed to help students better understand the reading assignment and to determine the extent to which they have mastered the material.

5. *Application practices* in which the students apply the fundamentals they have just studied. The exercise content and difficulty are sufficiently varied to challenge a wide range of student ability and interest. Application practices relate to specific content areas. Drills for writing, vocabulary building, and spelling are also included.

6. *Scoring guides and review notes* which instruct students to review particular sections when weaknesses exist.

7. *Periodic review exercises* that cover the subject matter presented in each unit and material studied at an earlier time.

A test package accompanies this text. Included are a pretest, a test for each unit, a review test, and a posttest.

ENGLISH THE EASY WAY, Fifth Edition, has utilized many improvements suggested by teachers who have tested the material in actual classrooms in a number of schools. In response to their recommendations and ideas, additional exercises dealing with synonyms and antonyms, spelling, and definitions are included. Unit 9, "Writing Sentences and Paragraphs," allows students an opportunity to demonstrate their writing ability in short, meaningful ways. All *examples* and *application practices* have been revised to make each exercise more stimulating for students regardless of age or academic ability.

The authors hope that ENGLISH THE EASY WAY, Fifth Edition, will contribute substantially to the improvement of the communicative skills of students.

Norman Schachter

Alfred T. Clark, Jr.

CONTENTS

| Section 1 | **The Sentence Defined** | **Unit 1**
 The Sentence |

OBJECTIVES:
1. To understand that a sentence expresses a complete thought.
2. To recognize the different kinds of sentences.
3. To identify the eight parts of speech.

A *sentence* expresses a complete thought through a series or a group of words. A simple sentence consists of two important parts, the *subject* (a *noun* or *pronoun*) and the *verb*. The subject noun is a person, place, or thing spoken of, and the verb is the word that tells what the subject does or is. A group of words is not a sentence unless it contains both a subject and a verb.

Below are examples of complete and incomplete sentences with subjects underlined once and verbs underlined twice. Remember that a complete sentence must have a subject and a verb.

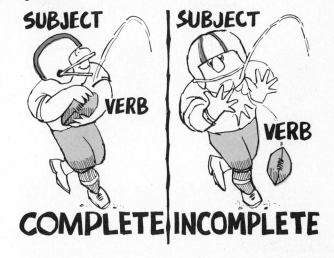

SUBJECT ... VERB ... SUBJECT ... VERB

COMPLETE | INCOMPLETE

EXAMPLE 1

Betty flew to Washington, D.C.

Analysis:
  Betty—person spoken of—subject
  flew—tells what Betty did—verb

EXAMPLE 2

Her sister paid for the plane ticket.

Analysis:
  sister—person spoken of—subject
  paid—tells what her sister did—verb

EXAMPLE 3

Bruce in the nation's capital last year.

Analysis:
  Bruce—person spoken of—subject
  no verb to tell what Bruce did— The sentence is incomplete. (A verb such as *visited, worked,* or *lived* is needed to complete the sentence.)

| **TRYOUT EXERCISE** | **Directions:** Identify the subjects of the following sentences by underlining them once. Identify the verbs by underlining them twice. Check your answers with your teacher before continuing with your assignment. |

1. The manager hired a new typist.
2. She enrolled in a business school last fall.
3. Mrs. Mitchell owned the company.
4. Her son mowed our lawn last Saturday.
5. Our neighbors bought a yellow car.
6. Margaret drove the new car to Cincinnati.

Complete Application Practices 1-3, pages 3-5, at this time.

DECLARATIVE | INTERROGATIVE | EXCLAMATORY | IMPERATIVE

The *declarative* sentence states a fact. It ends with a period.

My family traveled across the United States.
We visited the different national parks.

The *interrogative* sentence asks a question. It ends with a question mark.

Did you ever see the Grand Canyon?
"How," we asked, "did you ever climb Mount Ranier?"

The *exclamatory* sentence expresses surprise, disbelief, or deep feeling. It ends with an exclamation point.

What a volcanic eruption that was!
I saw it!
Stand back right now!

The *imperative* sentence gives a command, requests someone to do something, or begs. It usually ends with a period, but a strong command may be ended with an exclamation point (see the last example above). The subject *you* is often omitted, but understood.

Listen to the bird calls. (*You* understood)
You must walk only on the trails.
Please watch out for falling rocks. (*You* understood)
Don't feed the bears! (imperative and exclamatory)

TRYOUT EXERCISE	**Directions:** Classify the following sentences by placing a check mark in the proper blank at the right. *D* stands for declarative, *Int* for interrogative, *Excla* for exclamatory, and *Imp* for imperative. Check your answers with your teacher before continuing with your assignment.

	D	Int	Excla	Imp
1. Help protect your parks.	___	___	___	___
2. John Muir loved the redwood forests.	___	___	___	___
3. Did you ever visit Muir Woods?	___	___	___	___
4. Watch out for that snake!	___	___	___	___

Complete Application Practices 4-6, pages 6-8, at this time.

1-A: Practice Procedure. Identify the subjects of the following sentences by underlining them once. Identify the verbs by underlining them twice. Score one point for each correctly identified subject and one point for each correctly identified verb.

Your Score

1. Certain jobs require special skills.   1. _____
2. Mr. Martinez met with the interested students.   2. _____
3. Ann found the perfect job.   3. _____
4. She enjoyed the great outdoors.   4. _____
5. The path covered many miles.   5. _____
6. Her uncle walked over many of the hidden trails.   6. _____
7. Oscar studied for the test with Ann.   7. _____
8. The salary included many health benefits.   8. _____
9. Some students decided on careers in the circus.   9. _____
10. Rita Thomas acted the part of the clown.   10. _____

1-B: Practice Procedure. Follow the procedures given for 1-A.

1. A hobby gives great pleasure.   1. _____
2. People develop strange hobbies.   2. _____
3. Ricardo collected stamps.   3. _____
4. They provided many hours of fun.   4. _____
5. His sister found a few music boxes in the attic.   5. _____
6. The store sold many old postcards.   6. _____
7. Mrs. Silva bought a shell collection.   7. _____
8. Their neighbor enjoyed his Civil War relics.   8. _____
9. Music provides hours of pleasant listening.   9. _____
10. Walt bought dozens of popular records.   10. _____
11. My uncle received several stamps from Ireland.   11. _____
12. Mr. Hanson collects stamps from all countries.   12. _____
13. Alice designed some interesting jewelry.   13. _____
14. Our class produced a small model space station.   14. _____
15. The project required much patience and skill.   15. _____

Your Total Score _____

If your score was 39 or less for 1-A and B, review page 1 before continuing.

2: Practice Procedure. Identify the subjects of the following sentences by underlining them once. Identify the verbs by underlining them twice. Score one point for each correctly identified subject and verb.

Your Score

1. The dry air pushed its way across the desert.   1. _____
2. Showers dampened various parts of the country.   2. _____
3. The weather service declared a flash flood watch.   3. _____
4. Miami expects early morning clouds.   4. _____
5. The weather vane pointed in the direction of the wind.   5. _____
6. The heavy rainfall was unusual.   6. _____
7. Birds fly south for many reasons.   7. _____
8. The storm started in Canada.   8. _____
9. The barometer predicted the change in the weather.   9. _____
10. The cyclone resulted from the low-pressure areas.   10. _____
11. Dr. Frick showed the group his different charts.   11. _____
12. The hurricane ripped into the coastal areas.   12. _____
13. They called it Hurricane Hannah.   13. _____
14. The sun affects the temperature.   14. _____
15. Some scientists understand weather patterns.   15. _____
16. Tornadoes form along a cold front.   16. _____
17. Eva reads the weather map every morning.   17. _____
18. The information pours into the weather center.   18. _____
19. Joseph Henry received the first weather report by telegraph.   19. _____
20. The United States organized its weather service.   20. _____
21. The storms created much excitement.   21. _____
22. Jim Bailey established a fertilizer company.   22. _____
23. Pam Brown bought the company from Jim Bailey.   23. _____
24. The company did a large business with farmers.   24. _____
25. Many officials work closely with the public weather service.   25. _____
26. Charlotte listens to the eleven o'clock news every night.   26. _____
27. Satellites send pictures by television transmitters.   27. _____
28. My family relies on its weather vane.   28. _____
29. The hurricane increased the height and force of the waves.   29. _____
30. The weather changes constantly and frequently.   30. _____

If your score was 47 or less, review page 1 before continuing.   Your Total Score _____

4

3–A: Practice Procedure. Identify the incomplete sentences by placing a check mark in the blank at the right. In the space provided below the sentences, rewrite each of the incomplete sentences, adding whatever words are necessary to make them complete. Remember that a sentence expresses a complete thought and has a subject and verb. Score one point for each incomplete sentence identified.

Answers

1. She opened the new typing book.   1. _____
2. The typewriter on the table.   2. _____
3. The calculator showed the correct answer.   3. _____
4. Miss Earle types very quickly and accurately.   4. _____
5. A secretarial career rewarding job.   5. _____
6. The company hired more accountants.   6. _____
7. Harry a great math student.   7. _____

_____

_____

_____

_____

_____

3–B: Practice Procedure. Follow the directions given for 3–A.

1. The teller opened the windows for depositors.   1. _____
2. He smiled at the first customer.   2. _____
3. Nina with her paycheck in her hand.   3. _____
4. The manager walked over to Nina at the window.   4. _____
5. The possibility for a large deposit.   5. _____
6. The guard at the door with his pistol in his pocket.   6. _____
7. The slips, the checks, and the tables.   7. _____
8. The president of the bank sat in a large, open office.   8. _____
9. With flowers, telephones, papers, and messages on his desk.   9. _____
10. Ms. Marcellus married my uncle, the bank president.   10. _____

_____

_____

_____

_____

_____

_____

_____

Your Total Score _____

If your score was 5 or less for 3–A and 3–B, review page 1 before continuing.

4-A: Practice Procedure. Indicate whether the following sentences are declarative, interrogative, exclamatory, or imperative by placing a check mark in the proper space at the right. *D* is used for declarative, *Int* for interrogative, *Excla* for exclamatory, and *Imp* for imperative. Score one point for each correct answer.

	D	Int	Excla	Imp
1. Sea World in San Diego features playful dolphins.	1. ___	___	___	___
2. Did you ever see a shark swim?	2. ___	___	___	___
3. Look at the penguins at the entrance.	3. ___	___	___	___
4. The one-hour cruise of Mission Bay leaves every hour.	4. ___	___	___	___
5. Have you looked through America's largest telescope?	5. ___	___	___	___
6. What a spectacular sight it is!	6. ___	___	___	___
7. Balboa Park includes the famous San Diego Zoo.	7. ___	___	___	___
8. Give me a chance to look.	8. ___	___	___	___
9. Look at the size of that whale!	9. ___	___	___	___
10. When did you leave for home?	10. ___	___	___	___

4-B: Practice Procedure. Follow the directions given in 4-A.

	D	Int	Excla	Imp
1. Hand me that book.	1. ___	___	___	___
2. What a time we had getting to Williamsburg!	2. ___	___	___	___
3. Colonial Williamsburg has many familiar landmarks.	3. ___	___	___	___
4. Make certain to see the college there.	4. ___	___	___	___
5. Watch the glass blowers!	5. ___	___	___	___
6. Our class drove to the Jamestown Festival Park.	6. ___	___	___	___
7. Was it America's first permanent settlement?	7. ___	___	___	___
8. Buy me a souvenir, please.	8. ___	___	___	___
9. The guides greet you at the door.	9. ___	___	___	___
10. How did you know that?	10. ___	___	___	___
11. How that thunder scared us!	11. ___	___	___	___
12. The rain drove us from the area.	12. ___	___	___	___
13. Check the old-fashioned cabinet shop.	13. ___	___	___	___
14. Is the admission fee very expensive?	14. ___	___	___	___
15. Did they land in 1607 or in 1609?	15. ___	___	___	___

Your Total Score _____

If your score was 19 or less for 4-A and B, review page 2 before continuing.

5: Practice Procedure. In the spaces provided below, compose five examples of each kind of sentence (declarative, interrogative, exclamatory, and imperative). Score one point for each correct sentence.

Declarative Sentences

1. _____
2. _____
3. _____
4. _____
5. _____

Interrogative Sentences

1. _____
2. _____
3. _____
4. _____
5. _____

Exclamatory Sentences

1. _____
2. _____
3. _____
4. _____
5. _____

Imperative Sentences

1. _____
2. _____
3. _____
4. _____
5. _____

Your Total Score _____

If your score was 15 or less, review page 2 before continuing.

6–A: Practice Procedure. Indicate whether the following sentences are complete or incomplete. Write a *C* for complete and an *I* for incomplete in the space provided to the right of the sentences. Remember that a complete sentence must have a subject and a verb. Score one point for each correct answer.

Answers

1. The magazine readers rated the restaurants.　　1. _____
2. Quality of food and service and the average prices.　　2. _____
3. The hostess seated us quickly.　　3. _____
4. We ordered steak and french fries.　　4. _____
5. The pickles, dressing, tomatoes, and lettuce.　　5. _____
6. My parents used their credit card.　　6. _____
7. One of the credit cards on the table.　　7. _____
8. Ernie's restaurant serves fancy food.　　8. _____
9. Reservations and dinner daily.　　9. _____
10. Many people enjoy different food.　　10. _____

6–B: Practice Procedure. Indicate whether the following sentences are declarative, interrogative, exclamatory, or imperative by writing a *D* for declarative, *Int* for interrogative, *Excla* for exclamatory, and *Imp* for imperative in the spaces provided at the right of the sentences. Score one point for each correct answer.

1. The waitress waited for our orders.　　1. _____
2. Have you eaten here before?　　2. _____
3. Stop fooling with your knife.　　3. _____
4. Look at the size of that shrimp!　　4. _____
5. Where did they ever find them?　　5. _____
6. Many movie stars go to Ma Maison restaurant.　　6. _____
7. That meal costs too much!　　7. _____
8. Finish your dessert.　　8. _____
9. Antoine's restaurant specializes in French-Creole dishes.　　9. _____
10. A fifth-generation descendant owns it.　　10. _____
11. Are you aware that Brennan's is well known for breakfast?　　11. _____
12. Eat there if possible.　　12. _____
13. No one charges that much!　　13. _____
14. Many books list popular eating places.　　14. _____
15. Why do young people always order hamburgers?　　15. _____

Your Total Score _____

If your score was 19 or less for 6-A and 6-B, review pages 1-2 before continuing.

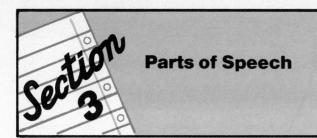

Most of the words which are used to make sentences can be sorted into eight classifications called *parts of speech*. The eight parts of speech are discussed briefly here. They will be treated in greater detail in later units.

PARTS OF SPEECH

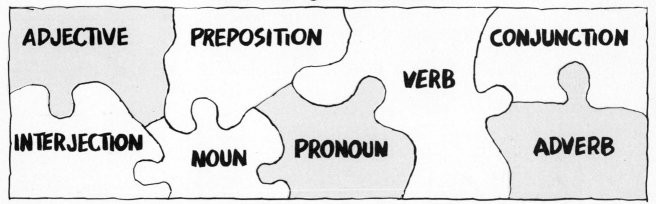

ADJECTIVE PREPOSITION CONJUNCTION

VERB

INTERJECTION NOUN PRONOUN ADVERB

3-A. NOUNS

A *noun* names a person, a place, or a thing. (See page 25 for a detailed treatment of nouns.)

EXAMPLE 1

Peggy jogs along the path in Prospect Park.

Analysis:
Peggy—names a person—noun
path—names a thing—noun
Prospect Park—names a place—noun

EXAMPLE 2

Dick Beeks ran in the marathon in Boston.

Analysis:
Dick Beeks—names a person—noun
marathon—names a thing—noun
Boston—names a place—noun

EXAMPLE 3

Citrus High School provided a few classes in the library.

Analysis:
Citrus High School—names a place—noun
classes—names things—noun
library—names a place—noun

EXAMPLE 4

Dr. Carter held a clinic in exercise at the Medical Center.

Analysis:
Dr. Carter—names a person—noun
clinic—names a thing—noun
exercise—names a thing—noun
Medical Center—names a place—noun

9

A *pronoun* is a word used as a substitute for a noun. (Pronouns are discussed in greater detail on page 41.)

EXAMPLE 1

I finished next to last in the five-mile run.

Analysis:

I—used in place of the name of the individual—pronoun

EXAMPLE 2

Miss Harris showed them a jogging film.

Analysis:

them—used in place of the names of the individuals—pronoun

EXAMPLE 3

They liked the grass jogging track.

Analysis:

They—used in place of the names of the individuals—pronoun

EXAMPLE 4

The coach bought her a new pair of shoes.

Analysis:

her—used in place of the name of the individual—pronoun

PRONOUNS TAKE THE PLACE OF NOUNS

TRYOUT EXERCISE	**Directions:** Identify the nouns, the verbs, and the pronouns in the following sentences. Underline the nouns once, the verbs twice, and the pronouns three times. Check your answers with your teacher before continuing with your assignment.

1. The shoes cost him $20.
2. She listened to Dr. Karlin.
3. They finished the race in two hours.
4. The crowd cheered for her with loud yells.

Complete Application Practices 7-8, pages 11-12, at this time.

7: **Practice Procedure.** Identify the nouns, the verbs, and the pronouns in the following sentences. Underline the nouns once, the verbs twice, and the pronouns three times. Score one point for each correct identification.

Your Score

1. They saw an exciting game last Thursday.   1. _____
2. The pitcher threw him a fastball.   2. _____
3. Baseball belongs to the fans.   3. _____
4. He and I go every Friday to the game at the stadium.   4. _____
5. The neighbor gave her a free ticket.   5. _____
6. Henry Aaron hit 715 home runs for a new record.   6. _____
7. We saw him many times over the years.   7. _____
8. The American League consists of 14 teams.   8. _____
9. He watches the Los Angeles Dodgers.   9. _____
10. The Houston Astros play games in the Astrodome.   10. _____
11. Mr. Jefferson took him and her to an exciting game.   11. _____
12. Judge Landis served as Commissioner of baseball.   12. _____
13. The New York Giants established a modern record of 26 consecutive wins.   13. _____
14. She and he stretched in the seventh inning.   14. _____
15. A bunt, a stolen base, and a home run excited us.   15. _____
16. Fujio prepared a lunch for him and us.   16. _____
17. We met them at the first gate.   17. _____
18. The players arrived ahead of us at the ball park.   18. _____
19. The manager flashed signals to them.   19. _____
20. She sat in the rain for an hour.   20. _____
21. He ran beneath the stands.   21. _____
22. A team consists of nine players.   22. _____
23. I once played shortstop at school.   23. _____
24. Ricky Henderson, of Oakland, shattered the record for stolen bases.   24. _____
25. The umpire glared at her and me.   25. _____

Your Total Score _____

If your score was 80 or less, review pages 1 and 9-10 before completing Application Practice 8.

8: **Practice Procedure.** Identify the nouns, the verbs, and the pronouns in the following sentences. Underline the nouns once, the verbs twice, and the pronouns three times. Score one point for each correct identification.

Your Score

1. They gave me a book on the different flags.   1. _____

2. We read the book during the holidays.   2. _____

3. They called the flag the Stars and Stripes.   3. _____

4. The addition of a new star on the flag appeared with every new state.   4. _____

5. Francis Scott Key wrote the national anthem during the War of 1812.   5. _____

6. He read the reason for the number of stripes to us.   6. _____

7. The President of the United States flies a personal flag.   7. _____

8. They bought us a large flag.   8. _____

9. We read about the different flags of the 50 states.   9. _____

10. Every July 4 Mr. Peters displays the flag for Mildred and him.   10. _____

11. I particularly like the state flags of Texas, Alaska, Rhode Island, and Indiana.   11. _____

12. The government issues detailed rules for the display of the flag.   12. _____

13. They prohibited any form of advertisement.   13. _____

14. Arkansas flies a flag with 25 stars.   14. _____

15. The information given to them and me was interesting.   15. _____

16. He shared the book with us.   16. _____

17. The flag stands for the hard work of millions of Americans.   17. _____

18. The seven red stripes and the six white stripes represent the 13 original colonies. 18. _____

19. They showed us a picture of the first flag.   19. _____

20. I learned about the colors from her.   20. _____

21. The man in the green house displays the flag every day.   21. _____

22. He carefully folds the flag at night.   22. _____

23. The flag stands for the land, the people, the government, and the ideals of the country. 23. _____

24. They represent the officials of the government.   24. _____

25. She and I recited the Pledge of Allegiance for them.   25. _____

Your Total Score _____

If your score was 93 or less, review pages 9-10 before continuing.

A *verb* tells what the subject does or is, or what happens to it. It can make a statement, ask a question, or give a command. (See page 67 for a detailed treatment of verbs.)

EXAMPLE 1

Mr. Edison invented the record player in 1877.

Analysis:

invented—tells what the subject *Mr. Edison* did—verb

EXAMPLE 2

Were roller skates an important invention?

Analysis:

Were—asks a question about the subject *roller skates*—verb

EXAMPLE 3

Read that book on inventors now!

Analysis:

Read—gives a command to the understood subject *you* (You read that book on inventors now!)—verb

A VERB IS AN *ACTION* WORD

An *adjective* modifies (describes) a noun or a pronoun. It answers such questions as these: How many? How big? What kind? Which? *A, an,* and *the* are adjectives. (See page 121 for a detailed treatment of adjectives. *Definite* (the) and *indefinite* (a, an) *adjectives* are referred to as articles.)

EXAMPLE 1

The speedy swimmer won a pretty trophy.

Analysis:

The—definite adjective
speedy—tells what kind of *swimmer*—adjective
a—indefinite adjective
pretty—tells what kind of *trophy*—adjective

EXAMPLE 2

Andrea was a happy and graceful diver.

Analysis:

a—indefinite adjective
happy, graceful—tells what kind of *diver*—adjectives

EXAMPLE 3

Mark Spitz won seven medals in the Olympics.

Analysis:

seven—tells how many *medals*—adjective
the—definite adjective

EXAMPLE 4

The five-foot diver won many medals.

Analysis:

The—definite adjective
five-foot—tells how big the *diver* is—adjective
many—tells how many *medals*—adjective

"PLAYFUL" "PRETTY" "COLORFUL" "CUTE" "SMALL" "CUDDLY" "UNUSUAL"
ADJECTIVES DESCRIBE NOUNS

An *adverb* modifies (describes) a verb, an adjective, or another adverb. It answers these questions: When? Where? How? Most words ending in *ly* are adverbs. Five common exceptions are *friendly, lively, lonely, lovely* and *ugly,* which are adjectives. (See page 129 for a detailed treatment of adverbs.)

EXAMPLE 1

The circus is <u>always</u> quiet during the animal act.

Analysis:
always—modifies *quiet* by telling *when* — adverb

EXAMPLE 2

The clown sneaked <u>quietly</u> behind the lions.

Analysis:
quietly—modifies *sneaked* by telling *how*—adverb

EXAMPLE 3

The sword thrower performed <u>carefully</u> and <u>accurately.</u>

Analysis:
carefully, accurately—modifies *performed* by telling *how*—adverbs

EXAMPLE 4

The circus truck drove <u>south.</u>

Analysis:
south—modifies *drove* by telling *where* or in what direction—adverb

ADVERBS DESCRIBE VERBS, ADJECTIVES, ADVERBS

TRYOUT EXERCISE	**Directions:** Identify the verbs, the adjectives, and the adverbs in the following sentences. Underline the verbs once, the adjectives twice, and the adverbs three times. Check your answers with your teacher before continuing the assignment.

1. The young girls eagerly reported for work.
2. The pretty manager greeted them pleasantly and cordially.
3. The youthful and red-headed ringmaster spoke briefly and clearly.
4. The older and experienced performers always acted in a proper manner.

Complete Application Practices 9-10, pages 15-16, at this time.

9-A: Practice Procedure. Identify the verbs, the adjectives, and the adverbs in the following sentences. Underline the verbs once, the adjectives twice, and the adverbs three times. Score one point for each correct verb, adjective, and adverb identified.

Your Score

1. Juanita finally learned about the computer at the school.   1. _____

2. The friendly counselor always told Helen about an exciting job.   2. _____

3. Kevin went early for an interview.   3. _____

4. He carefully completed the application form.   4. _____

5. Ten girls and five boys finally arrived for the same job.   5. _____

6. Twelve people seldom receive an early interview.   6. _____

7. Ramona waited patiently for the interesting interview.   7. _____

8. The unlucky people sadly left the crowded office.   8. _____

9. The careful manager officially received 16 applications.   9. _____

10. Electronic computers quickly processed the forms of the nervous applicants.   10. _____

11. The tall boy in the blue shirt unfortunately missed the pleasant interview.   11. _____

12. A small machine quietly printed the results.   12. _____

13. We frequently read of computers in the specialized field of medicine.   13. _____

14. Experienced doctors carefully use the information from sick people.   14. _____

15. The expensive computer here at school helps teachers and students.   15. _____

9-B: Practice Procedure. Indicate whether the following words are verbs, adjectives, or adverbs. Score one point for each correct answer.

1. gladly _____
2. buy _____
3. get _____
4. ugly _____
5. handsome _____

6. foolishly _____
7. yellow _____
8. pretend _____
9. quickly _____
10. unfortunately _____

Your Total Score _____

If your score was 67 or less for 9-A and 9-B, review pages 13-14 before completing Application Practice 10.

10–A: Practice Procedure. Identify the pronouns in the following sentences by underlining them once. Score one point for each correct answer.

Your Score

1. They used the new electronic computer.   1. _____
2. The author's wife bought him a word processor.   2. _____
3. She paid $3,000.   3. _____
4. We told her about the machine.   4. _____
5. Maria gave us a demonstration.   5. _____
6. He really learned how to operate the efficient computers.   6. _____
7. Don't they know when the first computers were developed?   7. _____
8. I gave her a book on data processing.   8. _____
9. Does he understand how they work?   9. _____
10. That company taught him and her the new process.   10. _____
11. She quickly showed us how to work the calculator.   11. _____
12. Let us realize that practice makes perfect.   12. _____
13. We told them how computers are used everywhere.   13. _____
14. I was sorry she lost the job.   14. _____
15. He and I received great training from her.   15. _____

10–B: Practice Procedure. Indicate whether the following words are nouns, pronouns, or verbs. Score one point for each correct answer.

1. machine	_____	8. she	_____
2. her	_____	9. business	_____
3. owner	_____	10. does	_____
4. language	_____	11. I	_____
5. believes	_____	12. shipped	_____
6. us	_____	13. they	_____
7. gave	_____	14. sells	_____

Your Total Score _____

If your score was 29 or less for 10–A and 10–B, review pages 9-10 and 13 before continuing.

A *preposition* shows the relationship between a noun or pronoun to some other word in the sentence. (See page 135 for a detailed treatment of prepositions.)

EXAMPLE 1

The ball rolled <u>down</u> the driveway <u>toward</u> the truck <u>near</u> the corner.

Analysis:
down—shows relationship between *rolled* and *driveway*—preposition
toward—shows relationship between *driveway* and *truck*—preposition
near—shows relationship between *truck* and *corner*—preposition

EXAMPLE 2

Sandy looked <u>at</u> the people <u>in</u> the water.

Analysis:
at—shows relationship between *looked* and *people*—preposition
in—shows relationship between *looked* and *water*—preposition

OVER

AROUND

THROUGH

PREPOSITIONS

A *conjunction* joins words, phrases, and clauses. (See page 139 for a detailed treatment of conjunctions.)

EXAMPLE 1

Henry <u>and</u> Dexter sell many video games.

Analysis:
and—joins *Henry* and *Dexter*—conjunction

EXAMPLE 2

Did you score higher than Leo <u>or</u> Sue?

Analysis:
or—joins *Leo* and *Sue*—conjunction

WORD AND PHRASE BUT CLAUSE

CONJUNCTIONS ARE JOINING WORDS

17

EXAMPLE 3

The owners of the Arcade <u>and</u> the parents of the students played <u>a</u> game.

Analysis:

and—joins phrases *The owners of the Arcade* with *the parents of the students* — conjunction

EXAMPLE 4

<u>If</u> you had the money, would you buy a video game?

Analysis:

If—connects the dependent clause with the main clause—conjunction

---

3-H. INTERJECTIONS

An *interjection* is a word or words used to express strong and sudden feeling, such as surprise, fear, suspense, anger, love, joy, and other emotions. Special words such as *wow, horrors, hurrah, ouch,* and *hooray* are often used, but words such as *help, beware,* and *stop* (usually verbs) may also be used as interjections.

EXAMPLE 1

<u>Oh!</u> I didn't know it closed at midnight.

Analysis:

Oh!—expresses a sudden feeling—interjection

EXAMPLE 2

<u>Yippee!</u> I finally won a game.

Analysis:

Yippee!—expresses a sudden feeling—interjection

INTERJECTION

TRYOUT EXERCISE

Directions: Identify the prepositions, the conjunctions, and the interjections in the following sentences. Underline the prepositions once, the conjunctions twice, and the interjections three times. Check your answers with your teacher before continuing with your assignment.

1. Hooray! The cafeteria installed a soft drink and ice cream machine for the students.

2. The manager of the student store or the assistant principal approved the purchase.

3. Because they played during their lunch period, Pete, Shirley, and Akeo didn't buy lunch.

4. Gosh! The principal worries about the students and their lunch.

5. Wow! Yolanda and Ramon worked hard after the lunch period was over.

Complete Application Practices 11-16, pages 19-24, at this time.

11-A: Practice Procedure. Identify the prepositions in the following sentences by underlining them once. Identify the conjunctions by underlining them twice. Score one point for each correct response.

Your Score

1. Is the zebra a white horse with black stripes or a black horse with white stripes?

   1. _____

2. The size and pattern of a zebra's stripes identify the different kinds for me.

   2. _____

3. Donkeys and zebras belong to the family of the domestic horse.

   3. _____

4. Giraffes in different parts of Africa vary in color and pattern.

   4. _____

5. Did Luis and Amando visit the San Diego Zoo in southern California during summer vacation?

   5. _____

6. The animal with jumping ability and speed is the gazelle.

   6. _____

7. Herds of animals often stand around water holes and drink during the early morning.

   7. _____

Your Total Score _____

If your score was 16 or less for 11-A, review pages 17 and 18.

11-B: Practice Procedure. Identify the interjections in the following sentences by underlining them once. Identify the verbs by underlining them twice. Score one point for each correct response.

1. Whoopee! I finally saw the American Bald Eagle.

   1. _____

2. Ouch! I stepped on a nail near the cage.

   2. _____

3. The seal act provided many laughs. Outstanding!

   3. _____

4. Whew! The roar of the lion scared me.

   4. _____

5. Gosh! The sick animal finally died yesterday.

   5. _____

Your Total Score _____

If your score was 7 or less for 11-B, review pages 13 and 18.

11-C: Practice Procedure. Identify the following words by writing the part of speech for each. Score one point for each correct answer.

1. animals	_____	7. or	_____
2. Golly!	_____	8. slowly	_____
3. during	_____	9. he	_____
4. roared	_____	10. always	_____
5. shh-h!	_____	11. cages	_____
6. pretty	_____	12. we	_____

Your Total Score _____

If your score was 9 or less for 11-C, review Section 3, pages 9-18, before continuing.

12–A: Practice Procedure. Identify the nouns, verbs, adjectives, and prepositions in the following sentences. Place *N* for noun, *V* for verb, *Adj* for adjective, and *Prep* for preposition above the word. Score one point for each correct response.

Your Score

1. Ed and Grace told me about the strange location and new date for the game.

  1. _____

2. The contest between the two teams started with a loud cheer from the noisy crowd.

  2. _____

3. The better team easily defeated the team from the school with the blue uniforms.

  3. _____

4. The daily newspapers published a funny story about the fans and players.

  4. _____

5. The band played familiar songs for the students in the stands.

  5. _____

6. The thrilling victory excited the students for several days.

  6. _____

7. The tickets to the game cost $2.50 for a good seat.

  7. _____

8. I noticed several students at the end of the field near the gymnasium.

  8. _____

9. The young referee in the striped shirt on the field fired the small gun at the end of the game.

  9. _____

10. The parents, the students, and the teachers sang a dignified song at the conclusion of the contest.

  10. _____

Your Total Score _____

If your score was 103 or less for 12-A, review pages 9, 13, and 17.

12–B: Practice Procedure. Identify the pronouns, conjunctions, interjections, and adverbs in the following sentences. Place *Pro* for pronoun, *C* for conjunction, *I* for interjection, and *Adv* for adverb above the word. Score one point for each correct response.

1. Whew! They finally hired Nick and Priscilla.

  1. _____

2. I quickly ran there for a job or an interview.

  2. _____

3. Yippee! The employer told me about a job in sales or accounting.

  3. _____

4. She sensibly mentioned the salary and hours of the job.

  4. _____

5. Wow! I secretly hoped for a position with the company or some other group.

  5. _____

6. The manager quickly wished me luck and success.

  6. _____

7. He silently watched the other salesperson and me.

  7. _____

8. Golly! They certainly treated us courteously and respectfully.

  8. _____

9. We happily and willingly learned the job from her and him.

  9. _____

10. Ugh! The heavy box landed on the desk and finally on me.

  10. _____

Your Total Score _____

If your score was 33 or less for 12-B, review pages 10, 14, and 17-18 before completing Application Practice 13.

13–A: Practice Procedure. Identify the nouns, verbs, adjectives, and prepositions in the following sentences. Place *N* for noun, *V* for verb, *Adj* for adjective, and *Prep* for preposition above the word. Score one point for each correct response.

Your Score

1. Raquel Diaz bought a colorful map of historic Washington, D.C., from the handsome guide.

    1._____

2. Mr. Dent got a ticket from the dignified Congresswoman for an exclusive tour of the Capitol.

    2._____

3. The guide told us about the bustling and fascinating city.

    3._____

4. The Smithsonian Association prepared the map of Washington, D.C., for visitors.

    4._____

5. Rich and Dennis traveled with a group from school to the famous Smithsonian Institute.

    5._____

6. An agreeable friend consulted the map for interesting places around the White House.

    6._____

7. We enjoyed the marvelous city with the many outstanding monuments.

    7._____

8. The agent of our tour arranged for a trip through the famous buildings and the Arlington Cemetery.

    8._____

13–B: Practice Procedure. Identify the pronouns, adverbs, conjunctions, and interjections in the following sentences. Place *Pro* for pronoun, *Adv* for adverb, *C* for conjunction, and *I* for interjection above the word. Score one point for each correct response.

1. Oh! We really missed the trip to the Space Museum and the Bureau of Engraving and Printing.

    1._____

2. She quickly suggested a drive to the Washington Monument or to John Kennedy's grave.

    2._____

3. Tremendous! The museum easily provided us many hours of fun and pleasure.

    3._____

4. They always planned a walking tour to Georgetown and Ford's Theater.

    4._____

5. We respectfully listened to the proud statements of the guide and driver.

    5._____

6. Shh-h! We walked quietly and happily through the rooms of the White House.

    6._____

7. We finally saw them at the Bureau of Engraving and Printing.

    7._____

8. Ugh! He later told us about a terrible accident near the Potomac Park by the Potomac River.

    8._____

Your Total Score _____

If your score was 97 or less for 13–A and 13–B, review Section 3, pages 9-18, before continuing.

14–A: Practice Procedure. Match the definitions listed in Column B with the right words in Column A. Write the letter that identifies the correct answer in the column provided at the right. Score one point for each correct answer.

Column A	Column B	Answers
1. noun	a. a word that tells what the subject does	1. _____
2. pronoun	b. names a person, place, or thing	2. _____
3. verb	c. expresses sudden feeling	3. _____
4. adjective	d. joins words, phrases, and clauses	4. _____
5. adverb	e. person, place, or thing spoken of	5. _____
6. preposition	f. modifies a verb, adjective, or adverb	6. _____
7. conjunction	g. describes a noun or a pronoun	7. _____
8. interjection	h. takes the place of a noun	8. _____
9. subject	i. shows relationship between words	9. _____
10. incomplete sentence	j. a sentence without a subject or verb	10. _____

Your Total Score _____

If your score was 7 or less, review Section 3, pages 9–18, before continuing.

14–B: Practice Procedure. Here are 52 words from Unit 1. They are frequently misspelled. Study them carefully and be prepared to write them from memory.

ability	computers	language	review
admission	courteously	machine	salary
animals	cruise	millions	serious
appeared	deposit	museum	several
believe	desert	neighbors	special
beneath	different	official	stadium
bureau	directions	patience	stretched
business	elephants	pleasant	television
calculator	exercise	prohibited	trails
careers	familiar	receive	unfortunately
cautiously	fascinating	recognize	unusual
college	frequent	remember	various
comfortable	government	restaurant	weather

15-A: Practice Procedure. Match the words in Column A with the definitions in Column B that are the closest in meaning. Write the letter that identifies the correct answer in the blank provided at the right. Score one point for each correct answer.

Column A	Column B	Answers
1. tranquil	a. unnoticeable	1. _____
2. astute	b. gloomy	2. _____
3. famished	c. genuine	3. _____
4. humble	d. peaceful	4. _____
5. tedious	e. dry	5. _____
6. apparent	f. fearful	6. _____
7. contempt	g. overbearing	7. _____
8. jovial	h. modest	8. _____
9. arid	i. shrewd	9. _____
10. timid	j. obvious	10. _____
11. omen	k. cheerful	11. _____
12. authentic	l. boring	12. _____
13. inconspicuous	m. scorn	13. _____
14. dreary	n. sign	14. _____
15. arrogant	o. hungry	15. _____

15-B: Practice Procedure. Alphabetize the words in Column A of 15-A in the spaces provided at the left. Then alphabetize the words in Column B of 15-A in the spaces provided at the right. Score one point for each correct answer.

Column A Words	Column B Words
1. apparent	1. boring
2. _____	2. _____
3. _____	3. _____
4. _____	4. _____
5. _____	5. _____
6. _____	6. _____
7. _____	7. _____
8. _____	8. _____
9. _____	9. _____
10. _____	10. _____
11. _____	11. _____
12. _____	12. _____
13. _____	13. _____
14. _____	14. _____
15. _____	15. _____

Your Total Score _____

23

16-A: Practice Procedure. Select the one word that is the closest in meaning to the numbered word. Write the letter that identifies the correct word in the blank provided at the right. Score one point for each correct answer.

Answers

1. *terminate*   (a) begin (b) end (c) return (d) frisk (e) employ   1. _____

2. *frigid*   (a) pensive (b) friendly (c) frank (d) serious (e) cold   2. _____

3. *skeptical*   (a) feverish (b) tender (c) insulting (d) doubting
(e) hateful   3. _____

4. *realistic*   (a) varied (b) romantic (c) lifelike (d) fragile
(e) pretending   4. _____

5. *fragile*   (a) breakable (b) sturdy (c) sweet (d) grouchy
(e) dishonest   5. _____

6. *candid*   (a) chocolate (b) frank (c) willing (d) sympathetic
(e) cute   6. _____

7. *unique*   (a) frightful (b) usual (c) improper (d) matched
(e) distinctive   7. _____

8. *reluctant*   (a) fresh (b) willing (c) unwilling (d) enthusiastic
(e) fashionable   8. _____

9. *potential*   (a) frail (b) weak (c) possible (d) frivolous (e) light   9. _____

10. *contradict*   (a) confirm (b) deny (c) regret (d) create (e) contrast   10. _____

11. *velocity*   (a) virtuous (b) risk (c) freight (d) speed (e) auto   11. _____

12. *rational*   (a) lazy (b) unreasonable (c) logical (d) frugal
(e) mournful   12. _____

13. *rectify*   (a) write (b) make (c) add (d) reduce (e) correct   13. _____

16-B: Practice Procedure. Alphabetize the following words from 16-A. Score one point for each correct answer.

1. frigid   1. _____

2. frisk   2. _____

3. fragile   3. _____

4. friendly   4. _____

5. frank   5. _____

6. frugal   6. _____

7. freight   7. _____

8. fresh   8. _____

9. frightful   9. _____

10. frail   10. _____

Your Total Score _____

Section 4

OBJECTIVES: 1. To recognize the three types of nouns.
2. To learn how to form noun plurals and noun possessives.

4-A. COMMON NOUNS

Common nouns are names given to words identifying persons, places, or things in a special class. A common noun does not refer to a *particular* person, place, or thing.

EXAMPLE 1

Thousands of boys and girls play sports during their spare time.

Analysis:

Thousands, boys, girls, sports, time—general terms not naming anyone or anything in particular—common nouns

EXAMPLE 2

The parents watched the children on the field.

Analysis:

parents, children, field—general terms not

naming anyone or anything in particular—common nouns

EXAMPLE 3

The players in the town often attend a professional game.

Analysis:

players, town, game—general terms not naming anyone or anything in particular—common nouns

EXAMPLE 4

The equipment is provided by the merchants and other interested citizens.

Analysis:

equipment, merchants, citizens—general terms not naming any particular thing or persons—common nouns

4-B. PROPER NOUNS

Proper nouns are names of particular persons, places, or things. Proper nouns should always be capitalized. (See page 189 for the section on capitalization.)

EXAMPLE 1

Willie Mays played for the Giants in San Francisco.

Analysis:

Willie Mays—name of a particular person—proper noun
Giants—name of a particular thing—proper noun
San Francisco—name of a particular place—proper noun

EXAMPLE 2

Fernando Valenzuela pitches in Los Angeles.

Analysis:

Fernando Valenzuela—name of a particular person—proper noun

Los Angeles—name of a particular place—proper noun

EXAMPLE 3

The World Series began on the second Tuesday in October.

Analysis:

World Series—name of a particular thing—proper noun

Tuesday, October—names of particular things—proper nouns

EXAMPLE 4

The National Baseball Hall of Fame and Museum was dedicated June 12, 1939, in Cooperstown, New York.

Analysis:

National Baseball Hall of Fame and Museum, June 12—names of particular things—proper nouns (1939 is a common noun.)

Cooperstown, New York—names of particular places—proper nouns

---

4-C. COLLECTIVE NOUNS

Collective nouns are names of groups or collections, such as *mob, crowd, committee.* Parts of numbers or sums of money are collective nouns *(three fifths, one third, $100).*

EXAMPLE 1

The jury voted in favor of the group from Arizona.

Analysis:

jury, group—names of groups of persons—collective nouns

EXAMPLE 2

The committee arranged for a bus for the band.

Analysis:

committee, band—names of groups of persons—collective nouns

EXAMPLE 3

The audience at the game gave the victory sign.

Analysis:

audience—name of a group of persons—collective noun

EXAMPLE 4

One fourth of the faculty remained for the dance.

Analysis:

One fourth—part of a number—collective noun

faculty—name of a group of persons—collective noun

Collective nouns may take either the singular or the plural form of the verb, depending on their use in the sentence. If a collective noun refers to a

JURY

COLLECTIVE NOUN

group acting as a whole, a singular verb is used. If a collective noun refers to a group in which the members act individually, a plural verb is used. However, collective nouns usually take the singular.

EXAMPLE 1

Our school is in favor of girls' sports.

Analysis:

school—collective noun. The singular form of the verb is used because the school is thought of as a group. Every member of the school is in favor of girls' sports.

EXAMPLE 2

The band is willing to play at the games.

Analysis:

band—collective noun. The singular form of the verb is used because the band is thought of as a group. Every member of the band is willing to play at the games.

EXAMPLE 3

The group were not pleased with their terrible tickets.

Analysis:

group—collective noun. The plural form of the verb is used because the members of the group are thought of as individuals.

EXAMPLE 4

The committee were talking about the dance among themselves.

Analysis:

committee—collective noun. The plural form of the verb is used because the members of the committee are thought of as individuals.

EXAMPLE 5

The class have been requested to write reports on their feelings about their tickets.

Analysis:

class—collective noun. The plural form of the verb is used because the members of the class are thought of as individuals.

Sometimes it may be difficult to determine whether the singular or plural form of the verb should be used with a collective noun. When in doubt, decide whether you want to refer to the group as a whole or to the individuals in the group, and then use a singular or a plural verb accordingly.

Common Collective Nouns			
army	company	herd	office force
assembly	congregation	jury	panel
audience	corps	legislature	platoon
band	crew	majority	police
cast	crowd	mass	public
choir	faculty	mob	school
chorus	family	nation	staff
class	flock	navy	swarm
club	gang	number	team
committee	group	orchestra	trio

Directions: Identify the nouns in the following sentences by underlining them once. Above each noun place the abbreviation *P* if it is a proper noun, *C* if it is a common noun, or *Col* if it is a collective noun. Check your answers with your teacher before continuing with your assignment.

1. A committee from the school elected John Whelan to be captain of the team.

2. The group planned a dinner and a dance for the third Saturday in November at the Aragon Ballroom.

3. Luisa Ortiz sang several songs with the orchestra at the party.

4. One fifth of the faculty presented a trophy to Diane McLane for the work of the committee.

5. The band from the navy conducted by Ensign Munson played *Anchors Aweigh* and the *Star-Spangled Banner.*

Complete Application Practices 17-18, pages 29-30, at this time.

17: Practice Procedure. Identify each noun and tell whether it is a proper, a common, or a collective noun. Place the abbreviation *P* for proper, *C* for common, or *Col* for collective above the noun. Score one point for each correct response.

Your Score

1. Martin Luther King was born in Atlanta, Georgia, in 1929.   1. _____

2. A committee of citizens have called Dr. King a crusader.   2. _____

3. One eighth of our class never read about the fight against discrimination.   3. _____

4. The crowd watched Rafael Septien kick the field goal for Dallas.   4. _____

5. Rafael was born in Mexico City, Mexico, in December, 1953.   5. _____

6. Dennis Chavez was a leader in the United States Senate.   6. _____

7. He was chairman of the committee for Public Works.   7. _____

8. The building was named after Alain L. Locke, a black philosopher.   8. _____

9. A native of Philadelphia, Alain Locke went to Oxford.   9. _____

10. Locke received a doctorate from Harvard University.   10. _____

11. Last July 4, the orchestra played many patriotic songs for the group.   11. _____

12. Men and women from the army and navy marched proudly on Veterans Day in Washington, D.C.   12. _____

13. Jane Holst gave a speech on the Nobel Prize to the club.   13. _____

14. Two thirds of our class knew Martin Luther King won the Nobel Peace Prize in 1964.   14. _____

15. The prize is worth about $225,000.   15. _____

16. Alfred Nobel was the inventor of dynamite.   16. _____

17. A choir sang for the winners of the different prizes.   17. _____

18. The awards are given regardless of nationality in physics, chemistry, medicine, economics, peace, and literature.   18. _____

19. The police of the city kept the mob behind the roped area.   19. _____

20. Armen Terzian was the pilot of the crew of the airplane.   20. _____

21. A candidate for an award may not apply directly for a prize.   21. _____

22. The theaters and restaurants in Stockholm welcomed the group.   22. _____

23. A platoon of soldiers controlled the mass of visitors in the city.   23. _____

24. A number of the tourists left Stockholm for the Baltic Sea.   24. _____

25. Ms. Olson and her family enjoyed the crew of the ship.   25. _____

Your Total Score _____

If your score was 79 or less, review pages 25-28 before completing Application Practice 18.

18: Practice Procedure. Identify each noun and tell whether it is a proper, a common, or a collective noun. Place the abbreviation *P* for proper, *C* for common, or *Col* for collective above the noun. Score one point for each correct response.

Your Score

1. The class took a poll on the number of different sports. 1. _____

2. Only one fifth of the students ever bowled. 2. _____

3. A reference to bowling in America appears in the novel *The Sketch Book.* 3. _____

4. Washington Irving was the author of "Rip Van Winkle." 4. _____

5. Rip Van Winkle heard the sound of falling pins. 5. _____

6. Women have become enthusiastic bowlers in all parts of the country. 6. _____

7. A number of women from our office bowl with intense concentration. 7. _____

8. Don Carter, Andy Varipapa, and Dick Weber are all members of the American Bowling Congress Hall of Fame. 8. _____

9. A group of experts consider football the most popular sport. 9. _____

10. Another group believes baseball or basketball is the most popular. 10. _____

11. George Halas organized the National Football League in 1920. 11. _____

12. A majority of fans around the country admire the ability of the players. 12. _____

13. A flock of pigeons fly over Candlestick Park in San Francisco. 13. _____

14. Princeton and Rutgers played the first game of football in 1869. 14. _____

15. Jim Thorpe, an American Indian, was one of the greatest football players in the nation. 15. _____

16. The Professional Football Hall of Fame is located in Canton, Ohio. 16. _____

17. A panel selected Jim Thorpe and Red Grange for the Hall of Fame. 17. _____

18. The crew of workers prepared the field for the Super Bowl. 18. _____

19. Millions of people watch the Rose Bowl and Super Bowl on television. 19. _____

20. Track and field are two important athletic features of the Olympic Games. 20. _____

21. The band played the national anthem for each winner. 21. _____

22. Gertrude Ederle was the first woman to swim the English Channel. 22. _____

23. The company sponsored a group for the Olympic Games. 23. _____

24. The band from the army entertained the spectators. 24. _____

25. The corps of medical people treated the mass of fans for sunstroke. 25. _____

Your Total Score _____

If your score was 75 or less, review pages 25-28 before continuing.

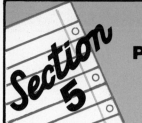

Section 5

Plural Nouns

Remember that a noun names a person, a place, or a thing. It is a *singular noun* when it names one person, one place, or one thing. It is a *plural noun* when it names more than one. You must know whether a noun is singular or plural. To form the plural of nouns, remember a few rules.

5-A. FORMING THE PLURAL OF NOUNS

Simple Plurals

Rule 1: Most nouns become plural by adding the letter *s* to the singular noun. Study the following examples.

Singular	Plural
car	cars
lion	lions
hat	hats
girl	girls
rock	rocks

Rule 2: For words ending in *s, x, z, sh,* or *ch,* you must add *es* to form the plural. Study the examples below.

Singular	Plural
bench	benches
dish	dishes
bus	buses
box	boxes
church	churches
class	classes
tax	taxes
waltz	waltzes

Plurals of Words with Special Endings

Rule 3: *Y*-Ending Plurals. If a noun ends in *y* and is preceded by a consonant, change the *y* to *i* and add *es*. Study the examples below.

Singular	Plural
story	stories
city	cities
puppy	puppies
lady	ladies

Rule 4: *O*-Ending Plurals. If a noun ends in *o* and is preceded by a consonant, add *es* to form the plural. Study the examples below.

Singular	Plural
potato	potatoes
tomato	tomatoes
echo	echoes
hero	heroes

There are several exceptions to this rule: solo, solos; piano, pianos; soprano, sopranos; alto, altos; silo, silos.

If a noun ends in *o* and is preceded by a vowel (a, e, i, o, u), add *s* to form the plural. Study the examples below.

Singular	Plural
rodeo	rodeos
radio	radios
patio	patios
stereo	stereos
shampoo	shampoos

Rule 5: *F*- or *Fe*-Ending Plurals. To form the plural of a noun ending in *f* or *fe,* change the *f* or *fe* to *v* and add *es*. Study the examples below.

Singular	Plural
shelf	shelves
knife	knives
half	halves
life	lives

Note these common exceptions to the above rule: roof, roofs; safe, safes; belief, beliefs; sheriff, sheriffs; chief, chiefs.

5-B. WORDS WITH IRREGULAR PLURALS

The following twelve words have no set rules for forming their plurals. Some of these words do not change at all from the singular to the plural. Study these words carefully for they are often used incorrectly.

Singular	Plural
man	men
woman	women
sheep	sheep
mouse	mice
foot	feet
goose	geese
ox	oxen
tooth	teeth

Singular	Plural
moose	moose
deer	deer
child	children
trout	trout

Note: Some nouns have unusual plural forms. Here are a few of them:

Singular	Plural
spoonful	spoonfuls
birdhouse	birdhouses
bookcase	bookcases
man-of-war	men-of-war
mother-in-law	mothers-in-law

5-C. NOUNS ALWAYS IN PLURAL FORM

Some nouns are always written in the plural form. The more commonly used ones are shown at the right.

athletics	pants	scissors
earnings	proceeds	shears
economics	riches	thanks

5-D. PLURAL FORMS WITH SINGULAR MEANING

Several nouns have a plural form but a singular meaning. Watch verb agreement with these nouns. These nouns require a singular verb.

civics	news
measles	physics
mumps	politics

TRYOUT EXERCISE	**Directions:** Write the plural form of the following singular nouns. Check your answers with your teacher before continuing with your assignment.

1. book _____

2. penny _____

3. bush _____

4. tomato _____

5. sheep _____

6. thief _____

Complete Application Practices 19-20, pages 33-34, at this time.

19: Practice Procedure. Write the plural form of each of the following singular nouns. Score one point for each correct response.

Singular	Plural	Singular	Plural
1. letter	_____	26. receipt	_____
2. teacher	_____	27. party	_____
3. company	_____	28. soprano	_____
4. class	_____	29. delivery	_____
5. client	_____	30. paper	_____
6. reply	_____	31. ribbon	_____
7. address	_____	32. wolf	_____
8. inquiry	_____	33. foot	_____
9. school	_____	34. object	_____
10. community	_____	35. cupful	_____
11. gentleman	_____	36. sheep	_____
12. activity	_____	37. earnings	_____
13. hotel	_____	38. tiger	_____
14. security	_____	39. dress	_____
15. college	_____	40. jacket	_____
16. quality	_____	41. toy	_____
17. puppet	_____	42. tooth	_____
18. duty	_____	43. knife	_____
19. quarrel	_____	44. piano	_____
20. victim	_____	45. tomato	_____
21. woman	_____	46. bench	_____
22. toaster	_____	47. echo	_____
23. calf	_____	48. spy	_____
24. business	_____	49. silo	_____
25. church	_____	50. half	_____

Your Total Score _____

If your score was 39 or less, review pages 31-32 before completing Application Practice 20.

20: Practice Procedure. Write the plural form of the following singular nouns. (Refer to the plural lists on pages 31-32 if necessary.) Score one point for each correct response.

Singular	Plural	Singular	Plural
1. man	_____	26. tax	_____
2. life	_____	27. birdhouse	_____
3. match	_____	28. gas	_____
4. ox	_____	29. navy	_____
5. thief	_____	30. shampoo	_____
6. baby	_____	31. stereo	_____
7. shelf	_____	32. puppy	_____
8. box	_____	33. moose	_____
9. radio	_____	34. bus	_____
10. kangaroo	_____	35. trophy	_____
11. loaf	_____	36. strawberry	_____
12. cameo	_____	37. key	_____
13. piano	_____	38. potato	_____
14. ratio	_____	39. daisy	_____
15. roof	_____	40. sketch	_____
16. series	_____	41. hero	_____
17. father-in-law	_____	42. rodeo	_____
18. quiz	_____	43. leaf	_____
19. glassful	_____	44. copy	_____
20. goose	_____	45. sheriff	_____
21. bookcase	_____	46. deer	_____
22. topaz	_____	47. spoonful	_____
23. mouse	_____	48. waltz	_____
24. child	_____	49. taboo	_____
25. chief	_____	50. trout	_____

Your Total Score _____

If your score was 39 or less, review pages 31-32 before continuing.

Section 6

Nouns and the Possessive Form

Nouns used in the *possessive form* show ownership or possession. The *apostrophe* (') is used to show the possessive form. Guides for forming possessives are given below. (For use of the apostrophe in a contraction, see page 184.)

6-A. SINGULAR POSSESSIVE

To show the possessive form of a singular noun, merely place the apostrophe (') after the last letter of the word and add *s*.

EXAMPLE 1

The girl's radio was broken.

Analysis:

girl's—singular noun—apostrophe after *girl* and before *s* tells whose radio it is (the radio of the girl)

EXAMPLE 2

The neighbor's stereo was expensive.

Analysis:

neighbor's—singular noun—apostrophe after *neighbor* and before *s* tells whose stereo it is (the stereo of the neighbor)

To show the singular possessive form of a noun of *one syllable* ending in a *s, x, ch,* or *sh* sound, place the apostrophe after the last letter and add *s*. However, to show the singular possessive form of a noun of *more than one syllable* ending in a *s, x, ch,* or *sh* sound, add only the apostrophe.

EXAMPLE 1

Miss Haas's voice was beautiful, but Mr. Dickens' song was off-key.

Analysis:

Haas's—singular proper noun of one syllable—apostrophe and *s* added to show possession

Dickens'—singular proper noun of two syllables—apostrophe alone added to show possession

---

6-B. PLURAL POSSESSIVE

To show the possessive form of a plural noun not ending in *s*, add the apostrophe (') and the *s*.

EXAMPLE 1

The men's business went bankrupt.

Analysis:

men's—plural form of *man*—apostrophe is placed before the *s* because the noun does not end in *s* (the business of the men)

EXAMPLE 2

The children's pets included a turtle, a hamster, and a white rat.

Analysis:

children's—plural form of *child*—apostrophe is placed before the *s* because the noun does not end in *s* (the pets of the children)

To show the possessive form of a plural noun ending in *s*, merely place the apostrophe after the *s*.

EXAMPLE 1

The <u>nurses'</u> uniforms were attractive.

Analysis:

nurses'—plural form of *nurse*—apostrophe is placed after the *s* to indicate plural possession (the uniforms of the nurses)

EXAMPLE 2

The <u>Pattersons'</u> garden won the flower award.

Analysis:

Pattersons'—plural form of *Patterson*—apostrophe is placed after the *s* to indicate plural possession (the garden of the Pattersons)

EXAMPLE 3

Our <u>friends'</u> dogs were very noisy.

Analysis:

friends'—plural form of *friend*—apostrophe is placed after the *s* to indicate plural possession (the dogs of our friends)

EXAMPLE 4

The <u>Smiths'</u> piano was a genuine antique.

Analysis:

Smiths'—plural form of *Smith*—apostrophe is placed after the *s* to indicate plural possession (the piano of the Smiths)

TRYOUT EXERCISE

Directions: Write the singular possessive and the plural possessive of each of the following expressions. Make both nouns plural in the plural possessive. Check your answers with your teacher before continuing with your assignment.

Example: the phone of the girl _____ the girl's phone
_____ the girls' phones

1. the pie of the cook _____

_____

2. the car of the owner _____

_____

3. the typewriter of the clerk _____

_____

Directions: Find the possessive nouns in the following sentences and place the apostrophe in the right spot. Check your answers with your teacher before continuing with your assignment.

1. The happy workers left the papers on the managers desk.
2. My aunts stories were repeated by her sisters.
3. The womens phone was used by many waiters.

Complete Application Practices 21-24, pages 37-40, at this time.

21: **Practice Procedure.** Use the apostrophe (') to form the possessives of the following nouns. Form the singular possessive and the plural possessive of each singular expression. Make both nouns plural in the plural possessive. Score one point for each correct response.

Examples	Singular Possessive	Plural Possessive
a. book of the writer	a. writer's book	a. writers' books
b. house of the teacher	b. teacher's house	b. teachers' houses
c. hat of the woman	c. woman's hat	c. women's hats
d. tooth of the child	d. child's tooth	d. children's teeth
1. pen of the girl	1. _____	1. _____
2. nose of the monkey	2. _____	2. _____
3. toy of the baby	3. _____	3. _____
4. knife of the neighbor	4. _____	4. _____
5. test of the pupil	5. _____	5. _____
6. headlight of the bus	6. _____	6. _____
7. guide of the hunter	7. _____	7. _____
8. box of the child	8. _____	8. _____
9. church of the minister	9. _____	9. _____
10. cry of the wolf	10. _____	10. _____
11. echo of the singer	11. _____	11. _____
12. gown of the princess	12. _____	12. _____
13. string of the piano	13. _____	13. _____
14. duty of the coach	14. _____	14. _____
15. sheep of the rancher	15. _____	15. _____
16. color of the box	16. _____	16. _____
17. mouse of the cat	17. _____	17. _____
18. gun of the police officer	18. _____	18. _____
19. tooth of the ox	19. _____	19. _____
20. radio of the spy	20. _____	20. _____
21. silo of the farmer	21. _____	21. _____
22. wish of the hero	22. _____	22. _____
23. bench of the thief	23. _____	23. _____
24. life of the sheriff	24. _____	24. _____
25. bus of the army	25. _____	25. _____

Your Total Score _____

If your score was 39 or less, review pages 35-36 before completing Application Practice 22.

22: Practice Procedure. Find the nouns that require the apostrophe ('). In the answer column, rewrite the correct possessive form of the nouns with the apostrophe in the correct place. Score one point for each correct answer.

Examples:

Answers

a. That girls hobbies were stamps and coins.

a. girl's

b. Janes interest was in the history of bells.

b. Jane's

c. The oxens horns were fascinating to many people.

c. oxen's

1. My junk may be another mans treasures. 1. _____

2. Many of those girls hobbies were displayed at the convention. 2. _____

3. That teachers postcards came from Ireland. 3. _____

4. Two of our friends guns were purchased in a surplus store. 4. _____

5. All of Mr. Burgess books were first editions. 5. _____

6. The third persons antiques were purchased by the Johnsons. 6. _____

7. Doris buttons and bows created much excitement at the show. 7. _____

8. Many parents vases showed great skill. 8. _____

9. The mens clocks were the most unusual of them all. 9. _____

10. Lyle Jones stamps were arranged by countries. 10. _____

11. Karen Smiths insects needed larger display cases. 11. _____

12. Miss Harris shells were used as dishes. 12. _____

13. Her schools chess tournaments received much publicity. 13. _____

14. The mens cakes sold for $5 apiece. 14. _____

15. Carols brothers helped box the cookies. 15. _____

16. Several of the companies flowers were beautiful and decorative. 16. _____

17. The secretaries registers kept ringing up the sales. 17. _____

18. The ladys flowers ranged from the monstrous to the exotic. 18. _____

19. Basketry and beadwork were my fathers specialties. 19. _____

20. Charles folks build birdhouses from different material. 20. _____

21. Jeans friends found satisfaction in rug making. 21. _____

22. The childrens exhibits at the Hobby Convention consisted of baseball cards. 22. _____

23. Englands Queen Victoria gave glass bells as wedding gifts. 23. _____

24. The history of bells is music to hobbyists ears. 24. _____

25. Pete Johnsons chimes were music to my ears. 25. _____

If your score was 19 or less, review pages 35-36 before continuing.

Your Total Score _____

23-A: Practice Procedure. Match each item in Column B with the item it describes in Column A. Write the identifying letter from Column B in the blank provided at the right. Score one point for each correct answer.

Column A	Column B	Answers
1. Ronald Reagan	**a.** names of groups or parts of numbers	**1.** _____
2. typewriter	**b.** possessive noun	**2.** _____
3. common nouns	**c.** names one person, one place, or one thing	**3.** _____
4. collective noun	**d.** nouns which should always be capitalized	**4.** _____
5. plural noun	**e.** collective noun	**5.** _____
6. singular noun	**f.** proper noun	**6.** _____
7. the *baby's* rattle	**g.** do not refer to particular person, place, or thing	**7.** _____
8. one fourth	**h.** shows ownership	**8.** _____
9. proper nouns	**i.** common noun	**9.** _____
10. possessive noun	**j.** names more than one person, place, or thing	**10.** _____

Your Total Score _____

If your score was 7 or less, review pages 25-28, 31-32, and 35-36 before continuing.

23-B: Practice Procedure. Here are 48 words that are frequently misspelled. Study them carefully and be prepared to write them from memory.

absence	business	friend	movies
absent	column	genius	negative
address	comb	grammar	operate
affair	contractor	health	perform
alphabet	creature	horrible	question
altar	crowd	hospital	rather
alter	curious	identify	really
among	desert	its	salary
angel	dessert	it's	several
angle	electric	jacket	smooth
ankle	excellent	lessen	spread
beginning	forty	lesson	straight

24–A: Practice Procedure. Select the correct *synonym* (word which means about the same) from the lettered words to match the italicized word in the sentence. Write the letter representing your answer in the blank at the right. Score one point for each correct answer.

Answers

1. A *pampered* baby is (a) teased (b) changed (c) praised (d) spoiled.
   1. _____
2. A *remote* area is (a) restricted (b) neglected (c) faraway (d) expensive.
   2. _____
3. A *gigantic* mountain is (a) hilly (b) pretty (c) rocky (d) huge.
   3. _____
4. An *artificial* smile is (a) sad (b) fake (c) happy (d) genuine.
   4. _____
5. An *amiable* person is (a) insolent (b) foreign (c) amazing (d) friendly.
   5. _____
6. A *gruesome* sight is (a) beautiful (b) pretentious (c) horrible (d) genuine.
   6. _____
7. A *forlorn* youngster is (a) argumentative (b) foolish (c) unhappy (d) athletic.
   7. _____
8. An *inflammatory* remark is (a) soothing (b) dirty (c) inflexible (d) inciting.
   8. _____
9. An *obnoxious* neighbor is (a) pleasant (b) objectionable (c) tactful (d) unconcerned.
   9. _____
10. An *incredible* video game is (a) indecent (b) ordinary (c) unbelievable (d) realistic.
    10. _____

24–B: Practice Procedure. Follow the procedure given for 24–A. Notice how all the italicized words begin with the letters *im*. Look at the words carefully.

1. An *immaculate* person is (a) spotless (b) spotted (c) painted (d) restricted.
   1. _____
2. An *immoral* movie is (a) expensive (b) unusual (c) unethical (d) virtuous.
   2. _____
3. An *imminent* danger is (a) delayed (b) approaching (c) great (d) fleeting.
   3. _____
4. An *impartial* view is (a) prejudiced (b) excited (c) nervous (d) fair
   4. _____
5. An *impassive* attitude is (a) emotional (b) unemotional (c) solid (d) forceful.
   5. _____
6. An *impertinent* youth is (a) polite (b) sensitive (c) ridiculous (d) rude.
   6. _____
7. An *impetuous* person is (a) hasty (b) cautious (c) naughty (d) poor.
   7. _____
8. An *impudent* child is (a) respectful (b) untidy (c) rude (d) wise.
   8. _____
9. An *imposing* building is (a) old (b) ordinary (c) impregnable (d) impressive.
   9. _____
10. An *immaterial* piece of evidence is (a) significant (b) developed (c) unimportant (d) restricted.
    10. _____

Your Total Score _____

Personal Pronouns

Unit 3
Pronouns

OBJECTIVES: 1. To know that pronouns are words used as substitutes for nouns.
2. To recognize and use different types of pronouns.

Personal pronouns are used in place of the person *speaking (I, me, we, us)*, in place of the person *spoken to (you)*, and in place of the person spoken of *(he, him, she, her, they, them)*. Personal pronouns replace nouns. The old second-person singular *(thou, thy, thee)* is still used in poetry.

Personal Pronouns

	Singular	**Plural**
1st person	I, me, my, mine	we, us, our, ours
2nd person	you, your, yours	you, your, yours
3rd person	he, him, his, she, her, hers, it, its	they, them, their, theirs

Person speaking: *I* visited a television studio.
Person spoken to: *You* drove the car to the theater.
Person spoken of: *She* saw many movie stars.

7-A. PRONOUN AGREEMENT IN PERSON AND NUMBER

A pronoun must agree with its antecedent in person, number (singular or plural), and gender (masculine, feminine, or neuter sex). The *antecedent* is the word for which the pronoun stands. If the antecedent is singular, a singular form of the pronoun is used. If the antecedent is plural, a plural form of the pronoun is used.

EXAMPLE 1

Sally went to <u>her</u> acting class.

Analysis:
> her—singular pronoun—agrees in person, number, and gender with antecedent *Sally*

EXAMPLE 2

Dan enjoyed <u>his</u> trip to Hollywood.

Analysis:
> his—singular pronoun—agrees in person, number, and gender with antecedent *Dan*

EXAMPLE 3

One of the writers was on the stage, but <u>he</u> didn't speak.

Analysis:
> he—agrees in person and in number with antecedent *One* (*She* could be used in place of *he* as antecedent *One* does not indicate gender.)

41

EXAMPLE 4

Mr. Chan and Mr. Diaz were excellent in their performances.

Analysis:

their—plural pronoun—agrees in person and number with antecedents *Mr. Chan* and *Mr. Diaz*

EXAMPLE 5

The actors have studied their parts for weeks.

Analysis:

their—plural pronoun—agrees in person and in number with antecedent *actors*

7-B. CASE FORMS OF PERSONAL PRONOUNS

The three case forms of personal pronouns are nominative, objective, and possessive.

The *nominative case* pronouns *(I, you, he, she, it, we, they)* are used as the subject or the predicate pronoun (in place of the predicate noun) of the sentence.

The *objective case* pronouns *(me, you, him, her, it, us, them)* are used as the object of the verb, indirect object, or object of a preposition.

The *possessive case* pronouns *(my, mine, your, yours, his, her, hers, its, our, ours, their, theirs)* are used to denote ownership.

Nominative Case

Pronouns (and nouns) used as subjects are in the *nominative* case. Remember that the *subject noun* is the person, place, or thing spoken of. The *subject pronoun*, however, may be the person, place, or thing spoken of, spoken to, or speaking.

EXAMPLE 1

I rode the bus to New Hampshire.

Analysis:

I—person speaking—subject—nominative case

EXAMPLE 2

You made excellent reservations at the ski lodge.

Analysis:

You—person spoken to—subject—nominative case

EXAMPLE 3

He took lessons from the ski instructor.

Analysis:

He—person spoken of—subject—nominative case

Personal pronouns may be used as *compound subjects. Compound* means more than one. Use a plural verb form with compound subjects. (See page 77 for plural form with compound subjects.)

EXAMPLE 1

She and her sisters won medals in the ski race.

Analysis:

She—singular pronoun. Since it is used with the word *sisters* as part of the compound subject, a plural verb is required.

When a pronoun (or noun) is used after a verb and refers to the same person or thing as the subject of the verb, it is called a *predicate pronoun* (or noun). A predicate pronoun means the same thing as the subject to which it refers and is in the nominative case.

EXAMPLE 1

The mystery skier was she.

Analysis:

she—predicate pronoun—nominative case —follows the verb *was* and refers to the subject *skier*

EXAMPLE 2

It is I.

Analysis:

I—predicate pronoun—nominative case—follows the verb *is* and refers to the subject *It*

EXAMPLE 3

James Michener is a famous <u>author</u>.

Analysis:

> <u>author</u>—predicate noun—nominative case
> —follows the verb *is* and refers to the subject *James Michener*

Most predicate pronouns (or nouns) follow a form of the verb *be (is, am, are, be, was, were, has been, have been, had been)* and are called *linking verbs*. Other linking verbs which take a predicate pronoun or noun are parts of the verbs *seem, feel* and *become*. (See page 70 for use of verbs with predicate nouns, pronouns, and adjectives.)

EXAMPLE 1

James Michener became a <u>writer</u> at an early age.

Analysis:

> <u>writer</u>—predicate noun—nominative case
> —follows the verb *became* and refers to the subject *James Michener*

Objective Case

Pronouns (and nouns) are in the *objective* case if they are used as objects of verbs, indirect objects, or objects of prepositions. If a pronoun (or noun) answers the question "what" or "whom" after the verb and receives the action, it is the object of the verb.

EXAMPLE 1

The snowmobile missed <u>him</u>.

Analysis:

> <u>him</u>—personal pronoun—objective case
> —answers the question "whom" after the verb *missed*—missed whom?

EXAMPLE 2

The snow patrol rescued <u>them</u>.

Analysis:

> <u>them</u>—personal pronoun—objective case
> —answers the question "whom" after the verb *rescued*—rescued whom?

EXAMPLE 3

The professional skater demonstrated <u>it</u>.

Analysis:

> <u>it</u>—personal pronoun—objective case—answers the question "what" after the verb *demonstrated*—demonstrated what?

A pronoun (or noun) which follows a preposition (see page 136 for a list of prepositions) is the *object of the preposition*. These pronouns or nouns must be in the objective case. (See page 42 for a list of objective pronouns.)

EXAMPLE 1

He wrote a story for <u>them</u>.

Analysis:

> <u>them</u>—personal pronoun—objective case
> —object of the preposition *for*

EXAMPLE 2

Mr. Akira skated with <u>her</u>.

Analysis:

> <u>her</u>—personal pronoun—objective case
> —object of the preposition *with*

Pronouns used as *compound* (more than one) *objects* of verbs or prepositions cause some confusion. Omit one of the compound objects, and it becomes very easy.

EXAMPLE 1

The highway patrol showed them and me the right road.

Analysis:
them—objective case—object of the verb *showed*—showed them
me—objective case—object of the verb *showed*—showed me

EXAMPLE 2

Mr. Wilkens returned with her and me.

Analysis:
her—objective case—object of the preposition *with*—with her
me—objective case—object of the preposition *with*—with me

An *indirect object* tells *to* or *for whom* something is done, or *to* or *for what* something is done. The pronoun used as an indirect object is always in the objective case.

EXAMPLE 1

Ben handed me the new skates.

Analysis:
me—indirect object—objective case—tells that the skates were handed to me (preposition *to* is omitted)

EXAMPLE 2

The instructor sold them tickets to the ski lift.

Analysis:
them—indirect object—objective case—tells that the tickets were sold to them (preposition *to* is omitted)

A pronoun (or noun) which follows *than* or *as* can be in the nominative or the objective case, depending on its use. When the rest of the clause has been left out, the clause must be reproduced mentally in order to determine the correct use of the pronoun or noun.

EXAMPLES

He knows her as well as I (know her).
He knows her as well as (he knows) me.

He swims faster than I (swim).
She sang to him more than I (sang to him).
She sang to him more than (she sang to) me.

In both nominative and objective case, pairs of pronouns can be used in teams. The following is a list of common pairs of pronouns:

Nominative	Objective
he and she	him and her
he and we	him and us
she and I	her and me
she and they	her and them
we and they	us and them
they and I	them and me

Possessive Case

Pronouns denoting ownership are in the *possessive* case. Do not use an apostrophe with the personal pronouns. *Its* (no apostrophe) is the possessive form of the personal pronoun *it*. (See page 52 for more explanation of possessive pronouns.)

EXAMPLE 1

Check the dictionary for its pronunciation.

Analysis:
its—personal pronoun—possessive case—shows ownership to *pronunciation*

Verbs ending in *ing* and used as nouns are called *verbal nouns* or *gerunds*. Pronouns modifying verbal nouns are in the possessive case *(my, his, her, its, our, their, your)*.

EXAMPLE 1

The announcer told of my winning the big race.

Analysis:
my—personal pronoun—possessive case—modifies verbal noun *winning*

EXAMPLE 2

She developed great endurance because of her jogging.

Analysis:
her—personal pronoun—possessive case—modifies verbal noun *jogging*

44

Directions: Complete each of the following sentences by writing in the blank provided at the right the correct form of the pronoun in the parentheses.

1. She and (I, me) listened to the job counselor.   1. _____

2. Sumio knew his job better than (I, me).   2. _____

3. Our neighbor sold Felix and (she, her) his old bikes.   3. _____

4. The best dancer is (he, him).   4. _____

5. (Them, Their) receiving an award surprised us.   5. _____

Directions: In the sentences below, underline all pronouns in the nominative case once and all pronouns in the objective case twice. Check your answers with your teacher before continuing with your assignment.

1. I went with her and him to the new movie.

2. We wanted her to go with us.

Complete Application Practices 25-26, pages 47-48, at this time.

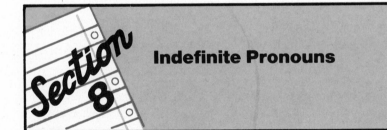

Section 8

Indefinite Pronouns

An *indefinite pronoun* is a pronoun that does not define or stand for a particular person or thing. Some common indefinite pronouns are *all, each, either, one, everyone, several, some, other, another, both, none, many*. Indefinite pronouns are often used as adjectives.

EXAMPLE 1

Some went to the game, but few bought tickets.

Analysis:
> Some—indefinite pronoun used as subject of the verb *went*—refers to no particular person
> few—indefinite pronoun used as subject of the verb *bought*—refers to no particular person

EXAMPLE 2

Some people enjoyed the game, and many happy fans cheered loudly.

Analysis:
> Some—indefinite pronoun used as an adjective—modifies the noun *people*
> many—indefinite pronoun used as an adjective—modifies the noun *fans*

EXAMPLE 3

Each player practiced every day for two hours.

Analysis:
> Each—indefinite pronoun used as an adjective—modifies the noun *player*

Pronouns must agree in number with their antecedents. (Remember that the antecedent is the word for which the pronoun stands.) When an indefinite pronoun is used as an antecedent, the personal pronoun must agree in number with the indefinite pronoun. Use a singular pronoun with the following indefinite pronoun antecedents.

another	either	nobody
anybody	everybody	one
anyone	everyone	somebody
each	neither	someone

EXAMPLE 1

Neither Gloria nor Dolores knew her speech.

Analysis:

her—singular personal pronoun—refers to singular antecedent *Neither*

EXAMPLE 2

Each of the boys did his work.

Analysis:

his—singular personal pronoun—refers to singular antecedent *Each*

EXAMPLE 3

Everybody wants his share of praise.

Analysis:

his—singular personal pronoun—refers to singular antecedent *Everybody* (*Her* could be used in place of *his* since the antecedent *Everybody* does not indicate gender.)

Use a plural pronoun with the following indefinite pronoun antecedents: *both, few, many, others,* and *several.* Be careful of the indefinite pronouns *all, any, most, none,* and *some.* These indefinite pronouns can take a singular or plural verb. They depend upon the antecedent. (See page 75 for verb agreement.)

EXAMPLE 1

Few of them bought their lunch.

Analysis:

their—plural personal pronoun—refers to plural antecedent *Few*

EXAMPLE 2

Several teachers sang their songs for the students.

Analysis:

their—plural personal pronoun—refers to plural antecedent *Several*

TRYOUT EXERCISE	**Directions:** Complete each of the following sentences by writing in the blank provided at the right the correct form of the pronoun in the parentheses. Check your answers with your teacher before continuing with your assignment.

1. Few of the players did (her, their) best.   1. _____

2. Someone has lost (his, their) glove.   2. _____

3. Neither Emilio nor Alfonso brought (his, their) friends to the game.   3. _____

4. Many of the reporters left (his, their) typewriters in the press box.   4. _____

5. Can anyone give (her, their) notes to the writers?   5. _____

6. Several of the men brought (his, their) children to the event.   6. _____

Complete Application Practices 27-28, pages 49-50, at this time.

25: Practice Procedure. Complete each of the following sentences by writing in the blank provided at the right the correct answer in the parentheses. Remember that the pronoun must agree in person and number with its antecedent. Score one point for each correct response.

Answers

1. Clara, Carl, and (her, she) listened to the writers.   1. _____

2. Anna helped (they, them) with the story.   2. _____

3. Wells and Burton gave (his, their) best performances in *Hamlet.*   3. _____

4. (Him, His) winning the Academy Award didn't surprise the critics.   4. _____

5. Marilyn and (I, me) interviewed the stars.   5. _____

6. Mario told them and (us, we) about his experiences.   6. _____

7. Was it really (he, him)?   7. _____

8. The set designer arrived with Ms. McCoy and (he, him).   8. _____

9. Was he amazed about (you, your) leaving early?   9. _____

10. They thought it was (her, she) who developed the film script.   10. _____

11. The producer explained the script to his son and (we, us).   11. _____

12. My aunt enjoys the movies, especially if (she, they) gets free tickets.   12. _____

13. (Me, My) being late to the show cost my father $5.   13. _____

14. The actress pretended to like her more than (I, me).   14. _____

15. Did they notice (him, his) entering the studio?   15. _____

16. The sound mixer gave them and (she, her) a look at the sound machines.   16. _____

17. That was an exciting movie written by Mrs. Phillips and (he, him).   17. _____

18. The guide told Iris and (they, them) about the wide-screen process.   18. _____

19. It is a wise director who understands (her, their) actors and writers.   19. _____

20. Paul Newman, one of the outstanding actors, did (his, their) best work in his later films.   20. _____

21. Do Lois and Ellen know how to complete (her, their) film review forms?   21. _____

22. Producers seldom hire new directors if (he, they) can get experienced ones.   22. _____

23. They seated Mark between Pam and (I, me).   23. _____

24. Instead of (him, his) going into the theater, he went to the store next door.   24. _____

25. They and (us, we) derive great pleasure from mystery movies   25. _____

Your Total Score _____

If your score was 19 or less, review Sections 7–A and B, pages 41-44, before continuing.

26–A: Practice Procedure. In the sentences listed below, underline all pronouns in the nominative case (subject or predicate pronoun). Score one point for each correct response.

Your Score

1. She told Dave and me about the sound stages.   1. _____
2. They showed us the permanent outdoor sets.   2. _____
3. Mr. Taylor and he wanted them to be on time.   3. _____
4. I listened carefully to the explanation from him.   4. _____
5. It was a carefully prepared talk given by her.   5. _____
6. We wrote of the visit to Mrs. Rivas and them.   6. _____
7. I received a funny letter from her and Mrs. Rivas.   7. _____
8. The director and I had lunch with the producer and her. 8. _____
9. We heard about the production from him.   9. _____
10. She and Oscar left their names with the casting office and them. 10. _____

Your Total Score _____

If your score was 7 or less, review Section 7–B, page 42, before continuing.

26–B: Practice Procedure. In the sentences below, underline all pronouns in the objective case (objects of verbs, objects of prepositions, and indirect objects). Score one point for each correct response.

1. Juan, Tony, and she went with us to the special-effects department. 1. _____
2. They presented him with a book on special effects.   2. _____
3. Mr. Delgado and I thanked them for their gift.   3. _____
4. We were grateful to her for the courtesy shown to the group. 4. _____
5. Lou and I presented our story to Mrs. Cruze and him. 5. _____
6. He thanked me and I left his office.   6. _____
7. They really helped all of us in our work.   7. _____
8. We listened to the techniques explained by Mrs. Mortimer and her. 8. _____
9. They gave us a better understanding of movie making. 9. _____
10. He and Rosa walked with Julio and me to the restaurant. 10. _____
11. Tom and I bought a book on the silent era of movies from Mr. Anthony and her. 11. _____
12. She, her brother, and I laughed at Charlie Chaplin and him. 12. _____
13. His sympathetic role in *The Tramp* made us understand his great talent. 13. _____

Your Total Score _____

If your score was 9 or less, review Section 7–B, pages 43-44, before continuing.

27: Practice Procedure. Complete each of the following sentences by writing in the blank provided at the right the correct pronoun in the parentheses. Remember that the pronoun must agree in number with its antecedent. Refer to the lists of singular and plural indefinite pronoun antecedents (page 46) before you decide on your answers. Score one point for each correct reponse.

Answers

1. Neither of the two girls had ever entered (her, their) dog in a show.   1. _____

2. One of them had paid (her, their) entrance fee.   2. _____

3. Many of the purebreds did (his, their) best.   3. _____

4. Everyone had to lead (his, their) dog into the arena.   4. _____

5. Few of the large dogs won (his, their) ribbons at this show.   5. _____

6. Some of the dogs were barking (its, their) loudest at the end of each event.   6. _____

7. Before anyone enters a dog show, (she, they) should read about the American Kennel Club.   7. _____

8. If someone knows how to train dogs, (he, they) might get a job.   8. _____

9. Many complained that (she, they) didn't hear about the show.   9. _____

10. Several of the dogs in this show won (her, their) ribbons regularly.   10. _____

11. None of the contestants was eager to lose (her, their) event.   11. _____

12. Nobody in this group likes to lose (his, their) event.   12. _____

13. Several of the dog shows were interesting, as (it, they) had many different breeds of dogs.   13. _____

14. Both of the Irish wolfhounds placed (his, their) feet on the trainer.   14. _____

15. Has everyone entered (his, their) pet in the show?   15. _____

16. One of the three cocker spaniels kept (his, their) eyes on the judge.   16. _____

17. Several of the dogs sat quietly and looked at (her, their) owners.   17. _____

18. Nobody in the entire class read much about (her, their) breed of hound.   18. _____

19. Many of the toy dogs were groomed by Mrs. Gilligan in order to look (her, their) best.   19. _____

20. One of the judges at the show left (her, their) scores with the official scorer.   20. _____

21. Audrey's dog was one of the fox terriers which won (its, their) top award.   21. _____

22. Others among the owners are proud of (his, their) memberships with the SPCA and The Humane Society.   22. _____

23. All of the dogs, like cats, have five claws on (its, their) front feet.   23. _____

Your Total Score _____

If your score was 17 or less, review Section 8, pages 45-46, before continuing.

28–A: Practice Procedure. In the answer column at the right, indicate whether the underlined pronouns are in the nominative or objective case. Be prepared to give a reason for your choice. Score one point for each correct response.

Answers

1. Max and <u>I</u> read how dogs help people.   1. _____

2. The animals gave <u>us</u> much pleasure.   2. _____

3. Dr. Casals, a veterinarian, explained to <u>them</u> why dogs need affection.   3. _____

4. Some veterinarians are better informed than Dr. Rodriquez or <u>she</u>.   4. _____

5. She helped you more than <u>me</u>.   5. _____

6. The six main groups of purebred dogs fascinated Mr. Tiant, Mrs. Sakata, and <u>us</u>.   6. _____

7. <u>We</u> arrived early and left late.   7. _____

8. <u>They</u> told Hilda and Mabel about the "dog days."   8. _____

9. <u>He</u> told the group that dogs lived about 15 million years ago.   9. _____

10. Many of <u>them</u> didn't believe what he said.   10. _____

28–B: Practice Procedure. Complete each of the following sentences by writing in the blank at the right the correct form of the pronoun in the parentheses. Be prepared to give a reason for your choice. Score one point for each correct response.

1. Let Roy and (I, me) discuss the different dogs.   1. _____

2. A year ago Dr. Jordan went to the dog pound with my mother and (we, us).   2. _____

3. (Him, His) guarding the house helped the old woman.   3. _____

4. Most dogs can be trained to guard (its, their) master's house.   4. _____

5. My golden retriever was placed between a Brittany spaniel and (he, him).   5. _____

6. Tina, Mae, and (she, her) had Siberian huskies.   6. _____

7. She and (I, me) prefer large dogs.   7. _____

8. It seemed as though she liked Burl better than (I, me).   8. _____

9. The old sheep dog watched Cathy and (he, him) most of the day.   9. _____

10. Between us and (they, them) there is an understanding.   10. _____

11. All dogs appeal to Liz, Todd, and (I, me).   11. _____

12. When did you learn it was (I, me) who voted for the mastiff?   12. _____

13. The entry form from Mr. Pierce and (her, she) arrived today.   13. _____

14. (Me, My) calling The Humane Society was necessary.   14. _____

15. The women and (us, we) know about the legendary dogs in history.   15. _____

Your Total Score _____

If your score was 19 or less, review pages 41-46 before continuing.

Relative pronouns relate or refer to nouns or other pronouns in a sentence. The nouns or pronouns referred to are called antecedents. The relative pronouns are *who, whom, whose, which,* and *that.*

Who and *whom* refer to persons. *Who* is used as the subject or predicate pronoun of a sentence and is in the nominative case. *Whom* is used as the object of a verb or the object of a preposition and is in the objective case. (See pages 54-55 for further explanations of *who* and *whom.*)

EXAMPLE 1

Thomas Jefferson, <u>who</u> was the third president, was born in 1743.

Analysis:
who—subject of the verb *was*—refers to *Jefferson,* person

EXAMPLE 2

He was a president <u>whom</u> the people trusted.

Analysis:
whom—object of the verb *trusted*—refers to *president,* person

Which refers to animals or things. *That* and *whose* refer to persons, animals, or things.

EXAMPLE 1

The cat, <u>which</u> is a popular house pet, is one of the smartest animals.

Analysis:
which—refers to *cat,* animal

EXAMPLE 2

Our cat played with her toy <u>which</u> was a long string.

Analysis:
which—refers to *toy,* thing

EXAMPLE 3

My aunt was the woman <u>that</u> gave me the Siamese cat.

Analysis:
that—refers to *aunt,* particular person

EXAMPLE 4

We knew the woman <u>whose</u> cat won first prize.

Analysis:
whose—refers to *woman,* person

51

Section 10 — Demonstrative Pronouns

Demonstrative pronouns are used to point out, to designate, or to demonstrate the particular antecedent to which they refer. The singular demonstrative pronouns are *this* and *that*. The plural demonstrative pronouns are *these* and *those*. When demonstrative pronouns are used as adjectives, they are called *demonstrative adjectives*.

EXAMPLE 1

This is my cat, and she is a very smart animal.

Analysis:

This—demonstrative pronoun—designates *cat*

EXAMPLE 2

Was that a meow from the cat?

Analysis:

that—demonstrative pronoun—designates *meow*

EXAMPLE 3

These kittens were lucky to find nice homes.

Analysis:

These—demonstrative adjective—tells which *kittens*

Section 11 — Possessive Pronouns

Possessive pronouns are pronouns used to denote ownership or possession. They are often used as adjectives, and when so used are called *possessive adjectives*. (See page 122 for more on possessive adjectives.)

	Singular	Plural
1st person	my, mine	our, ours
2nd person	your, yours	your, yours
3rd person	his, her, hers, its	their, theirs

EXAMPLE 1

Hers is a rare tortoise-shell cat.

Analysis:

Hers—possessive pronoun—denotes ownership

EXAMPLE 2

Yours is a Manx cat without a tail.

Analysis:

Yours—possessive pronoun—denotes ownership

EXAMPLE 3

Ours is a loving long-haired breed.

Analysis:

Ours—possessive pronoun—denotes ownership

EXAMPLE 4

Their food consisted of fish and milk.

Analysis:

Their—possessive pronoun used as an adjective—tells whose *food* it is

EXAMPLE 5

His mother feeds my kittens twice a day.

Analysis:

His—possessive pronoun used as an adjective—tells whose *mother* it is

my—possessive pronoun used as an adjective—tells whose *kittens* they are

Section 12

Interrogative Pronouns

The *interrogative pronouns* are used in asking questions. They are *who* (nominative), *whom* (objective, referring to persons), *which* (referring to persons or things and telling one object from another), *what* (referring to things), and *whose* (referring to persons or things).

EXAMPLE 1

Who knew that a cat's eyes may be blue, hazel, brown, or orange?

Analysis:
Who—asks question—refers to people—subject of the verb *knew*

EXAMPLE 2

Whom do you see if your cat gets sick?

Analysis:
Whom—asks question—refers to people—object of the verb *do see*

EXAMPLE 3

Which is prettier—the Siamese cat or the Burmese cat?

Analysis:
Which—asks question—refers to things and tells one object from another

EXAMPLE 4

What are the duties of an animal trainer?

Analysis:
What—asks question—refers to things

EXAMPLE 5

What have you read about the different cat foods?

Analysis:
What—asks question—refers to things

EXAMPLE 6

The Burmese cat isn't mine. Whose is it?

Analysis:
Whose—asks question—refers to people

TRYOUT EXERCISE	**Directions:** Complete each of the following sentences by writing in the blank provided at the right the correct form of the pronoun in the parentheses. Check your answers with your teacher before continuing with your assignment.

1. He knew several people (who, which) trained cats.   1. _____

2. (Which, What) is cuter—the kitten or the older cat?   2. _____

3. (Who, Whom) was the owner of the pet store?   3. _____

4. (Who, Whom) do you call when your veterinarian is out of town?   4. _____

5. (What, Which) is the address of her office?   5. _____

6. (Which, Who) of the parents thought the animals were ugly?   6. _____

Complete Application Practices 29-30, pages 57-58, at this time.

Who and Whom

Perhaps the two pronouns which cause the most confusion are *who* and *whom*. Although the pronoun *who* is used most frequently in daily conversation, it is worthwhile knowing when it should be used and when it is better to use *whom*.

Most of the difficulty lies in the sentences of inverted order like this one:

Who do the people think will become president in the next election?

If you rearrange the sentence as a statement, it is easier to see that *who* is correct.

The people think *who* will become president in the next election.

Remember that *who* is used as the subject or the predicate pronoun of the sentence and is in the nominative case. *Whom* is used as the object of a verb or the object of a preposition and is in the objective case. Look at the clause in this sentence:

The president whom he respected lost the election.

Again, change the order of the clause to see whether *whom* is correct.

he respected *whom*

Whom is the object of the verb *respected* and is therefore correct.

EXAMPLE 1

Who visited the home of Thomas Jefferson?

Analysis:
Who—subject of verb *visited*—nominative case

EXAMPLE 2

George Washington, who spent his childhood on a farm, was born February 22, 1732.

Analysis:
who—subject of verb *spent*—nominative case

EXAMPLE 3

Was it who I thought it was?

Analysis:
who—predicate pronoun—nominative case

EXAMPLE 4

With whom did you visit Monticello?

Analysis:
whom—object of the preposition *with*—objective case

EXAMPLE 5

To whom did he send the money?

Analysis:

whom—object of preposition *to*—objective case

EXAMPLE 6

From whom shall I get the book?

Analysis:

whom—object of preposition *from*—I shall get the book from whom.—objective case

EXAMPLE 7

Whom did you tell about the Declaration of Independence?

Analysis:

Whom—object of verb *did tell*—You did tell whom about the Declaration of Independence.—objective case

EXAMPLE 8

The woman whom we met at Monticello was a descendant of Jefferson.

Analysis:

whom—object of verb *met*—We met whom at Monticello.—objective case

Common Mistakes with Who and Whom

A number of mistakes are usually made with *who* and *whom* when they are used in sentences with unrelated clauses or parenthetical expressions such as *I know, in my judgment, in my opinion, we believe, we hope*. To determine whether *who* or *whom* is correct, drop the unrelated or parenthetical expression from the sentence. The meaning or construction of the sentence will not change.

EXAMPLE 1

Miss Paules, who, in my opinion, speaks very softly, won first prize in typing.

Analysis:

who—subject of verb *speaks*—nominative case. Remove the unrelated expression *in my opinion* and the meaning of the sentence is not changed. With the expression *in my opinion* omitted, the sentence reads as follows: Miss Paules, who speaks very softly, won first prize in typing.

EXAMPLE 2

John, who, we believe, took his examinations, had filed his college application form.

Analysis:

who—subject of verb *took*—nominative case. Remove the unrelated expression *we believe* and the sentence reads as follows: John, who took his examinations, had filed his college application form.

EXAMPLE 3

Andy, who, I know, types accurately and carefully, was hired by the telephone company.

Analysis:

who—subject of verb *types*—nominative case. Remove the unrelated expression *I know* and the meaning of the sentence is not changed. With the expression *I know* omitted, the sentence reads as follows: Andy, who types accurately and carefully, was hired by the telephone company.

EXAMPLE 4

Liz Sheffield, whom, we hope, you selected, can start work immediately.

Analysis:

whom—object of verb *selected*. Remove the unrelated expression *we hope* and the meaning of the sentence is not changed. With the expression *we hope* omitted, the sentence reads as follows: Liz Sheffield, whom you selected, can start work immediately.

EXAMPLE 5

It was he who, in my judgment, was the outstanding student in class.

Analysis:

who—subject of verb *was*—nominative case. Remove the parenthetical expression *in my judgment* and the sentence reads as follows: It was he who was the outstanding student in class.

Who-Whom, Whoever-Whomever in Noun Clauses

A common mistake is often made with *who-whom* in noun clauses (see pages 148-150). When you use a noun clause as an object of a verb or preposition, remember *who-whom* is not the object of the main clause but is used as either the subject or object of the noun clause.

EXAMPLE 1

Do you realize <u>who</u> received the most votes?

Analysis:
> who received the most votes—dependent clause used as a noun—object of verb *do realize. Who* is used as the subject of the clause *who received the most votes.*

EXAMPLE 2

The girls selected <u>whom</u> you wanted.

Analysis:
> whom you wanted—dependent clause used as a noun—object of verb *selected. Whom* is the object of the verb *wanted* in the clause *whom you wanted.*

EXAMPLE 3

<u>Who</u> did you think scored the winning goal?

Analysis:
> Who scored the winning goal—dependent clause used as a noun—object of verb *did think. Who* is used as the subject of the clause *Who scored the winning goal.*

Remember to use *whoever* or *whomever* the way it is used in the noun clause, not as the object of the preposition.

EXAMPLE 1

Students will be dismissed by the class president or by <u>whoever</u> is selected by the teacher.

Analysis:
> whoever—nominative case—subject of the noun clause *whoever is selected by the teacher.* (The entire clause *whoever is selected by the teacher* is the object of the preposition *by.*)

EXAMPLE 2

Players of the team will be chosen by the coach or by <u>whomever</u> you decide.

Analysis:
> whomever—objective case—object of verb *decide* in the noun clause *whomever you decide.* (The entire clause *whomever you decide* is the object of the preposition *by.*)

TRYOUT EXERCISE	**Directions:** Complete each of the following sentences by writing in the blank provided at the right the correct pronoun in the parentheses. Check your answers with your teacher before continuing with your assignment.

1. F. D. Roosevelt, (who, whom), in my judgment, worked very hard, was elected president four times.   1. _____

2. Did you know (who, whom) succeeded him?   2. _____

3. Harry Truman, (who, whom), in my opinion, people sometimes forget, did an outstanding job as president.   3. _____

4. She will send the absentee ballot to (whoever, whomever) mails in a request.   4. _____

5. Miss Moreno mailed out the ballots to (whoever, whomever) you listed.   5. _____

Complete Application Practices 31-38, pages 59-66, at this time.

APPLICATION PRACTICE 29
Relative, Demonstrative,
Possessive, and
Interrogative Pronouns

Name _____ Date _____

Teacher _____ Score _____

29: Practice Procedure. Complete each of the following sentences by writing in the blank provided at the right the correct pronoun in the parentheses. Make sure the pronouns agree with their antecedents. Score one point for each correct response.

Answers

1. Art Skrumbis was the one (that, which) told us about Greece. 1. _____

2. His father, (who, whom) was born in Athens, came to the United States as a child. 2. _____

3. (That, Those) is the country of Greece. 3. _____

4. (She, Her, Hers) film on Greece showed us the different cities. 4. _____

5. Our uncle is the person (which, whose) pictures showed the island of Santorin. 5. _____

6. Where are your friends (who, whom) you told about Plato and Socrates? 6. _____

7. They were statesmen (who, whom) we respected. 7. _____

8. With (who, whom) did you go? 8. _____

9. Mel Caras, (who, whom) you met at my house, traveled to Delphi last summer. 9. _____

10. Ms. Angie Pakadakis, (who, whom) was my history teacher, was born on the island of Rhodes. 10. _____

11. (This, These) is the boat you took to Crete. 11. _____

12. Santorin was the Greek island (who, that) provided them a ride on a donkey. 12. _____

13. The donkey, (which, who) I rode, was called Homer. 13. _____

14. Cato and Cicero were two famous Roman statesmen (who, whom) are still remembered. 14. _____

15. (This, These) statesmen lived exciting lives. 15. _____

16. The Acropolis in Athens is near (that, those) body of water. 16. _____

17. (Who, Which) of the Greek islands is the most popular? 17. _____

18. Plutarch wrote (he, him, his) books about the Greeks and Romans. 18. _____

19. (Which, What) is more expensive—the Greek or Asian stamp? 19. _____

20. I went to see a travel agent (who, whom) handles Grecian holiday tours. 20. _____

21. Are (that, those) the people that left with Mr. Grady and Miss Culpepper? 21. _____

22. Plutarch's book, *Lives,* (who, which) was in our library, is interesting reading. 22. _____

Your Total Score _____

If your score was 16 or less, review Sections 9-12, pages 51-53, before continuing.

30-A: Practice Procedure. Complete each of the following sentences by writing in the blank space provided at the left the correct interrogative pronoun *(who, whom, which, what, whose)*. Score one point for each correct response.

Your Score

1. (   ) should a person do who wants to travel?   1. _____
2. (   ) has the address of World Tours?   2. _____
3. (   ) of the two companies is the better one?   3. _____
4. (   ) do you know at the Greek Embassy?   4. _____
5. (   ) can buy me a discounted plane ticket?   5. _____
6. (   ) do I see when I get the ticket?   6. _____
7. (   ) of the companies is the most reliable?   7. _____
8. (   ) agent sold you the cruise ticket?   8. _____
9. (   ) is a good bargain for the entire trip?   9. _____
10. (   ) idea was it to cook Greek food?   10. _____

30-B: Practice Procedure. Complete each of the following sentences by writing in the blank provided at the right the correct pronoun in the parentheses. Score one point for each correct response.

Answers

1. Mr. Maupin and (her, she) arranged our trip.   1. _____
2. His fee was acceptable to Pete and (they, them).   2. _____
3. A group of them and (us, we) sold magazines to pay for part of the trip.   3. _____
4. She and (I, me) enjoyed the story of the Olympic Games which started in Greece.   4. _____
5. Mr. Abrams, our teacher, arranged a tour for Grace, Belinda, and (I, me).   5. _____
6. For (who, whom) did you buy that beautiful Greek coin?   6. _____
7. Marcia and her parrot, (who, which) was very colorful, repeated several words.   7. _____
8. That tour director knew his schedules better than (I, me).   8. _____
9. Ms. Bolin and (he, him) waited three hours for the plane.   9. _____
10. Mike and Cam showed Susan and (we, us) pictures of the ship.   10. _____

Your Total Score _____

If your score was 15 or less for 30-A and B, review pages 42-44 and pages 51-53 before continuing.

31: Practice Procedure. Complete each of the following sentences by writing in the blank provided at the right the correct form of *who* or *whom*. Score one point for each correct response.

Answers

1. Mr. Nagakama, (who, whom) is from the Bureau of Labor Statistics, spoke to us.

    1. _____

2. With (who, whom) did you go to the meeting?

    2. _____

3. A student (who, whom) is self-motivated can get a job.

    3. _____

4. Mr. Lassler, (who, whom), we hope, will list the various job prospects, came early.

    4. _____

5. (Who, Whom) do you think will be the first one hired?

    5. _____

6. Wasn't it your cousin (who, whom) had the first interview?

    6. _____

7. They told us that there is a job for (whoever, whomever) is trained.

    7. _____

8. (Who, Whom) do I see for an interview?

    8. _____

9. Frank Perez brought his uncle, an employment consultant, to (who, whom) we directed our questions.

    9. _____

10. I don't know (who, whom) you brought to the meeting.

    10. _____

11. (Who, Whom) has the best chance to get a job?

    11. _____

12. A job seeker who is eager can get facts from (whoever, whomever) is in charge.

    12. _____

13. Some firms, (who, whom), in my opinion, hire regularly, do a great service.

    13. _____

14. Christine Judge is the person (who, whom) is in charge of hiring.

    14. _____

15. (Who, Whom) do I see for a sales job?

    15. _____

16. He hired clerical workers (who, whom), in my judgment, did a great job.

    16. _____

17. Applicants will be interviewed by the personnel director or by (whoever, whomever) you say.

    17. _____

18. (Who, Whom) have you asked for references?

    18. _____

19. I don't know another student (who, whom) is better qualified.

    19. _____

20. Here is Mrs. Molina (who, whom), I know, is interested in finding a secretary.

    20. _____

21. I don't know (who, whom) you told about the opening.

    21. _____

22. The employers (who, whom) place the ads can improve advertising.

    22. _____

23. (Who, Whom) did you say arrived first on the job?

    23. _____

24. With (who, whom) do you like to work?

    24. _____

25. Stan Freberg was the person (who, whom) developed the clever TV jingles.

    25. _____

If your score was 19 or less, review pages 51, 53, and 54-56.   Your Total Score _____

32: Practice Procedure. Complete each of the following sentences by writing in the blank provided at the right the correct pronoun in the parentheses. Score one point for each correct answer.

Answers

1. Ms. Kendall taught good work habits to Josie and (us, we).   1. _____

2. There was great competition between Lucia and (I, me).   2. _____

3. Helen and (he, him) are self-assured and poised.   3. _____

4. Cheerful and pleasant speech is practiced by Lorna and (he, him).   4. _____

5. My younger brother has more confidence than (I, me).   5. _____

6. (Him, His) getting a job inspired all of us.   6. _____

7. Julian or (he, him) will be selected for the job.   7. _____

8. Punctuality and cooperation are practiced by Sergio and (they, them).   8. _____

9. Thelma and (he, him) met us at the employment agency.   9. _____

10. There was a good relationship between my brother and (I, me).   10. _____

11. Lionel works faster than (I, me).   11. _____

12. The class received the information needed for the job from Greg and (they, them).   12. _____

13. Mr. Brewer and (us, we) found the work exciting.   13. _____

14. The *Occupational Outlook Handbook* helped Pat and (she, her).   14. _____

15. Just between you and (I, me), were you ready for work?   15. _____

16. Duane and (her, she) know what a good job means.   16. _____

17. Did Myrna and (she, her) find a job?   17. _____

18. Roxanna and she helped Jim and (he, him).   18. _____

19. (Their, Them) finding work helped the entire family.   19. _____

20. Our parents' assistance meant a great deal to Matt and (I, me).   20. _____

21. Many students and (I, me) desire an interesting job.   21. _____

22. We went with Avery and (she, her) to the employment agency.   22. _____

23. Ms. Munson and (they, them) gave us temporary work.   23. _____

24. (Me, My) getting paid for the first time was a real thrill.   24. _____

25. Edith, Rory, and (I, me) were pleased with the company.   25. _____

Your Total Score _____

If your score was 19 or less, review pages 42-44 before continuing.

33: Practice Procedure. Complete each of the following sentences by writing in the blank provided at the right the correct pronoun in parentheses. Score one point for each correct answer.

Answers

1. Miss Purvine, our guidance adviser, (who, whom) knows many of the top executives in business, invited Mr. Settle to our class.   1. _____

2. Mr. Settle spoke to our group and (they, them).   2. _____

3. (Him, His) being president of the Settle Employment Agency made it worthwhile.   3. _____

4. The interviewer chose between Mary Brown and (he, him).   4. _____

5. An interviewer (who, whom) can put you at ease is important.   5. _____

6. References are important for (whoever, whomever) is looking for a job.   6. _____

7. Salary is sometimes the most important factor in (him, his) considering a job.   7. _____

8. With (who, whom) should you go for an interview?   8. _____

9. "Want Ads" in the newspapers gave Yuki and (he, him) several leads for jobs.   9. _____

10. She and (I, me) read about possibilities for a job.   10. _____

11. (What, Which) is more important—good looks or a good résumé?   11. _____

12. Nell Simpson and Audrey Strock will show us how (she, they) prepared a résumé.   12. _____

13. The discussion on résumés between Mr. Flores and (he, him) was very helpful.   13. _____

14. Sheila, (who, whom), in my opinion, you helped, prepared a positive résumé.   14. _____

15. (Me, My) learning to list references in reverse chronological order made my résumé better.   15. _____

16. Miss de la Torre is more qualified for the job than (she, her).   16. _____

17. Mr. Settle was the first one (who, whom) we heard speak.   17. _____

18. He is the person (that, which) gave us the best advice.   18. _____

19. Our teacher set up a "mock" interview with Mr. Settle and (he, him).   19. _____

20. Interviews were set up by the teacher or by (whoever, whomever) she told.   20. _____

21. With (who, whom) did Mr. Settle discuss job opportunities and salary?   21. _____

22. Our teacher told Austin, Russ, and (she, her) not to get too emotional.   22. _____

Your Total Score _____

If your score was 16 or less, review pages 41-45 and 51-56 before continuing.

34: Practice Procedure. Complete each of the following sentences by writing in the blank provided at the right the correct pronoun in the parentheses. Score one point for each correct answer.

Answers

1. Ms. Davis, editor of *The Quarterly,* (who, whom) is my aunt, spoke to our writing class.   1. _____

2. Everyone of the girls brought (her, their) story to read.   2. _____

3. (Who, Whom) will read the first story?   3. _____

4. The editor told Jody and (them, they) about the short story.   4. _____

5. Sonia received much help from the teacher and (he, him).   5. _____

6. He and (I, me) never realized that the short story was really developed in America.   6. _____

7. Plot, character, and setting are the three essentials of any short story (that, who) is well constructed.   7. _____

8. José and Jennie received a free copy of the magazine from me and (he, him).   8. _____

9. Our teacher read a story by Edgar Allan Poe to Ms. Davis and (we, us).   9. _____

10. Poe, (who, whom), we believe, started the detective story, was a fascinating writer.   10. _____

11. Many writers have tried to imitate Poe, but they are not quite as perfect as (he, him).   11. _____

12. The editor placed one of Poe's books between Tom and (she, her).   12. _____

13. Some of the early short stories are fascinating for (its, their) descriptive value.   13. _____

14. Washington Irving, one of the first writers in America, (who, whom) you mentioned, began the style of short story writing.   14. _____

15. (Who, Whom) will read their story aloud?   15. _____

16. (His, Him) checking out a book of short stories from the library helped.   16. _____

17. Please tell him and (we, us) something about Hawthorne, Mark Twain, and O. Henry.   17. _____

18. (Who, Whom) do I see for a new library card?   18. _____

19. William Faulkner, (who, whom), in my judgment, wrote good short stories, also won the Nobel Prize in literature.   19. _____

20. Many critics believe that Faulkner's novels were (his, their) best writings.   20. _____

21. To (who, whom) did he dedicate his book?   21. _____

22. Paula read the story to Jack and (he, him).   22. _____

Your Total Score _____

If your score was 16 or less, review pages 41-46 and 51-56 before continuing.

35: Practice Procedure. Complete each of the following sentences by writing in the blank provided at the right the correct pronoun in the parentheses. Score one point for each correct answer.

Answers

1. It was William Sidney Porter (who, whom) wrote under the pen name of O. Henry.

    1. _____

2. (Who, Whom) do you think was Mark Twain?

    2. _____

3. Samuel Clemens, (who, whom), I believe, you enjoy, wrote under the name of Mark Twain.

    3. _____

4. (Him, His) working as a river pilot gave him valuable experience.

    4. _____

5. A copy of *The Adventures of Tom Sawyer* was given to Glenn and (I, me) by my aunt.

    5. _____

6. Patty and (he, him) remember the movie about Huck Finn.

    6. _____

7. (What, Which) is the better character—Tom Sawyer or Huck Finn?

    7. _____

8. Anna, Maria, and (she, her) read two books a week.

    8. _____

9. This book will be discussed by him or by (whoever, whomever) you tell.

    9. _____

10. John Steinbeck and Saul Bellow also wrote (his, their) short stories before winning Nobel Prizes.

    10. _____

11. Sinclair Lewis, the famous novelist, was the first American (who, whom) won a Nobel Prize in literature.

    11. _____

12. The short stories of Kay Boyle and Scott Fitzgerald were read to Linda Zapata and (them, they).

    12. _____

13. Some of them handed (his, their) copies of Irwin Shaw to us.

    13. _____

14. Virginia, Sandra, and (he, him) worked two hours a day in the library.

    14. _____

15. The author (who, whom) you brought to class yesterday has written many novels.

    15. _____

16. With (who, whom) did you go to the bookstore?

    16. _____

17. One of the three boys lost (his, their) book yesterday.

    17. _____

18. He gave the address of the publisher to (whoever, whomever) asked for it.

    18. _____

19. There are few magazines today which publish short stories for (us, we) to enjoy.

    19. _____

20. Victor and Alberto are two of the best readers in (his, their) class.

    20. _____

21. Many of the librarians in town say that Hemingway's and Faulkner's short stories were (his, their) best writings.

    21. _____

22. She and (he, him) bought an old copy of the early short story writers' works.

    22. _____

If your score was 16 or less, review pages 41-46 and 51-56 before continuing. Your Total Score _____

36–A: Practice Procedure. Underline each noun and tell whether it is a proper, a common, or a collective noun. Place the abbreviation *P* for proper, *C* for common, or *Col* for collective above each noun. Score one point for each correct response.

Your Score

1. Art McNally is the supervisor of officials in the National Football League.

   1. _____

2. A committee of referees explained the rules of the game to the class.

   2. _____

3. Burl Toler, the first black official in professional football, told us about his experiences.

   3. _____

4. Our coaching staff listened to the coaches from the New York Giants.

   4. _____

5. Tom Flores, an expert in the business, showed the school some films of his games.

   5. _____

6. A panel of writers from the newspapers suggested ways to prepare the statistics.

   6. _____

7. The crew of officials wore their uniforms to show the group how they looked.

   7. _____

8. A crowd formed outside the field, and the police arrived to help the coaches and teachers.

   8. _____

9. Our faculty enjoyed the demonstration and also the music provided by the band.

   9. _____

10. The club that sponsors the cheerleaders and orchestra provided entertainment for the parents.

    10. _____

36–B: Practice Procedure. Complete each of the following sentences by writing in the blank provided at the right the correct pronoun(s) in the parentheses. Score one point for each correct response.

1. The publicity director of the Denver Broncos went with (him and me, he and I) to the stadium.

   1. _____

2. (Him, His) showing me a jersey illustrated the vivid colors of the uniforms.

   2. _____

3. Don Shula, of the Miami Dolphins, told the writer and (us, we) about the Super Bowl.

   3. _____

4. Nobody wanted to give up (his, their) tickets to the game.

   4. _____

5. (Me, My) getting a ticket from the trainer was an unexpected pleasure.

   5. _____

6. (They and I, Them and him) saw Miami beat Buffalo last year.

   6. _____

7. Sell the two tickets to (whoever, whomever) has $60.

   7. _____

8. Marcus Allen, (who, whom), in my opinion, is one of the best runners, scored three touchdowns last week.

   8. _____

9. Jim Tunney knows the commissioner to (who, whom) fans send their complaints.

   9. _____

10. Gale Sayers, one of the truly great runners of professional football, gave a football to (they and we, us and them).

    10. _____

If your score was 43 or less, review Units 2 and 3 before continuing. Your Total Score _____

37–A: Practice Procedure. Match the word or words in Column A with the identifying item in Column B. Place the most correct answer in the blank at the right. Score one point for each correct answer.

Column A	Column B	Answers
1. beach, sand	a. possessive form of noun	1. _____
2. either, anyone, many	b. personal pronouns	2. _____
3. this, that, these, those	c. relative pronouns	3. _____
4. children, teeth	d. possessive pronouns	4. _____
5. child's	e. common nouns	5. _____
6. my, his, our	f. proper nouns	6. _____
7. who, whom	g. plural nouns	7. _____
8. I, she, we	h. indefinite pronouns	8. _____
9. Ronald Reagan, Martin Luther King	i. collective nouns	9. _____
10. crowd, audience, jury	j. demonstrative pronouns	10. _____

37–B: Practice Procedure. In the blank provided at the right, place the letter that best identifies the *synonym* (same meaning) as the italicized word. Use your dictionary to verify your answers. Score one point for each correct answer.

1. *obscene* picture	(a) modern (b) troubled (c) vulgar (d) fearful	1. _____
2. *insolent* stranger	(a) courteous (b) interesting (c) unreal (d) rude	2. _____
3. *intrepid* hunter	(a) involved (b) fearless (c) timid (d) stubborn	3. _____
4. *frugal* person	(a) thrifty (b) wasteful (c) lively (d) humorous	4. _____
5. *morbid* story	(a) gloomy (b) optimistic (c) dull (d) entertaining	5. _____
6. *humid* day	(a) muggy (b) cold (c) gloomy (d) injured	6. _____
7. *raucous* laughter	(a) mellow (b) sensible (c) harsh (d) affected	7. _____
8. *ominous* sign	(a) encouraging (b) natural (c) threatening (d) unyielding	8. _____
9. *hostile* clerk	(a) hopeless (b) unfriendly (c) peaceful (d) sympathetic	9. _____
10. *obsolete* toy	(a) ordinary (b) outdated (c) colorful (d) expensive	10. _____
11. *valid* reason	(a) false (b) ridiculous (c) simple (d) cogent	11. _____
12. *hazardous* condition	(a) safe (b) smoggy (c) dangerous (d) disgusting	12. _____
13. *precarious* position	(a) uncertain (b) dependable (c) definite (d) previous	13. _____
14. *dismal* attitude	(a) cheerful (b) excitable (c) gloomy (d) concerned	14. _____
15. *fictitious* story	(a) genuine (b) brutal (c) exact (d) false	15. _____

Your Total Score _____

38–A: Practice Procedure. Select the correct *antonym* (word which means the opposite) from each group of words to match the italicized word. Write your answer in the blank provided at the right. Use your dictionary to verify your answers. Score one point for each correct answer.

Answers

1. *stately* house   (a) impressive (b) humble (c) tidy (d) unclean   1. _____

2. *ambiguous* remark   (a) clever (b) rude (c) clear (d) vague   2. _____

3. *ingenious* scheme   (a) stupid (b) clever (c) shrewd (d) appealing   3. _____

4. *facetious* tone   (a) solemn (b) humorous (c) unfair (d) eloquent   4. _____

5. *odious* smell   (a) familiar (b) unique (c) foul (d) pleasant   5. _____

6. *inflexible* attitude   (a) firm (b) yielding (c) fast (d) amusing   6. _____

7. *malicious* person   (a) mature (b) kindhearted (c) foolish (d) vicious 7. _____

8. *discreet* question   (a) careful (b) ruffled (c) rash (d) sensitive   8. _____

9. *obscure* town   (a) hidden (b) obvious (c) old-fashioned (d) dirty 9. _____

10. *extravagant* clothes (a) expensive (b) unique (c) stylish
                           (d) economical   10. _____

11. *audacious* fighter   (a) brave (b) stupid (c) hopeful (d) careful   11. _____

12. *turbulent* waters   (a) calm (b) stirred up (c) difficult (d) trusting 12. _____

13. *surly* guard   (a) rude (b) pleasant (c) suspicious
                           (d) understanding   13. _____

14. *vivacious* child   (a) vital (b) lively (c) listless (d) vocal   14. _____

15. *ludicrous* story   (a) ridiculous (b) sensible (c) tragic (d) short 15. _____

Your Total Score _____

38–B: Practice Procedure. The 40 words below are frequently misspelled. Study them carefully and be prepared to write them from memory.

across	democracy	journal	parcel
advice	different	lawyer	picnic
advisable	doctor	lead	practice
advise	enemy	led	remember
around	error	lonely	reply
article	fault	medicine	similar
bandage	figure	mountain	stitch
beauty	finally	nickel	stopped
capital	handle	off	surely
capitol	instance	owned	surprise

Section 13 — Uses of Verbs

Unit 4

Verbs

OBJECTIVES:
1. To recognize and use verbs correctly when making a statement, asking a question, or giving a command.
2. To identify principal helping verbs and linking verbs.
3. To use verbs so that they agree with the subject of a sentence.

A *verb* tells what the subject does or is, or what happens to it. Verbs can make a statement, ask a question, or give a command.

The verb is one of the two required words in every sentence. The other required word is the subject. All sentences must have a subject and a verb. When you use verbs properly, your speech will be improved, your writing skills good, and your sentences correct. The proper use of verbs requires great care. Watch your use of verbs, and you will be amazed at how much more your sentences will communicate.

13-A. VERBS MAKE STATEMENTS

EXAMPLE 1

Lucy <u>uses</u> a word processor.

Analysis:
   <u>uses</u>—a verb. It tells what the subject *Lucy* does. It makes a statement.

EXAMPLE 2

Mr. Sato <u>bought</u> a computer for the office.

Analysis:
   <u>bought</u>—a verb. It tells what the subject *Mr. Sato* did. It makes a statement.

13-B. VERBS ASK QUESTIONS

EXAMPLE 1

Who <u>understands</u> computers?

Analysis:
   <u>understands</u>—a verb. It asks a question of the subject *Who.*

EXAMPLE 2

<u>Is</u> the computer large?

Analysis:
   <u>Is</u>—a verb. It asks a question about the subject *computer.*

13-C. VERBS GIVE COMMANDS

EXAMPLE 1

<u>Check</u> the power on the machine.

Analysis:
   <u>Check</u>—a verb. It gives a command to the subject *you* (understood).

EXAMPLE 2

<u>Put</u> the letter on the word processor.

Analysis:
   <u>Put</u>—a verb. It gives a command to the subject *you* (understood).

Helping Verbs and Linking Verbs

Section 14

14-A. USES OF HELPING VERBS

Helping verbs are well named because they help the main verbs tell what the subjects are doing by asking a question, giving a command, or making a statement. (Helping verbs are also known as *auxiliary verbs*.) Remember them as words which help connect the subject and the main verb. *Principal helping verbs* include *is, be, am, are, was, were, have, has, had, may, must, ought, can, might, could, would, should, shall, will, do, does,* and *did*.

EXAMPLE 1

Computers <u>are</u> used in many businesses.

"GET YOUR HELPING VERBS HERE!"

Analysis:

  <u>are</u>—helping verb. It helps the main verb *used* tell about the subject *Computers*.

EXAMPLE 2

Much research in medicine <u>is</u> done by computers.

Analysis:

  <u>is</u>—helping verb. It helps the main verb *done* tell about the subject *research*.

EXAMPLE 3

Computers <u>can</u> draw pictures.

Analysis:

  <u>can</u>—helping verb. It helps the main verb *draw* tell about the subject *Computers*.

EXAMPLE 4

Optical character readers <u>will</u> print prices and descriptions of grocery items on a cash register tape.

Analysis:

  <u>will</u>—helping verb. It helps the main verb *print* tell about the subject *readers*.

EXAMPLE 5

Bus riders <u>may</u> purchase tickets from a computer vending machine.

Analysis:

  <u>may</u>—helping verb. It helps the main verb *purchase* tell about the subject *riders*.

EXAMPLE 6

Computers <u>did</u> track the launching of even the first space vehicles.

Analysis:

  <u>did</u>—helping verb. It helps the main verb *track* tell about the subject *Computers*.

Often the helping verb is separated from the main verb by a *modifier* (a word used to describe another word). You can find the main verb because it still tells what the subject is doing or what is being done to the subject.

EXAMPLE 1

Computer technology is often used in education.

Analysis:
is often used—verb separation. Helping verb *is* and main verb *used* are separated by modifier *often*.

EXAMPLE 2

Electronic devices have definitely changed the appearance of today's office.

Analysis:
have definitely changed— verb separation.

Helping verb *have* and main verb *changed* are separated by modifier *definitely*.

EXAMPLE 3

How have computers improved inventory records in supermarkets?

Analysis:
have computers improved—verb separation. Helping verb *have* and the main verb *improved* are separated by modifier *computers*.

EXAMPLE 4

Criminals are frequently identified through a computer fingerprint search.

Analysis:
are frequently identified—verb separation. Helping verb *are* and the main verb *identified* are separated by the modifier *frequently*.

TRYOUT EXERCISE

Directions: Identify the helping verbs in the following sentences by underlining them once. Identify the main verbs by underlining them twice. In the blank provided at the right, write S if the verb makes a statement, Q if it asks a question, or C if it gives a command. Check your answers with your teacher before continuing with your assignment.

1. The main computer switch is easily located.   1. _____
2. Will a computer keep a jet plane on course?   2. _____
3. The computer tour will start at noon.   3. _____
4. Computer equipment can monitor a car's operation.   4. _____
5. In education, computers do help students learn.   5. _____
6. How are computers used to sell bus tickets?   6. _____
7. Should computers take jobs away from people?   7. _____
8. A word processor could improve office productivity.   8. _____
9. You will lead the next computer room tour.   9. _____
10. Robots were utilized to assemble products in factories.   10. _____

Complete Application Practices 39-40, pages 71-72, at this time.

14-C. USE OF LINKING VERBS WITH PREDICATE NOUNS, PRONOUNS, AND ADJECTIVES

When a form of the verb *be (be, am is, are, was, were, have been, has been, had been, shall be, will be)* is used alone, the word used to complete the meaning of the verb is called a *predicate noun,* a *predicate pronoun,* or a *predicate adjective.* These forms of the verb *be* are called *linking verbs.*

The predicate noun or pronoun is in the nominative case, as it refers to and describes the subject of the sentence. Other linking verbs which take predicate adjectives or predicate nouns or pronouns in the nominative case are *become, seem, appear, taste, smell, feel, sound,* and *look.* (See page 42 for a review of the nominative case and linking verbs.)

Predicate Nouns

EXAMPLE 1

The computer has been an important business machine.

Analysis:
machine—a noun. It completes the meaning of the verb *has been.* It is a predicate noun because it refers to the subject *computer.*

EXAMPLE 2

A typewriter is a data processing tool.

Analysis:
tool—a noun. It completes the meaning of the verb *is.* It is a predicate noun because it refers to the subject *typewriter.*

Predicate Pronouns

EXAMPLE 1

It was he.

Analysis:
he—a pronoun. It completes the meaning of the verb *was.* It is a predicate pronoun because it refers to the subject *It.*

EXAMPLE 2

The best programmer is she.

Analysis:
she—a pronoun. It completes the meaning of the verb *is.* It is a predicate pronoun because it refers to the subject *programmer.*

Predicate Adjectives

EXAMPLE 1

Early computers were huge.

Analysis:
huge—an adjective. It completes the meaning of the verb *were.* It is a predicate adjective because it describes the subject *computers.*

EXAMPLE 2

Computer printouts will be complicated.

Analysis:
complicated—an adjective. It completes the meaning of the verb *will be.* It is a predicate adjective because it describes the subject *printouts.*

TRYOUT EXERCISE	**Directions:** Identify the predicate noun, predicate pronoun, or predicate adjective in each of the following sentences by underlining them once. In the space provided, tell whether it is a predicate noun (N), a pronoun (P), or an adjective (A). Check your answers with your teacher before continuing with your assignment.

1. The computer room seemed cold.   1. _____

2. The operator of the personal computer was she.   2. _____

3. Robots are computer-controlled machines.   3. _____

Complete Application Practices 41-42, pages 73-74, at this time.

39-A: Practice Procedure. Identify the verbs in the following sentences by underlining them once. In the answer column at the right, write an S if the verb makes a statement, Q if it asks a question, or C if it gives a command. Score one point for each correct verb and one point for each correct sentence type identified.

Answers

1. Baseball started in the United States.   1. _____

2. Who wrote the first baseball rules?   2. _____

3. Fred Thayer invented the catcher's mask.   3. _____

4. Which teams played in the first World Series?   4. _____

5. Read the book about baseball history.   5. _____

6. The first Polo Grounds opened on July 8, 1889.   6. _____

7. Who hit 60 home runs in 1927?   7. _____

8. Look at that ball go!   8. _____

9. The American League won the first All-Star Game.   9. _____

10. Search the record book for baseball firsts.   10. _____

39-B: Practice Procedure. Follow the procedure given for 39-A.

1. Who appointed the first baseball commissioner?   1. _____

2. When was "Happy" Chandler the commissioner?   2. _____

3. Jackie Robinson became the first black in major league baseball.   3. _____

4. The Dodgers moved to Los Angeles in 1958.   4. _____

5. Play ball!   5. _____

6. The National League expanded to 12 teams in 1968.   6. _____

7. Record the wins and losses in columns for the official record book.   7. _____

8. Mickey Mantle retired in 1969.   8. _____

9. What pitcher broke Walter Johnson's record in 1968?   9. _____

10. Name the winner of the 1980 World Series.   10. _____

Your Total Score _____

If your score was 31 or less for 39-A and B, review Section 13, page 67, before continuing.

39-C: Practice Procedure. Demonstrate your understanding of verbs by writing five sentences on a separate sheet of paper. Underline the verb in each sentence once. Score one point for each correct sentence and one point for each correctly identified verb.

Your Total Score _____

40–A: Practice Procedure. Identify the helping verbs in the following sentences by underlining them once. Identify the main verbs by underlining them twice. Score one point for each correct helping verb and one point for each correct main verb.

Your Score

1. Sometimes jobs are taken for experience.   1. _____

2. Pat should find a career in space technology very exciting.   2. _____

3. When will you decide about a career?   3. _____

4. The interview was interrupted by the telephone.   4. _____

5. James is interested in film work.   5. _____

6. Martha and Steve were interviewed together.   6. _____

7. The job might open for new applicants soon.   7. _____

8. The salary could always help our finances.   8. _____

9. Her mother has greatly influenced her career decision.   9. _____

10. The students were eventually hired by the store.   10. _____

40–B: Practice Procedure. Follow the procedure given for 40–A.

1. Starting as a salesperson has sometimes improved a person's promotion chances.   1. _____

2. A salesperson should satisfy a customer's needs.   2. _____

3. Sales slips often are lost by customers.   3. _____

4. Did the customer ever explain the problems?   4. _____

5. Ron was considered for a promotion.   5. _____

6. He must prove himself to be selected.   6. _____

7. Customers are impressed by a salesperson's courtesy.   7. _____

8. Harry was assigned to the housewares department.   8. _____

9. New employee benefits were approved by the company.   9. _____

10. Tina can work after school and Saturdays.   10. _____

Your Total Score _____

If your score was 31 or less for 40–A and B, review Section 14–A and B, page 68-69, before continuing.

40–C: Practice Procedure. Demonstrate your understanding of helping verbs by writing five sentences on a separate sheet of paper. Underline helping verbs once and main verbs twice. Score one point for each correct sentence, one point for each correctly identified helping verb, and one point for each correctly identified main verb.

Your Total Score _____

41-A: Practice Procedure. Identify the predicate nouns, predicate pronouns, or predicate adjectives in the following sentences by underlining each once. In the answer column, tell whether it is a predicate noun (N), pronoun (P), or adjective (A). Score one point for each correct word and one point for each correct identification.

Answers

1. Lillian Leitzel was a famous aerialist in the American circus.   1. _____

2. It was she who held audiences spellbound.   2. _____

3. At one time, the Wallendas were the best aerialists.   3. _____

4. Their aerial act often seemed dangerous.   4. _____

5. Joey was a world-famous clown.   5. _____

6. The line of circus customers appeared long.   6. _____

7. "Buffalo Bill" became a circus performer.   7. _____

8. The best horseman in his show was he.   8. _____

9. The circus operated by Ringling Brothers was huge.   9. _____

10. The wild animal trainers are brave.   10. _____

41-B: Practice Procedure. Identify the predicate nouns, predicate pronouns, and predicate adjectives in the following paragraph by underlining them once. In the space provided, write the word you have underlined and indicate whether it is a predicate noun (N), pronoun (P), or adjective (A). Score one point for every correct word and one point for each correct identification.

The circus is a wonderland to the spectator with imagination. All the world becomes a tipsy carousel, and the lights and music are tempting lures to those outside the Big Top. The cotton candy smells warm and sweet, the lemonade and cola drinks taste refreshingly cool, and hot dogs are a delightful treat. Circus magic is apparent everywhere, as elephants become dancers, monkeys become bareback riders, and performers in sparkling costumes appear suspended in the air. Tales of dancers and freaks sound enchanting to the stranger in this paradise of fantasy. The happiest onlooker is one who can believe that magic and sorcery are real and present in this starry world of glitter.

_____   _____   _____   _____

_____   _____   _____   _____

_____   _____   _____   _____

_____   _____   _____

Your Total Score _____

If your score was 39 or less for 41-A and B, review Section 14-C, page 70, before continuing.

42-A: **Practice Procedure.** Identify the linking verbs by underlining them once. Identify the predicate nouns, predicate pronouns, and predicate adjectives by underlining them twice. In the answer column, write S if the verb makes a statement, Q if it asks a question, or C if it gives a command. Score one point for each underlined verb and one point for each predicate noun, pronoun, or adjective. Score one point for each sentence type identified correctly.

Answers

1. The personnel office was one large room.   1. _____
2. The available position sounded interesting.   2. _____
3. The interviewers were they.   3. _____
4. Eileen had been an interviewer, too.   4. _____
5. Does the salary appear satisfactory?   5. _____
6. The best candidate was she.   6. _____
7. Is Henry the new applicant?   7. _____
8. The final applicant will be she.   8. _____
9. The test was easy.   9. _____
10. The company's offer seemed fair.   10. _____

42-B: **Practice Procedure.** Follow the procedure given for 42-A.

1. The oranges tasted good.   1. _____
2. Is Barry a grocery checker?   2. _____
3. You will be the checker today!   3. _____
4. The employees are we.   4. _____
5. The gourmet section of the store seems small.   5. _____
6. The fruit looked delicious.   6. _____
7. The new product from China looked exotic.   7. _____
8. The next customers will be they.   8. _____
9. Is the contest prize a car?   9. _____
10. The bakery counter was long.   10. _____
11. The baked goods smelled delicious.   11. _____
12. She became the owner of the store.   12. _____
13. The new bakery will be huge.   13. _____
14. Are you a customer?   14. _____
15. The last customers were we.   15. _____

Your Total Score _____

If your score was 59 or less, review Section 13 and 14-C, pages 67 and 70, before continuing.

Verb Agreement with Subject

A verb should agree with its subject in person and number. A *singular* (one) *subject* takes a singular form of a verb. A *plural* (more than one) *subject* takes the plural form of a verb. An exception is the pronoun *you* which takes the plural form of the verb in both singular and plural.

EXAMPLE 1

Isabel <u>is</u> from Spain.

Analysis:

<u>is</u>—singular form of the verb agrees with the singular subject *Isabel.* A singular subject takes a singular verb.

EXAMPLE 2

She <u>was</u> a child when she arrived in New York.

Analysis:

<u>was</u>—singular form of the verb agrees with the singular subject *She.* A singular subject takes a singular verb.

EXAMPLE 3

They <u>are</u> from Madrid, Spain.

Analysis:

<u>are</u>—plural form of the verb agrees with the plural subject *They.* A plural subject takes a plural verb.

EXAMPLE 4

You <u>are</u> a native-born New Yorker.

Analysis:

<u>are</u>—plural form of the verb. The subject *You* always takes the plural form of the verb.

15-A. FORMS OF THE VERB *BE*

Am, is, and *was* are the singular forms of the verb *be* and require singular subjects. *Are* and *were* are the plural forms and require plural subjects. Study the verb forms of *be* so they will become a strong part of your speech. These verb forms are so common that by learning them thoroughly, your language skills will be greatly improved.

AGREEMENT OF SUBJECT AND VERB

EXAMPLE 1

I <u>was</u> a visitor to the United Nations.

Analysis:

<u>was</u>—singular form of the verb agrees in number with the singular subject *I*

EXAMPLE 2

She <u>is</u> a security guard at the United Nations Building.

Analysis:

<u>is</u>—singular form of the verb agrees in number with the singular subject *She*

EXAMPLE 3

I <u>am</u> interested in a diplomatic career.

Analysis:

<u>am</u>—singular form of the verb agrees in number with the singular subject *I*

EXAMPLE 4

He <u>was</u> a graduate of Howard University.

Analysis:

<u>was</u>—singular form of the verb agrees in number with the singular subject *He*

EXAMPLE 5

Those members of the committee <u>were</u> noisy.

Analysis:

<u>were</u>—plural form of the verb agrees in number with the plural subject *members*

EXAMPLE 6

Maureen <u>is</u> an aide to the committee.

Analysis:

<u>is</u>—singular form of the verb agrees in number with the singular subject *Maureen*

EXAMPLE 7

They <u>were</u> friends of Maureen's father.

Analysis:

<u>were</u>—plural form of the verb agrees in number with the plural subject *They*

EXAMPLE 8

We <u>were</u> in school with Isabel and Maureen.

Analysis:

<u>were</u>—plural form of the verb agrees in number with the plural subject *We*

EXAMPLE 9

Many people <u>were</u> visitors to the United Nations last year.

Analysis:

<u>were</u>—plural form of the verb agrees in number with the plural subject *people*

EXAMPLE 10

Guides <u>are</u> available to help visitors.

Analysis:

<u>are</u>—plural form of the verb agrees in number with the plural subject *Guides*

EXAMPLE 11

Most visitors <u>are</u> well behaved.

Analysis:

<u>are</u>—plural form of the verb agrees in number with the plural subject *visitors*

Contrary-to-Fact Conditions

When stating a *condition contrary to fact,* use *were* with all subjects, singular or plural. Such a condition does not presently exist, but the speaker plans it or wishes it to be true.

EXAMPLE 1

She wishes that she <u>were</u> a delegate to the United Nations.

Analysis:

<u>were</u>—plural form of the verb is used with a singular subject when stating a condition contrary to fact

EXAMPLE 2

She acts as if she <u>were</u> a delegate.

Analysis:

<u>were</u>—plural form of the verb used with a singular subject when stating a condition contrary to fact

EXAMPLE 3

If they <u>were</u> delegates, it would be a sad day.

Analysis:

<u>were</u>—plural form of the verb used with a plural subject when stating a condition contrary to fact

15-B. FORMS OF THE VERB *HAVE*

The second most used verb is *have*. To express something which is happening at the present time, use *have* with all singular and plural subjects. The exception is third person singular nouns and pronouns (he, she, it). Third person singular requires the use of *has*.

To express something which happened in the past, use *had* with all subjects, both singular and plural.

EXAMPLE 1

Cable cars <u>have</u> a place in San Francisco's history.

Analysis:
> have—plural verb agrees with the plural subject *Cable cars*

EXAMPLE 2

Each car <u>has</u> a conductor and a person operating the brake.

Analysis:
> has—singular verb agrees with the singular subject *car*

EXAMPLE 3

She <u>has</u> a ticket to ride the cable car.

Analysis:
> has—singular verb agrees with the subject *She*—third person singular

EXAMPLE 4

We <u>have</u> a date to ride the cars tonight.

Analysis:
> have—plural verb agrees with the plural subject *We*

EXAMPLE 5

He <u>had</u> his tickets stolen from his pocket.

Analysis:
> had—verb expressing past time agrees with the singular subject *He*

EXAMPLE 6

They <u>had</u> their tickets stolen also.

Analysis:
> had—verb expressing past time agrees with the plural subject *They*

EXAMPLE 7

She <u>had</u> a great time riding the cable car.

Analysis:
> had—verb expressing past time agrees with the singular subject *She*

15-C. PLURAL FORM WITH COMPOUND SUBJECTS

Compound subjects (more than one subject) take the plural form of the verb.

EXAMPLE 1

Gary and Debbie, a brother and sister, <u>are</u> on the same team.

Analysis:
> are—plural verb agrees with the compound subject *Gary and Debbie*

EXAMPLE 2

The Americans, British, and Australians <u>were</u> on separate teams.

Analysis:
> were—plural verb agrees with the compound subject *Americans, British, and Australians*

15-D. SINGULAR SUBJECTS AND PLURAL MODIFIERS

Sometimes the singular subject is separated from the verb by a *plural modifier,* which is often a phrase. (Remember that modifiers are words which describe.) Look for the subject and make the verb agree with it. Do not make the mistake of making the verb agree with the modifier.

EXAMPLE 1

Raquel, as well as Luisa, <u>is</u> Mexican-American.

Analysis:

is—singular verb agrees with the singular subject *Raquel*

EXAMPLE 2

The barrio, with its many inhabitants, <u>was</u> her home.

Analysis:

was—singular verb agrees with the singular subject *barrio*

EXAMPLE 3

East Los Angeles, which is part of Greater Los Angeles, <u>is</u> largely Mexican-American.

Analysis:

is—singular verb agrees with the singular subject *East Los Angeles*

TRYOUT EXERCISE

Directions: Complete each of the following sentences by writing in the blank provided at the right the correct form of the verb in the parentheses. Check your answers with your teacher before continuing your assignment.

1. He (is, are) a friend of Alan.   1. _____
2. The women (was, were) making bread.   2. _____
3. If he (was, were) the singer, you would know it.   3. _____
4. Olivia (has, have) a party every year.   4. _____
5. Jerry, instead of Mark, (was, were) elected.   5. _____

Complete Application Practices 43-44, pages 79-80, at this time.

43-A: Practice Procedure. Complete each of the following sentences by writing in the blank provided at the right the correct form of the verb in the parentheses. Make the verb agree in person and in number with the subject. Score one point for every correct verb.

Answers

1. Log houses (is, are) still seen in rural communities.   1. _____

2. They (is, are) part of America's past.   2. _____

3. Many old log buildings (was, were) covered with new exteriors.   3. _____

4. Historians (is, are) interested in finding old log houses.   4. _____

5. To build a log house, neighbors (was, were) divided into teams.   5. _____

6. Each person (was, were) given a particular job.   6. _____

7. The family (was, were) able to move into the house at the end of the day.   7. _____

8. Log cabins (is, are) different from log houses.   8. _____

9. Log cabins (was, were) built from whole tree trunks.   9. _____

10. Log houses (was, were) fitted with glass window panes.   10. _____

43-B: Practice Procedure. Follow the procedure given for 43-A.

1. The one tool owned by most pioneers (was, were) the adz.   1. _____

2. The space between logs (was, were) filled with chinking.   2. _____

3. Inside walls (was, were) whitewashed or plastered.   3. _____

4. Log houses in Kentucky (was, were) usually 1½ stories high.   4. _____

5. A single log house (was, were) known as a pen.   5. _____

6. Sometimes, two pens (was, were) connected by a roofed passageway.   6. _____

7. The roofed passageway of the two pens (was, were) known as a dogtrot.   7. _____

8. The dogtrot (was, were) shelter for the family animals.   8. _____

9. Family sleeping quarters (was, were) in the upper half story.   9. _____

10. In today's log houses, the foxtrot (is, are) a foyer.   10. _____

11. Poplar (was, were) the favorite wood for a log house.   11. _____

12. In the early days, nails (was, were) not used to build a house.   12. _____

13. In place of nails, logs (was, were) notched to stay together.   13. _____

14. As a family prospered, improvements on a house (was, were) made.   14. _____

15. Today, raw logs on a house exterior (is, are) fashionable.   15. _____

Your Total Score _____

If your score was 19 or less for 43-A and B, review pages 75-77 before continuing.

44-A: Practice Procedure. Complete each of the following sentences by writing in the blank provided at the right the correct form of the verb in the parentheses. Make the verb agree in number with the subject. Score one point for every correct verb.

Answers

1. The Mayflower (is, are) a ship which brought English settlers to North America.

   1. _____

2. Religious problems (was, were) experienced by some people.

   2. _____

3. Puritans (was, were) one such group who came to the colonies.

   3. _____

4. Other groups (has, had) other reasons for coming.

   4. _____

5. The time when the 13 colonies belonged to Britain (is, are) known as the Colonial Period.

   5. _____

6. Groups other than the English (is, are) part of our nation's past, too.

   6. _____

7. The Scotch-Irish, Germans, French, and Dutch (is, are) some who also came to the colonies.

   7. _____

8. On the west coast, the Spanish and Mexicans (was, were) early settlers.

   8. _____

9. The English colonies (was, were) given some self-government.

   9. _____

10. Three types of colonies (is, are) known to have existed.

   10. _____

44-B: Practice Procedure. Follow the procedure given for 44-A.

1. Virginia, Georgia, and New York (was, were) royal colonies.

   1. _____

2. Connecticut and Rhode Island (is, are) the only ones that were self-governing.

   2. _____

3. Patriotism (was, were) important in each colony.

   3. _____

4. Cooperation among the colonies (was, were) rare.

   4. _____

5. The English colonies (was, were) known to have united against the Indians, French, and Dutch.

   5. _____

6. The New England Confederation of 1643 (is, are) an example of that cooperation.

   6. _____

7. The Albany Congress of 1754 (is, are) another example.

   7. _____

8. Benjamin Franklin, not William Penn, (is, are) the author of the Albany Plan of Union.

   8. _____

9. Franklin's plan (was, were) rejected by the colonies and the British.

   9. _____

10. Frontier farmers (was, were) opposed to the colonial legislatures as well as the British.

   10. _____

Your Total Score _____

If your score was 15 or below for 44-A and B, review pages 75-78 before continuing.

44-C: Practice Procedure. On a separate sheet of paper, demonstrate your understanding of verb and subject agreement in five well-written sentences. Score one point for each correct sentence.

Your Total Score _____

15-E. VERB AGREEMENT WITH INDEFINITE PRONOUNS

Whenever you use an indefinite pronoun as the subject of a sentence, the verb must agree in number with the subject. The following indefinite pronouns are used with a singular verb: (Refer to pages 45-46 for a review of indefinite pronouns.)

another	either	nobody
anybody	everybody	one
anyone	everyone	somebody
each	neither	someone

EXAMPLE 1

Each of the scientists <u>is</u> outstanding.

Analysis:
> <u>is</u>—singular verb agrees in number with the singular subject *Each*

EXAMPLE 2

Everyone <u>was</u> interested in his report.

Analysis:
> <u>was</u>—singular verb agrees in number with the singular subject *Everyone*

EACH, NEITHER, EITHER, ANYBODY

FEW, MANY, OTHERS, SEVERAL

INDEFINITE PRONOUNS

The following indefinite pronouns are used with a plural verb:

both	many	several
few	others	

EXAMPLE 1

Several of the scientists <u>are</u> Nobel Prize winners.

Analysis:
> <u>are</u>—plural verb agrees in number with the plural subject *Several*

EXAMPLE 2

Both of the visitors <u>were</u> from Italy.

Analysis:
> <u>were</u>—plural verb agrees in number with the plural subject *Both*

The following indefinite pronouns may be used with either a singular or a plural verb:

all	most	some
any	none	

When indicating *how much,* use a singular verb. When indicating *how many,* use a plural verb.

EXAMPLE 1

Some of the test <u>was</u> easy.

Analysis:
> <u>was</u>—singular verb indicates *how much*

EXAMPLE 2

All of the experiments <u>were</u> successful.

Analysis:
> <u>were</u>—plural verb indicates *how many*

15-F. VERB AGREEMENT WITH *THERE*

There is an *expletive* (meaning to fill out) which introduces a sentence. The verb agrees with the subject which follows the verb when *there* is used to start the sentence. Ignore the word *there* when looking for the subject. It is never used as the subject of a sentence.

EXAMPLE 1

There <u>is</u> a new play in town.

Analysis:
  is—singular verb agrees in number with the singular subject *play*

EXAMPLE 2

There <u>are</u> seats available for the play tonight.

Analysis:
  are—plural verb agrees in number with the plural subject *seats*

EXAMPLE 3

There <u>is</u> a price of $20 for orchestra seats.

Analysis:
  is—singular verb agrees in number with the singular subject *price*

EXAMPLE 4

There <u>are</u> good reviews for the play.

Analysis:
  are—plural verb agrees in number with the plural subject *reviews*

15-G. VERB AGREEMENT WITH *OR*

Singular Use of Verb with *Or*

Or, when used to combine two or more subjects, takes a singular verb if the subject nearest the verb is singular.

EXAMPLE 1

My brothers or my sister <u>is</u> available to help.

Analysis:
  is—singular verb agrees in number with the nearest subject *sister* which is singular

EXAMPLE 2

The elephant, the clowns, or the high-wire aerialist <u>was</u> to be introduced next.

Analysis:
  was—singular verb agrees in number with the nearest subject *aerialist* which is singular

Plural Use of Verb with *Or*

Or, when used to combine two or more subjects, takes a plural verb if the subject nearest the verb is plural.

EXAMPLE 1

The accident victim or the automobile drivers <u>are</u> to be questioned by the police first.

Analysis:
  are—plural verb agrees in number with the nearest subject *drivers* which is plural

EXAMPLE 2

His father or her parents <u>are</u> arriving at the accident scene in that blue car.

Analysis:
  are—plural verb agrees in number with the nearest subject *parents* which is plural

A *collective noun* that refers to a group acting as a whole requires a singular verb. A collective noun that refers to a group in which the members act individually requires a plural verb. In most sentences, the collective noun is a unit requiring a singular verb. (See pages 26-27 for a review of collective nouns.)

EXAMPLE 1

That group of books <u>was</u> on sale.

Analysis:
> was—singular verb. The collective noun *group* is thought of as one.

EXAMPLE 2

The orchestra <u>is</u> playing here tonight.

Analysis:
> is—singular verb. The collective noun *orchestra* is thought of as one.

EXAMPLE 3

The class <u>is</u> having its dance Friday night.

Analysis:
> is—singular verb. The collective noun *class* is thought of as one.

EXAMPLE 4

The committee <u>was</u> meeting at the school.

Analysis:
> was—singular verb. The collective noun *committee* is thought of as one.

EXAMPLE 5

The team <u>is</u> in the locker room.

Analysis:
> is—singular verb. The collective noun *team* is thought of as one.

EXAMPLE 6

The team <u>were</u> putting on their uniforms.

Analysis:
> were—plural verb. The collective noun *team* is thought of as individuals acting independently of the group.

EXAMPLE 7

The jury <u>is</u> making its decision.

Analysis:
> is—singular verb. The collective noun *jury* is thought of as one.

EXAMPLE 8

The trio <u>was</u> singing a popular song.

Analysis:
> was—singular verb. The collective noun *trio* is thought of as one.

EXAMPLE 9

The gas company <u>is</u> raising its rates.

Analysis:
> is—singular verb. The collective noun *company* is thought of as one.

EXAMPLE 10

The police <u>are</u> surrounding the building in which the suspect lives.

Analysis:
> are—plural verb. The collective noun *police* is thought of as individuals acting independently of the group.

TRYOUT EXERCISE

Directions: Complete each of the following sentences by writing in the blank provided at the right the correct form of the verb in the parentheses. Check your answers with your teacher before continuing with your assignment.

1. The orchestra (was, were) hired to play Sunday.   1. _____
2. The jury (was, were) polled by the judge.   2. _____
3. Everyone (is, are) at the concert.   3. _____
4. There (is, are) four persons seeking that job.   4. _____
5. The roses or the orchid (was, were) the same price.   5. _____
6. The cat or the dogs (is, are) always hungry.   6. _____
7. Neither (was, were) a good athlete.   7. _____
8. Many of the students (is, are) from out of town.   8. _____
9. The group (has, have) changed their minds.   9. _____
10. The committee (is, are) having its meeting now.   10. _____

Complete Application Practices 45-48, pages 85-88, at this time.

45-A: **Practice Procedure.** Complete each of the following sentences by writing in the blank provided at the right the correct word in the parentheses. Score one point for each correct answer.

Answers

1. Television (is, are) a favorite of most Americans.   1. _____

2. Everyone (is, are) eagerly awaiting the new TV show.   2. _____

3. Many TV stars (has, have) huge fan clubs.   3. _____

4. Some performers (has, have) become overnight hits.   4. _____

5. Both (is, are) well paid as writers.   5. _____

6. Commercial sponsors (is, are) important to the TV industry.   6. _____

7. Some of the variety shows (was, were) big hits.   7. _____

8. They (is, are) still favorites with millions of people.   8. _____

9. TV satellites (has, have) made world-wide TV reception possible.   9. _____

10. There (is, are) weather reports in most TV news shows.   10. _____

45-B: **Practice Procedure.** Follow the procedure given for 45-A.

1. As a nation, (we, us) are attracted to TV.   1. _____

2. TV performers (is, are) paid high salaries.   2. _____

3. The TV industry (is, are) international in scope.   3. _____

4. The performers or the director (is, are) responsible for the poor show.   4. _____

5. (Who, Whom) among the female performers is the best tennis player?   5. _____

6. Each viewer (is, are) important to a show's ratings.   6. _____

7. Neither of the two new TV dramas (was, were) good.   7. _____

8. (He, She) and her co-star are married.   8. _____

9. The Hitchcock movie festival (has, have) begun.   9. _____

10. The Public Broadcasting System (is, are) enjoyed by many.   10. _____

11. Soap operas (has, have) faithful followers.   11. _____

12. TV specials are enjoyed by (we, us).   12. _____

13. Television (had, has) a large viewing audience last winter.   13. _____

14. (Is, Are) there commercials on PBS?   14. _____

15. Too much TV watching is bad for (they, them).   15. _____

Your Total Score _____

If your score was 19 or less for 45-A and B, review Section 15, pages 75-78, before continuing.

46–A: Practice Procedure. Complete each of the following sentences by writing in the blank provided at the right the correct word in the parentheses. Score one point for each correct answer.

Answers

1. A cruise in Alaskan waters (is, are) an enjoyable experience. 1. _____
2. Each passenger on the ship has (her, their) reason for going on the trip. 2. _____
3. For some passengers, the food on the ship (was, were) the attraction. 3. _____
4. For others, the Alaskan scenery (is, are) the reason. 4. _____
5. It was a beautiful sight for (we, us) to leave Vancouver by ship. 5. _____
6. (We, Us) felt the roll of the ship when we reached the open sea. 6. _____
7. (Who, Whom) got seasick the first night out? 7. _____
8. (Was, Were) the first views of Ketchikan dreary? 8. _____
9. The city of Ketchikan (is, are) known for its rainy weather. 9. _____
10. It (was, were) wonderful to sail the Inside Passage to Alaska. 10. _____

46–B: Practice Procedure. Follow the procedure given for 46–A.

1. Frequently, islands (was, were) on both sides of the ship. 1. _____
2. Small villages (is, are) on some islands. 2. _____
3. As our ship sailed by, villagers (was, were) waving from the shore. 3. _____
4. The villagers (who, whom) were friendly taught us new words. 4. _____
5. The city of Juneau (was, were) our next stop. 5. _____
6. It (is, are) the capital of Alaska. 6. _____
7. The group that greeted us on the dock (was, were) all of native Alaskan heritage. 7. _____
8. (She, Her) and a friend flew in a floatplane over the glaciers. 8. _____
9. A view of glaciers from the air (is, are) spectacular! 9. _____
10. There (is, are) deep crevasses throughout the glaciers. 10. _____
11. The salmon bake by a wilderness lake (was, were) an unusual eating experience. 11. _____
12. The gnats at the lake bothered (she, her). 12. _____
13. Rain boots, a raincoat, or an umbrella (is, are) standard gear in Juneau. 13. _____
14. The collection of Eskimo art in the museum (was, were) extensive. 14. _____
15. Everybody who saw the collection (was, were) impressed. 15. _____

Your Total Score _____

If your score was 19 or less for 46–A and B, review Units 2, 3, and 4 before continuing.

47-A: Practice Procedure. Match the definitions in Column B with the correct word in Column A. Place the letter that identifies the correct definition in the column to the right of Column B. Use your dictionary to check your answers. Score one point for each correct answer.

Column A	Column B	Answers
1. poem	**a.** writing that tells about imaginary people or happenings	1. _____
2. ballad	**b.** a fictional story long enough to fill one or more volumes	2. _____
3. essay	**c.** a short composition on a single subject	3. _____
4. narrative	**d.** a popular, narrative type song	4. _____
5. novelette	**e.** a writing based on real people and events	5. _____
6. nonfiction	**f.** a short novel	6. _____
7. biography	**g.** a composition using meter, cadence, or rhythm	7. _____
8. literature	**h.** a life history	8. _____
9. fiction	**i.** a story of real or unreal events, usually told in order of their happening	9. _____
10. novel	**j.** an excellent writing of a period or of a country in prose or verse	10. _____

Your Total Score _____

47-B: Practice Procedure. Here are 40 words that are frequently misspelled. Study them carefully and be prepared to write them from memory.

absence	develop	neighbor	rhythm
all right	efficient	original	ridiculous
altogether	embarrass	pertain	safety
appetite	favorite	piece	seize
basically	fourth	pledge	separate
believe	imagine	practice	shining
choose	loose	pursue	sponsor
chose	lose	receive	therefore
coarse	maintenance	relief	thorough
desperate	morale	religion	weird

48–A: **Practice Procedure.** In the blank at the right, place the letter of the word that is a synonym for the numbered word. Score one point for each correct answer.

Answers

1. *bragged*   (a) boasted (b) laughed (c) belittled (d) arched
(e) smoothed   1. _____

2. *frugal*   (a) thrifty (b) free (c) extravagant (d) rhythmic
(e) brotherly   2. _____

3. *typical*   (a) normal (b) numerable (c) motley (d) exceptional
(e) special   3. _____

4. *despicable*   (a) capable (b) contemptible (c) helpful (d) reckless
(e) marked   4. _____

5. *rely*   (a) ignore (b) agree (c) distrust (d) alter (e) depend   5. _____

6. *veer*   (a) finish (b) halt (c) abate (d) swerve (e) snake   6. _____

7. *tirade*   (a) vitality (b) a spanking (c) beverage
(d) a scolding (e) speed   7. _____

8. *grisly*   (a) bearable (b) tough (c) horrid (d) pleasant (e) plump   8. _____

9. *obstinate*   (a) cruel (b) steady (c) faltering (d) stubborn
(e) impulsive   9. _____

10. *oafish*   (a) settled (b) clumsy (c) polished (d) beginning (e) fat   10. _____

48–B: **Practice Procedure.** Follow the procedure given for 48–A.

1. *prohibit*   (a) forbid (b) agree (c) decline (d) reject (e) consent   1. _____

2. *apprehend*   (a) understand (b) arrest (c) release (d) hit (e) leave   2. _____

3. *fabulous*   (a) limited (b) bright (c) petty (d) incredible (e) additional   3. _____

4. *squander*   (a) presume (b) dirty (c) waste (d) duck (e) double   4. _____

5. *superficial*   (a) small (b) haughty (c) sound (d) enormous (e) shallow   5. _____

6. *fascinate*   (a) endure (b) annoy (c) tolerate (d) calm (e) charm   6. _____

7. *prim*   (a) formal (b) informal (c) cautious (d) loose (e) forceful   7. _____

8. *regal*   (a) common (b) liquid (c) basic (d) royal (e) feminine   8. _____

9. *alleviate*   (a) worsen (b) control (c) relieve (d) hurt (e) break   9. _____

10. *franchise*   (a) reason (b) tax (c) clash (d) license (e) credit   10. _____

11. *ideal*   (a) perfect (b) important (c) useful (d) unsound
(e) correct   11. _____

12. *conformity*   (a) pride (b) control (c) agreement (d) body (e) rebellion   12. _____

13. *germane*   (a) relevant (b) bacterial (c) European (d) flashy (e) pert   13. _____

14. *objective*   (a) statue (b) goal (c) disagreement (d) speech
(e) constable   14. _____

15. *notorious*   (a) renowned (b) infamous (c) recluse (d) beloved
(e) quiet   15. _____

Your Total Score _____

OBJECTIVES:
1. To recognize and use the present, past, and future tenses of verbs.
2. To recognize and use the perfect tenses of verbs.
3. To recognize and use verbs according to person, number, tense, and voice.

Verbs are used to express the time at which events occur. Some events take place in the present, some took place in the past, and others will take place in the future.

The form of the verb that is used to indicate the time of an event is called *tense*. There are three primary tenses: the *present*, the *past*, and the *future*.

PAST

PRESENT

FUTURE

TENSES

16–A. PRESENT TENSE FORM OF VERBS

The *present tense* tells what is happening now. It is also used to express a general truth and to indicate habitual action.

EXAMPLE 1

Jowanda <u>sells</u> office equipment.

Analysis:
   <u>sells</u>—present tense because the subject *Jowanda* is doing it now

EXAMPLE 2

Our company <u>buys</u> equipment from her annually.

Analysis:
   <u>buys</u>—present tense because it expresses habitual action

To form the present tense of most verbs, use the verb in its original form for all persons except third person singular. In the third person singular, add the letter *s* to the verb.

	Singular	Plural
1st person	I talk	we talk
2nd person	you talk	you talk
3rd person	he, she, it talks	they talk

Study the verbs *sing* and *stand*, for example, to see how they are formed in the present tense.

I sing	we sing
you sing	you sing
he, she, it sings	they sing

I stand	we stand
you stand	you stand
he, she, it stands	they stand

16-B. PRESENT TENSE FORMS OF THE VERB *BE*

Perhaps the most commonly used verb in the English language is the verb *be*. Unlike the verbs mentioned on the preceding page, this verb changes forms in the first, second, and third person singular. Study these forms of the verb *be* to improve your use of this verb.

	Singular	Plural
1st person	I am	we are
2nd person	you are	you are
3rd person	he, she, it is	they are

(See pages 75-76 for agreement of subjects with the forms of the verb *be*.)

16-C. PRESENT TENSE FORMS OF THE VERB *HAVE*

Have is the next most-used verb. This verb is easy to learn because it is the same in almost all forms. The only change takes place in the third person singular when the form *has* is used. *Have* is used with all other singular and plural subjects.

	Singular	Plural
1st person	I have	we have
2nd person	you have	you have
3rd person	he, she, it has	they have

(See page 77 for agreement of subjects with forms of the verb *have*.)

16-D. PRESENT TENSE FORMS OF THE VERB *DO*

A common mistake is using the wrong form of the verb *do* in the third person singular. Always be sure to use *does* with third person singular subjects. Do not use *he don't*. Use the correct form *he doesn't*.

	Singular	Plural
1st person	I do	we do
2nd person	you do	you do
3rd person	he, she, it does	they do

HE DON'T   **HE DOESN'T**

EXAMPLE 1

Incorrect: She <u>don't</u> know the house.
Correct: She <u>doesn't</u> know the house.

Analysis:
    doesn't—singular verb agrees with the subject
    She—third person singular

EXAMPLE 2

Incorrect: He <u>don't</u> type.
Correct: He <u>doesn't</u> type.

Analysis:
    doesn't—singular verb agrees with the subject
    He—third person singular

EXAMPLE 3

Incorrect: It <u>don't</u> need a battery.
Correct: It <u>doesn't</u> need a battery.

Analysis:
    doesn't—singular verb agrees with the subject
    It—third person singular

Section 17

Past Tense

17-A. PAST TENSE FORM OF VERBS

The *past tense* tells what has already happened. The past tense of regular verbs is formed by adding *ed* to the verb regardless of number (singular or plural) or person. If the verb ends with the letter *e*, just add *d* to form the past tense. Be careful of the irregular verbs which are listed on pages 101-102. They are different in form.

EXAMPLE 1

We <u>ordered</u> the pizza dinner.

Analysis:

> <u>ordered</u>—past tense of the verb *order*—tells that the subject *We* has already completed the act of ordering

EXAMPLE 2

Eileen <u>talked</u> to Lonnie on the telephone.

Analysis:

> <u>talked</u>—past tense of the verb *talk*—tells that the subject *Eileen* has already completed the act of talking

EXAMPLE 3

Toni <u>marched</u> in the band.

Analysis:

> <u>marched</u>—past tense of the verb *march*—tells that the subject *Toni* has already completed the act of marching

EXAMPLE 4

I <u>broke</u> the track record yesterday.

Analysis:

> <u>broke</u>—past tense of the verb *break*—tells that the subject *I* has already completed the act of breaking the record (Note that the verb *break* is irregular, and the past tense does not add *d*.)

EXAMPLE 5

On vacation last week, they *slept* late.

Analysis:

> slept—past tense of the verb *sleep*—tells that the subject *they* has already completed the act of sleeping (Note that the verb *sleep* is irregular, and the past tense does not add *d*.)

17-B. PAST TENSE FORMS OF THE VERB *BE*

The verb form *was* is used with all singular subjects except *you*. Always say and write *you were*. The verb form *were* is used with all plural subjects.

	Singular	**Plural**
1st person	I was	we were
2nd person	you were	you were
3rd person	he, she, it was	they were

17-C. PAST TENSE FORMS OF THE VERB *HAVE*

The past tense of *have* has only one form. It is *had*. Use *had* with all subjects, singular and plural, in the past tense.

	Singular	**Plural**
1st person	I had	we had
2nd person	you had	you had
3rd person	he, she, it had	they had

Future Tense

The *future tense* tells what will happen in the time to come.

EXAMPLE 1

His vacation <u>will start</u> next Monday.

Analysis:

<u>will start</u>—future tense because the subject *vacation* will take place in the time to come

SHALL WE SIT DOWN?

(I, WE FOR QUESTIONS)

WE WILL SIT DOWN!

(I, YOU, HE, SHE, IT, WE, THEY)

To express the future, use *will* before the verb in all persons, except in questions. For the first person (I, we) in questions, use *shall* before the verb.

EXAMPLES

<u>Shall we</u> leave together?
<u>Shall I</u> go as well?
<u>Will you</u> help me start the car?

	Singular	Plural
1st person	I will eat	we will eat
(questions)	Shall I eat?	Shall we eat?
2nd person	you will eat	you will eat
3rd person	he, she, it will eat	they will eat

Note: Some persons use *shall* in the first person singular and plural in declarative sentences (I shall eat. We shall eat.). This usage, however, is seldom heard today in speech and is considered formal rather than general English usage.

TRYOUT EXERCISE

Directions: Write the present tense in all persons (singular and plural) of the verb *provide*.

I _____ we _____
you _____ you _____
he, she, it _____ they _____

Directions: Complete each of the sentences below by writing the correct form of the verb in parentheses. Check your answers with your teacher before continuing.

1. We (order, orders) tickets from Mrs. Ezer.   1. _____
2. I (use, used) those books before.   2. _____
3. She (shall, will) finish the text tomorrow.   3. _____
4. It (don't, doesn't) matter.   4. _____
5. They (sell, sold) the chairs and tables yesterday. 5. _____

Complete Application Practices 49-50, pages 93-94, at this time.

Present Tense   Teacher _____ Score _____

49-A: Practice Procedure. Complete each of the following sentences by writing in the blank provided at the right the correct form of the verb in the parentheses. Remember that the verb form is different only in the third person singular. Score one point for every correct verb.

Answers

1. The team (play, plays) softball on the vacant lot.   1. _____

2. They (practice, practices) on Saturday.   2. _____

3. Their coach (teach, teaches) at the high school, too.   3. _____

4. The merchants (provide, provides) team uniforms.   4. _____

5. Both boys and girls (play, plays) on the same team.   5. _____

6. Most of the parents (attend, attends) all the games.   6. _____

7. Team members usually (walk, walks) to practice.   7. _____

8. Each pitcher (work, works) one inning.   8. _____

9. Her mother (announce, announces) each game.   9. _____

10. The parents (sell, sells) refreshments during the game.   10. _____

Your Total Score _____

If your score was 7 or less, review Section 16–A, page 89, before continuing.

49-B: Practice Procedure. Complete each of the following sentences by writing in the blank provided at the right the correct form of the verb *do*. Score one point for every correct verb.

1. (Does, Do) the softball team perform well?   1. _____

2. It (don't, doesn't) practice enough to suit me.   2. _____

3. He (don't, doesn't) have a uniform yet.   3. _____

4. We (do, does) enjoy watching the game.   4. _____

5. (Do, Does) the game sell out often?   5. _____

6. The batting order (don't, doesn't) make sense.   6. _____

7. It (don't, doesn't) matter whether they win or not.   7. _____

8. The team record (don't, doesn't) speak well for the coach.   8. _____

9. They (don't, doesn't) win too many games.   9. _____

10. The new uniforms (don't, doesn't) fit well.   10. _____

Your Total Score _____

If your score was 7 or less, review Section 16–D, page 90, before continuing.

50-A: Practice Procedure. Complete each of the following sentences by writing in the blank provided at the right the past tense of the verb in parentheses. Remember to add *ed* to the verb form, unless the verb ends in *e* in which case you add just *d*. Score one point for each correct answer.

Answers

Example: The soldiers (march) long distances.   <u>marched</u>

1. The Romans (conquer) the Mediterranean.   1. _____
2. Their legions (travel) to Gaul.   2. _____
3. Julius Caesar (rule) Rome.   3. _____
4. Alexander the Great (unite) the Greek cities.   4. _____
5. The Greeks (add) India to their empire.   5. _____

50-B: Practice Procedure. Write the past tense of the following verbs in the blanks provided.

Example: play <u>played</u>

1. review _____	6. introduce _____	11. listen _____
2. prepare _____	7. perform _____	12. guide _____
3. ask _____	8. notice _____	13. land _____
4. divide _____	9. talk _____	14. visit _____
5. discuss _____	10. hire _____	15. enclose _____

If your score was 15 or less for 50-A and B, review Section 17, page 91, before continuing.

50-C: Practice Procedure. Complete each of the following sentences by writing in the blank provided at the right the correct helping verb. Remember that in the future tense, *I* and *we* are the only two subjects that take the form *shall* in questions. Score one point for each correct answer.

1. After the meeting, we (shall, will) eat lunch.   1. _____
2. He (will, shall) serve as chairperson.   2. _____
3. (Shall, Will) I take minutes?   3. _____
4. She (will, shall) make the motion.   4. _____
5. They (will, shall) support her motion.   5. _____

Your Total Score _____

If your score was 4 or less for 50-C, review Section 18, page 92, before continuing.

Section 19 — The Perfect Tenses

All the perfect tenses show action that is completed in relation to a later action, circumstance, or time. Although we use the perfect tenses less often, an understanding of them is essential to good English. As you study this text, you will find that the perfect tenses are easy to learn.

19-A. PRESENT PERFECT TENSE

The *present perfect tense* is formed by using the present tense of the verb *have* before the past participle of the main verb. With regular verbs, the *past participle* of the verb is formed by adding *ed* to the verb or just *d* if the verb ends in *e*. (Most of the irregular past participles can be found on pages 101-102.) Be careful to have subject and verb agreement. Use *has* only when the subject is third person singular. Use *have* with all other singular and plural subjects.

The present perfect tense is used to show that something has started in the past and has continued to the present. It is also used to show that an action has been completed at some indefinite time in the past.

Present Perfect Tense

	Singular	Plural
1st person	I have replied	we have replied
2nd person	you have replied	you have replied
3rd person	he has replied	they have replied

EXAMPLE 1

I <u>have played</u> tennis for two years.

Analysis:
> have played—singular verb agrees in number with the subject *I*—first person singular

EXAMPLE 2

He <u>has enjoyed</u> watching tennis on television.

Analysis:
> has enjoyed—singular verb agrees in number with the subject *He*—third person singular

EXAMPLE 3

They <u>have purchased</u> tickets to the tennis match.

Analysis:
> have purchased—plural verb agrees in number with the subject *They*—third person plural

EXAMPLE 4

We <u>have grown</u> stronger by exercising daily.

Analysis:
> have grown—irregular plural verb agrees in number with the subject *We*—first person plural

19-B. PAST PERFECT TENSE

The *past perfect tense* is formed in all numbers and persons by using *had* with the past participle of the main verb. The past perfect tense refers to something which was completed in the past before another past action or event.

Past Perfect Tense

	Singular	**Plural**
1st person	I had listened	we had listened
2nd person	you had listened	you had listened
3rd person	she had listened	they had listened

EXAMPLE 1

John <u>had worked</u> there before taking his present job.

Analysis:
> <u>had worked</u>—past perfect tense. The action

was completed before another past action. *Had* is always used to form the past perfect tense, regardless of singular or plural subjects.

EXAMPLE 2

She <u>had hoped</u> to improve her score over last week's game but failed to do so.

Analysis:
> <u>had hoped</u>—past perfect tense. The action was completed in the past before another past action.

19-C. FUTURE PERFECT TENSE

The *future perfect tense* is formed by using *will have* with the past participle of the main verb. Use *shall have* instead of *will have* for the first person in questions. The future perfect tense is used when an action begun at any time will be completed by some time in the future.

Future Perfect Tense

	Singular	**Plural**
1st person	I will have talked	we will have talked
2nd person	you will have talked	you will have talked
3rd person	he will have talked	they will have talked

EXAMPLE 1

Before noon we <u>will have decided</u> on a winner.

Analysis:
> <u>will have decided</u>—future perfect tense. The action will be completed before noon.

EXAMPLE 2

Shall I <u>have received</u> the package by the time the invoice arrives?

Analysis:
> <u>Shall have received</u>—future perfect tense in a first person question. The action will be completed before the invoice arrives.

TRYOUT EXERCISE	**Directions:** Complete each of the following sentences by writing in the blank provided at the right the correct form of the verb in the parentheses. Check your answers with your teacher before continuing with your assignment.

1. She (present perfect of play) the game for years.　　1. _____
2. Before too long, we (future perfect of complete) the job.　　2. _____
3. He (past perfect of decide) to leave earlier than we thought.　　3. _____
4. I (future perfect of see) the film three times already.　　4. _____
5. Cathie (past perfect of lift) the lid to let off the steam.　　5. _____

Complete Application Practices 51-52, pages 97-98, at this time.

Perfect Tense   Teacher _____ Score _____

51-A: **Practice Procedure.** Complete each of the sentences below by writing in the blank provided at the right the correct perfect tense of the verb in parentheses. Watch the past participle in irregular verbs. See the chart of irregular verbs on pages 101-102 when necessary. Score one point for each correct answer.

Answers

1. Carlos (present perfect of speak) English for several years.   1. _____

2. He (past perfect of learn) English before coming to the United States.   2. _____

3. Students in his class (future perfect of master) their lesson together.   3. _____

4. Max (past perfect of be) to the United States once before.   4. _____

5. His sister, Marlene, (future perfect of arrive) at school by the end of first period.   5. _____

6. By then, she (future perfect of see) the principal.   6. _____

7. We (present perfect of notice) new students enrolling daily.   7. _____

8. Some new students (past perfect of walk) many miles from their homes before eating breakfast.   8. _____

9. Many parents (present perfect of visit) the school.   9. _____

10. The principal (present perfect of respond) to the request for more bilingual classes.   10. _____

11. The new bilingual textbooks (past perfect of arrive) last week prior to classes beginning.   11. _____

12. Some students (present perfect of use) a tape recorder to practice their English.   12. _____

13. They (present perfect of practice) speaking over the telephone.   13. _____

14. Elena (past perfect of hope) to learn English last semester.   14. _____

15. By June, Elena (future perfect of achieve) her goal.   15. _____

51-B: **Practice Procedure.** Complete the following sentences using the correct perfect tense form of the verb in parentheses. Score one point for each correct sentence.

1. Melvin (past perfect of select) _____

_____

2. The students (present perfect of hear) _____

_____

3. She (future perfect of perform) _____

_____

4. Michi (past perfect of talk) _____

_____

Your Total Score _____

If your score was 14 or less for 51-A and B, review Section 19, pages 95-96, before continuing.

52–A: Practice Procedure. Complete the sentences below by writing in the blank at the right the correct form of the verb in parentheses. Remember that *present tense* tells what is happening now, *past tense* tells what has already happened, and *future tense* tells what will happen later. Score one point for each correct answer.

Answers

1. Last week, Priscilla and Dan (leave, left, will leave) for Hawaii.　　　1. _____

2. They (arrive, arrived, will arrive) in Honolulu right now.　　　2. _____

3. Before they leave they (ask, asked, will ask) Mary and Al to breakfast.　　　3. _____

4. They (eat, ate, will eat) before they boarded the plane.　　　4. _____

5. Dan (pays, paid, will pay) for breakfast before they departed.　　　5. _____

6. Next week Mary (calls, called, will call) the travelers in Kona, Hawaii.　　　6. _____

7. Their cruise ship (sails, sailed, will sail) every Saturday.　　　7. _____

8. Prices for the cruise ship (jumps, jumped, will jump) last month.　　　8. _____

9. If the volcano on Hawaii erupts, they (see, saw, will see) it from the ship.　　　9. _____

10. The hurricane (damage, damaged, will damage) Kauai last year.　　　10. _____

52–B: Practice Procedure. Follow the procedure given for 52–A.

1. Today, the lion population of the world (is, was) small.　　　1. _____

2. By count, only about 200 lions (live, lived, will live) in India last year.　　　2. _____

3. A scientific team (spends, spent, will spend) the last four years observing wild lions.　　　3. _____

4. The team (watch, watched, will watch) a pride of lions live in the bush a month ago.　　　4. _____

5. The team members (move, moved, will move) to a new location next year.　　　5. _____

6. They (record, recorded, will record) their notes into a book every day.　　　6. _____

7. They (see, saw, will see) more lions when they went to Africa.　　　7. _____

8. One time the team (waits, waited, will wait) in their vehicle for over two hours.　　　8. _____

9. If they wait two hours, the team (see, saw, will see) the lions at the water hole.　　　9. _____

10. Unfortunately, everyone (thinks, thought, will think) that lions will become extinct in time.　　　10. _____

11. One time, the team (see, saw, will see) a lion eat pounds of meat.　　　11. _____

Your Total Score _____

If your score was 15 or less for 52–A and B, review Sections 16-18, pages 89-92, before continuing.

Conjugation of Verbs

Conjugation means breaking the verb down into its different forms to show person, number, tense, and voice. All verbs have these forms called *principal parts*. By knowing which part of the verb to use, your sentences will be correct.

Remember that the main tenses of any verb are the present, past, and future. From these three forms, you can make up the tense of any verb. The present tense is formed by using the verb as it is, except in the third person singular when you add *s* to the verb. The past tense of regular verbs is formed by adding *ed* or *d*, and the same is true in forming the *past participle*. The *present participle* is formed by adding *ing* to the verb. Page 100 shows the complete conjugation of a regular verb.

The irregular verbs have ususual parts. They are, however, the most used verbs in the English language. Learning them involves practice and memorization. Pages 101 and 102 list irregular verbs and their variations. The charts on pages 100-102 will simplify conjugation as much as possible, but the only way to learn how to conjugate verbs is to use them repeatedly.

Verbs may be in either the *active voice* or the *passive voice*. A verb is in the active voice when the subject does the action. A verb is in the passive voice when the action is done to the subject by something or someone else. Some form of the helping verb *be* and a past participle are necessary with the passive voice.

EXAMPLE 1

The horses <u>ran</u> hard in the featured race.

Analysis:
   <u>ran</u>—active voice—action is done by the subject *horses*

EXAMPLE 2

The jockey <u>rode</u> a spectacular race.

Analysis:
   <u>rode</u>—active voice—action is done by the subject *jockey*

EXAMPLE 3

The trophy <u>was awarded</u> to the horse's owner.

Analysis:
   <u>was awarded</u>—passive voice—action is done to the subject *trophy*

EXAMPLE 4

The race <u>was won</u> by my favorite horse.

Analysis:
   <u>was won</u>—passive voice—action is done to the subject *race* by the horse

EXAMPLE 5

A good groom <u>walks</u> his horse daily.

Analysis:
   <u>walks</u>—active voice—action is done by the subject *groom*

JOE HIT A HOME RUN. (ACTIVE)

(PASSIVE) THE HOME RUN WAS HIT BY JOE.

The active voice (action done by the subject) is on the left-hand side of this page. The passive voice (action done to the subject) is on the right-hand side of this page. The verbs are used in the singular and the plural forms with the subject *he* used to illustrate the third person singular.

This chart can be used as a guide and check in deciding how a verb is broken down into its different parts. Use and refer to this chart often.

Verb	Present Participle	Past Tense	Past Participle
move	moving	moved	moved

Active Voice	**Passive Voice**
(Action done by subject)	(Action done to subject)

Present Tense

Singular	Plural	Singular	Plural
I move	we move	I am moved	we are moved
you move	you move	you are moved	you are moved
he moves	they move	he is moved	they are moved

Past Tense

Singular	Plural	Singular	Plural
I moved	we moved	I was moved	we were moved
you moved	you moved	you were moved	you were moved
he moved	they moved	he was moved	they were moved

Future Tense

Singular	Plural	Singular	Plural
I will (shall) move	we will (shall) move	I will (shall) be moved	we will (shall) be moved
you will move	you will move	you will be moved	you will be moved
he will move	they will move	he will be moved	they will be moved

Present Perfect Tense

Singular	Plural	Singular	Plural
I have moved	we have moved	I have been moved	we have been moved
you have moved	you have moved	you have been moved	you have been moved
he has moved	they have moved	he has been moved	they have been moved

Past Perfect Tense

Singular	Plural	Singular	Plural
I had moved	we had moved	I had been moved	we had been moved
you had moved	you had moved	you had been moved	you had been moved
he had moved	they had moved	he had been moved	they had been moved

Future Perfect Tense

Singular	Plural	Singular	Plural
I will have moved	we will have moved	I will have been moved	we will have been moved
you will have moved	you will have moved	you will have been moved	you will have been moved
he will have moved	they will have moved	he will have been moved	they will have been moved

20-B. PRINCIPAL PARTS OF IRREGULAR VERBS

These 50 irregular verbs differ from the rule in forming the past tense and the past participle. Many of them are used in daily speech. Review them now, and study any that are unfamiliar to you.

Commonly Used Irregular Verbs

Irregular Verb	Past Tense	Past Participle
be (am, is, are)	was (were)	been
become	became	become
begin	began	begun
bite	bit	bitten
blow	blew	blown
break	broke	broken
bring	brought	brought
build	built	built
come	came	come
do	did	done
draw	drew	drawn
drink	drank	drunk
drive	drove	driven
eat	ate	eaten
fall	fell	fallen
fight	fought	fought
fly	flew	flown
get	got	got or gotten
give	gave	given
go	went	gone
grow	grew	grown
hear	heard	heard
hit	hit	hit
know	knew	known
lay	laid	laid
lead	led	led
leave	left	left
let	let	let
lie (recline)	lay	lain
lose	lost	lost
put	put	put
ride	rode	ridden
ring	rang	rung
run	ran	run
say	said	said
see	saw	seen
show	showed	shown or showed
sing	sang	sung
sink	sank or sunk	sunk
sit	sat	sat
sleep	slept	slept
speak	spoke	spoken
swim	swam	swum
take	took	taken
teach	taught	taught
tell	told	told
think	thought	thought
throw	threw	thrown
wear	wore	worn
write	wrote	written

The list below contains 29 additional irregular verbs. They are important for you to learn, as well.

Less Frequently Used Irregular Verbs

Irregular Verb	Past Tense	Past Participle
arise	arose	arisen
awake	awaked or awoke	awaked or awoken
bear	bore	borne
beat	beat	beaten
burst	burst or bursted	burst or bursted
catch	caught	caught
choose	chose	chosen
cling	clung	clung
cost	cost	cost
dive	dived or dove	dived
fling	flung	flung
forget	forgot	forgotten or forgot
freeze	froze	frozen
hang	hung	hung
hang (death)	hanged	hanged
hurt	hurt	hurt
keep	kept	kept
pay	paid	paid
read	read	read
rise	rose	risen
set	set	set
shake	shook	shaken
shine	shone	shone
spring	sprang or sprung	sprung
steal	stole	stolen
swear	swore	sworn
swing	swung	swung
tear	tore	torn
wake	waked or woke	waked or woken

TRYOUT EXERCISE

Directions: Complete each of the following sentences by writing in the blank provided at the right the correct tense of the verb in the parentheses. Check your answers with your teacher before continuing with your assignment.

1. The cat (past of get) a new collar. 1. _____

2. The dog had (past participle of sleep) through the robbery. 2. _____

3. She (future of bring) the ladder. 3. _____

Complete Application Practices 53-54, pages 103-104, at this time.

53-A: Practice Procedure. Complete each of the following sentences by writing in the blank provided at the right the correct form of the verb in parentheses. Refer to the lists on pages 101-102 if necessary. Score one point for each correct answer.

Answers

1. This summer, our family (past of drive) to Virginia City, Nevada.   1. _____

2. On automobile trips we (present of leave) home early in the morning.   2. _____

3. We always (present of arise) early to pack the car.   3. _____

4. En route to Los Angeles, we (past of see) Disneyland.   4. _____

5. On a Los Angeles freeway, the car (past of blow) a tire.   5. _____

6. Dad (past of sleep) while Mother drove the car.   6. _____

7. At our lunch stop, I (past of tear) my shirt on a tree.   7. _____

8. Everyone (past of wear) light clothing because of the heat.   8. _____

9. My little brother (past of become) a good traveler on the trip.   9. _____

10. To pass the time, we (present of sing) songs.   10. _____

53-B: Practice Procedure. Follow the procedure given for 53-A.

1. We had (past participle of do) well to reach Mammoth Lakes by early evening.   1. _____

2. A friend had (past participle of give) us permission to stay in his cabin.   2. _____

3. Since we had (past participle of ride) a long way, we were tired.   3. _____

4. My mother and sister (past of swim) in a nearby swimming pool.   4. _____

5. All of us usually (present of take) walks before dinner.   5. _____

6. Our friends had (past participle of choose) the restaurant.   6. _____

7. On the way back to the cabin we (past of take) a shortcut.   7. _____

8. The next morning our friends (past of show) us the Devil's Postpile.   8. _____

9. We (past of hear) the ranger explain the origin of this strange lava monument.   9. _____

10. Later, we (past of come) to the John Muir Trail.   10. _____

11. My sister has (past participle of write) about the trail in her diary.   11. _____

12. We (past of lose) our way getting into Carson City.   12. _____

13. In Virginia City, we (past of pay) a fee to see a famous old opera house.   13. _____

14. Guides (present of draw) a vivid picture of the opera house.   14. _____

15. Virginia City's Comstock Lode had (past participle of give) the city great wealth.   15. _____

Your Total Score _____

If your score was 19 or less for 53-A and B, review pages 101-102 before continuing.

54-A: **Practice Procedure.** Complete each of the following sentences by writing in the blank provided at the right the correct form of the verb in the parentheses. See pages 101-102 for the forms of the irregular verbs if necessary. Score one point for each correct answer.   Answers

1. The British (past of start) the idea of the pleasure pier.   1. _____

2. Strollers (past of walk) out on the pier to view the ocean.   2. _____

3. They (past of enjoy) piers at several British seaside resorts.   3. _____

4. George Howard (past of build) Atlantic City's first pleasure pier.   4. _____

5. A storm (past of destroy) Howard's first pier.   5. _____

6. James Applegate (past of open) Atlantic City's first successful pier in 1884.   6. _____

7. Applegate's pier (past of draw) thousands of visitors.   7. _____

8. The visitors (past of see) fish exhibits on the pier.   8. _____

9. Pleasure piers (past of cost) a great deal of money to build.   9. _____

10. Famous bands (past of play) in the pier auditoriums.   10. _____

54-B: **Practice Procedure.** Follow the procedure given for 54-A. Refer to page 100 for tenses of verbs if necessary.

1. Star performers (past perfect passive of bring) to entertain pier visitors.   1. _____

2. Pier owners (past perfect active of operate) exciting rides.   2. _____

3. The pleasure pier (past of come) to southern California as well.   3. _____

4. Many couples (present perfect passive of know) to dance at the Santa Monica pier ballroom.   4. _____

5. The dancers (past passive of watch) by 5,000 spectators.   5. _____

6. At night, lights on the piers (past of give) them a fairy-tale appearance.   6. _____

7. Roller coaster riders (future passive of excite) by their ride.   7. _____

8. In Venice, California, the roller coaster ride (past tense of leave) passengers breathless.   8. _____

9. In Chicago, the Navy Pier (past of become) a working pleasure pier.   9. _____

10. Today pleasure piers (present perfect active of lose) their audience.   10. _____

11. The pleasure pier lights no longer (past of look) bright.   11. _____

12. The sea and marine animals (past of destroy) many piers.   12. _____

13. Today people's attitudes toward pleasure piers (present perfect passive of change).   13. _____

14. Surfers (past of ride) through the aging pier pilings.   14. _____

15. In the surf, pounding waves (present perfect active of crack) the pilings.   15. _____

Your Total Score _____

If your score was 19 or less for 54-A and B, review Sections 19 and 20 before going to Section 21.

Misused Verbs

A few verbs can be troublesome. Special attention should be given when you use them. Some of the most troublesome verbs are *lie* and *lay* and *sit* and *set*.

21-A. LIE AND LAY

Uses of the Verb *Lie*

The verb *lie* means to rest or recline. With *lie* the subject usually takes a position or is in a position. *Lie* never has an object (a word following the verb which answers the question "what" or "whom").

Present Tense: lie

I lie	we lie
you lie	you lie
he, she, it lies	they lie

Past Tense: lay

I lay	we lay
you lay	you lay
he, she, it lay	they lay

Past Participle: lain

I have lain	we have lain
you have lain	you have lain
he, she, it has lain	they have lain

Hint: If you cannot use *place* or *put* instead of the verb *lie*, you know some form of the verb *lie* is correct.

EXAMPLE 1

At the beach I <u>lie</u> on the sand to get a suntan.

Analysis:

lie—present tense—means to rest or recline on the sand—does not have an object

EXAMPLE 2

She <u>lies</u> on each side for fifteen minutes to get a good tan.

Analysis:

lies—present tense—means to rest or recline—does not have an object

EXAMPLE 3

I <u>lay</u> out too long without an umbrella and got a bad sunburn.

Analysis:

lay—past tense—means to rest or recline—does not have an object

EXAMPLE 4

They <u>lay</u> under the only palm tree on the beach.

Analysis:

lay—past tense—means to rest or recline—does not have an object

EXAMPLE 5

He <u>has lain</u> under the same tree all summer long.

Analysis:

has lain—past participle—means to rest or recline—does not have an object

LIE

TO REST OR RECLINE
NO OBJECT

LAY

TO PLACE OR PUT
TAKES OBJECT

Uses of the Verb *Lay*

The verb *lay* is often misused for the verb *lie*. *Lay* means to place or put something down. It always takes an object (a word following the verb which answers the question "what" or "whom").

Present Tense: lay

I lay	we lay
you lay	you lay
he, she, it lays	they lay

Past Tense: laid

I laid	we laid
you laid	you laid
he, she, it laid	they laid

Past Participle: laid

I have laid	we have laid
you have laid	you have laid
he, she, it has laid	they have laid

Hint: If you can use *place* or *put* instead of the verb *lay,* you know some form of the verb *lay* is correct.

EXAMPLE 1

I <u>lay</u> my books on that shelf.

Analysis:
    lay—present tense—means to place or put something down—has an object *books*

EXAMPLE 2

She <u>lays</u> pencils with the test papers.

Analysis:
    lays—present tense—means to place or put something down—has an object *pencils*

EXAMPLE 3

The students <u>laid</u> their papers on the desk.

Analysis:
    laid—past tense—means to place or put something down—has an object *papers*

EXAMPLE 4

He <u>laid</u> the pencil in the box.

Analysis:
    laid—past tense—means to place or put something down—has an object *pencil*

EXAMPLE 5

They <u>have laid</u> their books over there.

Analysis:
    have laid—past participle—means to place or put something down—has an object *books*

REVIEW

lie (to rest or recline)	lying	lay	lain	(no object)
lay (to put or place)	laying	laid	laid	(always an object)

The verbs *sit* and *set* are also troublesome verbs. Having learned the use of *lie* and *lay, sit* and *set* will be easy. *Sit* and *lie* are governed by the same rules while *set* and *lay* have the same rules.

Uses of the Verb *Sit*

Sit means to have a seat or occupy a position. It never has an object (a word following the verb which answers the question "what" or "whom").

Present Tense: sit

I sit	we sit
you sit	you sit
he, she, it sits	they sit

Past Tense: sat

I sat	we sat
you sat	you sat
he, she, it sat	they sat

Past Participle: sat

I have sat	we have sat
you have sat	you have sat
he, she, it has sat	they have sat

Hint: If you cannot use *place* or *put* instead of the verb *sit,* you know some form of *sit* is correct.

EXAMPLE 1

On a tour bus, usually I <u>sit</u> behind the bus driver.

Analysis:
    <u>sit</u>—present tense—means to have a seat or occupy a position—does not have an object

EXAMPLE 2

He <u>sits</u> in front to hear the tour guide better.

Analysis:
    <u>sits</u>—present tense—means to have a seat or occupy a position—does not have an object

EXAMPLE 3

They <u>sat</u> together so they could gossip.

Analysis:
    <u>sat</u>—past tense—means to have a seat or occupy a position—does not have an object

EXAMPLE 4

The tour guide <u>sat</u> with the young child.

Analysis:
    <u>sat</u>—past tense—means to have a seat or occupy a position—does not have an object

EXAMPLE 5

She <u>has sat</u> in that same seat the entire trip.

Analysis:
    <u>has sat</u>—past participle—means to have sat or occupied a position—does not have an object

EXAMPLE 6

You <u>have sat</u> beside her before.

Analysis:
    <u>have sat</u>—past participle—means to have sat or occupied a position—does not have an object

SIT — TO RECLINE OR REST

SET — TO PLACE OR PUT

Uses of the Verb *Set*

Set means to put or place. It always has an object. Remember the hint: If you substitute *place* or *put* for the verb *set,* you know some form of *set* is correct.

Present Tense: set

I set	we set
you set	you set
he, she, it sets	they set

Past Tense: set

I set	we set
you set	you set
he, she, it set	they set

Past Participle: set

I have set	we have set
you have set	you have set
he, she, it has set	they have set

EXAMPLE 1

He <u>sets</u> the plate on the table.

Analysis:

sets—present tense—means to place or put something down—has an object *plate*

EXAMPLE 2

She <u>sets</u> her fishing poles on the porch.

Analysis:

sets—present tense—means to place or put something down—has an object *fishing poles*

EXAMPLE 3

They <u>set</u> the chairs on the patio for the party.

Analysis:

set—past tense—means to place or put something down—has an object *chairs*

EXAMPLE 4

Yesterday you <u>set</u> your boots in the porch closet.

Analysis:

set—past tense—means to place or put something down—has an object *boots*

EXAMPLE 5

She <u>has set</u> the flowers on the table already.

Analysis:

has set—past participle—means to have placed or put something down—has an object *flowers*

REVIEW

sit (rest or occupy a position)	sitting	sat	sat	(no object)
set (place or put)	setting	set	set	(always an object)

TRYOUT EXERCISE

Directions: Complete each of the following sentences by writing in the blank provided at the right the correct form of the verb in parentheses. Check your answers with your teacher before continuing with your assignment.

1. She (sit, set) the soap on the sink. 1. _____
2. He (lies, lay) in bed too long. 2. _____
3. I (lay, laid) the key on the table. 3. _____
4. They (sat, set) on the porch last night. 4. _____

Complete Application Practices 55-56, pages 109-110, at this time.

APPLICATION PRACTICE 55   Name _____ Date _____

Lie-Lay Practice   Teacher _____ Score _____

55-A: Practice Procedure. Complete each of the following sentences by writing in the blank provided at the right the correct form of the verb indicated in parentheses. Score one point for each correct answer.

Answers

1. The orchestra conductor (past of lay) his baton in a travel case.   1. _____

2. The violinist (past of lie) down on the bus seat after the concert.   2. _____

3. A singer (past of lay) her music on the stand.   3. _____

4. The packers have (past participle of lay) the fragile instruments on top of the pile.   4. _____

5. The tired orchestra members (present of lie) back in the comfortable bus seats.   5. _____

6. The tall concertmaster (past of lie) over two seats.   6. _____

7. His right leg (past of lie) in the aisle of the bus.   7. _____

8. Ted, the orchestra's librarian, has (past participle of lay) the music scores in special folders.   8. _____

9. He (past of lay) the newest score on top.   9. _____

10. The young trumpet player (present of lie) down on the backseat.   10. _____

55-B: Practice Procedure. Follow the procedure given for 55-A.

1. Jamie ordered his dog to (lie, lay) down at once.   1. _____

2. Our cat, Kris, (has lain, has laid) on the bed before.   2. _____

3. Sandy, our fox terrier, (lay, laid) the newspaper at my feet this morning.   3. _____

4. Because of the storm last night, Julia (lay, laid) awake until morning.   4. _____

5. Julia will (lie, lay) down early tonight.   5. _____

6. I saw Steve (lying, laying) the dog leash on the shelf.   6. _____

7. She (lay, laid) the training book over there.   7. _____

8. Marta (lay, laid) in the lounge under the tree.   8. _____

9. The animals (have lain, have laid) there, too.   9. _____

10. She (lies, lays) in the lounge too much.   10. _____

11. I (have lain, have laid) the dog food on the floor.   11. _____

12. Peter (lay, laid) down near the fireplace.   12. _____

13. Peter's mother (lay, laid) a fire in the fireplace.   13. _____

14. We (have lain, have laid) there before.   14. _____

15. I always (lie, lay) on the couch to watch the fire.   15. _____

Your Total Score _____

If your score was 19 or less for 55-A and B, review Section 21-A, pages 105-106, before continuing.

56–A: Practice Procedure. Complete each of the following sentences by writing in the blank provided at the right the correct form of the verb indicated in parentheses. Score one point for each correct answer.

Answers

1. The porter (past of set) the luggage by the car.   1. _____
2. Marsha always (present of sit) in the front seat.   2. _____
3. On the plane, she (past of sit) by the window.   3. _____
4. I have (past participle of sit) there as well.   4. _____
5. I (present of sit) next to the pilot in order to see.   5. _____
6. The pilot (past of set) his empty coffee cup on the floor.   6. _____
7. He has (past participle of set) it there before.   7. _____
8. The flight attendant (present of set) her tray on the seat.   8. _____
9. On takeoff, the attendant (present of sit) in a jump seat.   9. _____
10. The staff have (past participle of set) the food trays in the oven.   10. _____

56–B: Practice Procedure. Follow the procedure given for 56–A.

1. The wedding guests will (sit, set) on both sides of the aisle.   1. _____
2. The bride's friends will (sit, set) on the left.   2. _____
3. The groom's friends (sat, set) on the right.   3. _____
4. The guests (sat, set) their gifts on tables.   4. _____
5. A waiter (sat, set) the glasses by a punch bowl.   5. _____
6. One elderly guest (sat, set) in a wheelchair.   6. _____
7. The usher (sat, set) the wheelchair in a special place.   7. _____
8. The florist (has sat, has set) flowers throughout the room.   8. _____
9. I (sat, set) next to a large bowl of orchids.   9. _____
10. They (have sat, have set) extra chairs in the aisle.   10. _____
11. Usually he (sits, sets) up in front so he can hear.   11. _____
12. The caterers (have sat, have set) the cake on a special table.   12. _____
13. The groom's aunt (sat, set) a knife by the cake.   13. _____
14. The bridal party will (sit, set) at the head table.   14. _____
15. The bride's parents (have sat, have set) down with their guests.   15. _____

Your Total Score _____

If your score was 19 or less for 56–A and B, review Section 21–B, pages 107-108, before continuing.

Less Troublesome Verbs

Now that you understand *lie, lay* and *sit, set,* we'll look at some less troublesome verbs. Most of these verbs you already know; however, all of us misuse them occasionally.

22-A. SHALL, SHOULD, WILL, AND WOULD

You have already learned to use the verb forms of *shall* and *will* in the future tense. If necessary, refer to page 92 for a review.

Should and *would* are used in conditional sentences. These sentences contain some doubt or uncertainty about the statement being made. *Should* is used with the subjects *I* and *we. Would* is used with all other subjects.

EXAMPLES

We should be ready to leave on a moment's notice.
Are you sure he would go in any event?

Should is used with all pronouns to indicate obligation. In such sentences, *should* is used in the sense of *ought.*

EXAMPLES

I should study for the test tonight.
She should know better.

Exceptions: Use *will* and *would* with the subjects *I* and *we* to show determination or emphasis. Determination is a strong and definite feeling. *Shall* is used with all other subjects in sentences that show determination.

EXAMPLES

I will come since you really want me there.
She shall be on time, or else!

Would is used in polite or unemphatic requests.

EXAMPLES

Would you answer the telephone please?
He would call if you asked.

22-B. MAY, MIGHT, CAN, AND COULD

May and *might* are used to express permission, possibility, or probability.

EXAMPLES

May I see the menu please?
You may like it when you taste it.

Can and *could* are used to express ability or power to do something.

EXAMPLES

Can you hear the telephone if it rings?
You could be quieter if you tried.

22-C. LEAVE AND LET

Leave is often confused with *let*. *Leave* means to depart from one place to go to another. It also means to allow to remain.

EXAMPLES

Did she <u>leave</u> the house yet?
Please <u>leave</u> the dog in the house.

Let means to permit or allow. Only with *alone* meaning "stop from disturbing" can either verb be used.

EXAMPLES

Will you <u>let</u> me leave early?
Her father <u>let</u> her go to the dance with Jim.
I will be happy to <u>leave</u> (or let) you alone!
Nancy <u>let</u> her little brother have an ice cream cone.

22-D. TEACH AND LEARN

Teach means to instruct or to show someone how something is done.

EXAMPLES

I <u>teach</u> English to the freshmen.
She will <u>teach</u> school in the fall.

Learn means to acquire or obtain knowledge and information.

EXAMPLES

He will <u>learn</u> to swim by summer's end.
We <u>learn</u> best by example.

22-E. BORROW AND LEND

Borrow means to take or to obtain something from someone else on loan. You do not have it, so you borrow it.

EXAMPLES

May I <u>borrow</u> your car tomorrow?
Will he <u>borrow</u> snow chains or buy them?

Lend means to let someone use something of yours for a period of time. You have it, and you allow the other person to use it.

EXAMPLES

You will <u>lend</u> me your skis, won't you?
Mark will <u>lend</u> you his snow chains.

Bring means to carry something toward a person, place, or thing or to *come* carrying something.

EXAMPLES

Charlotte will <u>bring</u> Norm to the party.
<u>Bring</u> me a loaf of bread, a quart of milk, and some eggs when you go to the store.

Take means to carry something away from a person, place, or thing or to *go* carrying something.

EXAMPLES

Please <u>take</u> my suitcase from the car.
Will you <u>take</u> the groceries home for me?

Fetch means to go after and bring back.

EXAMPLES

John will be happy to <u>fetch</u> your paper if you like.
Rover, <u>fetch</u> the ball!

BRING   **TAKE**

22-G. RISE AND RAISE

Rise means to get up, arise, or ascend. It never has an object.

EXAMPLES

You should <u>rise</u> when she comes into the room.
It will be warmer after the sun <u>rises</u>.

Raise means to lift something. It may have an object.

EXAMPLES

<u>Raise</u> the window please.
If you have a question, <u>raise</u> your hand.
The flag was <u>raised</u> to the top of the staff.

RISE

RAISE

TRYOUT EXERCISE

Directions: Complete each of the following sentences by writing in the blank provided at the right the correct form of the verb in the parentheses. Check your answers with your teacher before continuing with your assignment.

1. If I (would, should) drop it, will it break?   1. _____
2. (May, Can) I serve you now?   2. _____
3. (Leave, Let) me go!   3. _____
4. She will (teach, learn) me English.   4. _____
5. (Borrow, Lend) me a pencil?   5. _____
6. Please (bring, take) the package from her.   6. _____
7. (Rise, Raise) your head a little.   7. _____

Complete Application Practices 57-62, pages 115-120, at this time.

57–A: Practice Procedure. Complete each of the following sentences by writing *shall* or *will* in the blank provided at the right. Score one point for each correct answer.

Answers

1. (?) I buy a new camera for the trip?   1. _____
2. He (?) have extra rolls of film in his camera bag.   2. _____
3. The x-ray check at the airport (?) ruin sensitive film.   3. _____
4. If we are five minutes late, (?) we still make the plane?   4. _____
5. Bring your passport because the officials (?) need to see it.   5. _____
6. (?) I check us in at the flight desk?   6. _____
7. If you insist, I (?) help with the luggage!   7. _____
8. You (?) listen for our flight's departure time or else!   8. _____
9. The plane (?) not leave on time after all.   9. _____
10. We (?) sit in Row 14 which is behind the emergency door.   10. _____

57–B: Practice Procedure. Complete each of the following sentences by writing *should* or *would* in the blank provided at the right. Score one point for each correct answer.

1. If we (?) get separated on arrival, meet me at the taxi stand.   1. _____
2. He (?) call the hotel from the airport if he had the number.   2. _____
3. By rights, the airline (?) replace my damaged luggage.   3. _____
4. (?) you prepare a customs declaration form for me?   4. _____
5. I (?) appreciate your holding my place in line.   5. _____
6. We (?) be through customs in no time at all.   6. _____
7. If I (?) need help, I'll call for the luggage agent.   7. _____
8. I (?) know the Vancouver airport, but I don't.   8. _____
9. (?) you please call a taxi for me?   9. _____
10. We (?) have left the airport before now.   10. _____

Your Total Score _____

If your score was 15 or less for 57–A and B, review Sections 18 and 22–A, pages 92 and 111, before continuing.

57–C: Practice Procedure. On a separate sheet of paper, write five sentences using *shall* and *will* and five sentences using *should* and *would*. Try to make your writing interesting. Score one point for each correct sentence.

Your Total Score _____

58-A: Practice Procedure. Complete each of the following sentences by writing *may* or *can* in the blank provided at the right. Score one point for each correct answer.

Answers

1. In Vancouver, (?) we please visit Stanley Park? 1. _____
2. We (?) always see several totem poles there. 2. _____
3. (?) I buy tour tickets for you and your guests, too? 3. _____
4. If I (?) find one I like, I'll buy an Indian necklace. 4. _____
5. In Gastown, I know we (?) easily find the steam clock. 5. _____
6. (?) I take your picture in front of the steam clock? 6. _____
7. We (?) usually have a good lunch at that French cafe in Gastown. 7. _____
8. I (?) buy that souvenir for less money at the first shop. 8. _____
9. I'm told we (?) see the ships at anchor from the hotel. 9. _____
10. (?) I step in front of you to take a picture of the ships? 10. _____

58-B: Practice Procedure. Follow the procedure given for 58-A.

1. At the fish hatchery, you (?) usually see salmon jump the ladder. 1. _____
2. To get to the hatchery, people (?) always take a bus. 2. _____
3. The bus fare (?) be as much as a dollar. 3. _____
4. (?) Colin and Pat go with you on the bus? 4. _____
5. At the bird sanctuary, you (?) always buy seed for the birds. 5. _____
6. Children (?) visit the bird sanctuary only if they are with a parent. 6. _____
7. (?) you join me for a visit to the aquarium? 7. _____
8. Lemon sharks from Mexico (?) be seen at the aquarium if you have a special ticket. 8. _____
9. You (?) see the sharks daily but only with a special ticket. 9. _____
10. (?) we go to the zoo in Stanley Park on Friday? 10. _____

Your Total Score _____

If your score was 15 or less for 58-A and B, review Section 22-B, page 111, before continuing.

58-C: Practice Procedure. On a separate piece of paper, write five sentences using *may* and five sentences using *can*. Try to make your writing interesting. Score one point for each correct sentence.

Your Total Score _____

59-A: Practice Procedure. Complete the following sentences by writing in the blank at the right the correct form of the verb in the parentheses. Score one point for each correct answer.

Answers

1. Be sure to (lie, lay) your golf club off the green.   1. _____
2. (Set, Sit) your golf bag on the golf cart.   2. _____
3. If she (should, would) par this hole, she would win.   3. _____
4. (May, Can) she win without a par of that hole?   4. _____
5. Will you (leave, let) me carry your golf bag?   5. _____
6. The golf pro will (teach, learn) you, if you like.   6. _____
7. Marcus will (borrow, lend) her his putter.   7. _____
8. The last golfer to tee off is (lying, laying) down to rest.   8. _____
9. Be sure to (rise, raise) your club slowly.   9. _____
10. Each golfer must (bring, take) his scorecard to the judge.   10. _____

59-B: Practice Procedure. Follow the procedure given for 59-A.

1. I probably will (lie, lay) awake all night before the game.   1. _____
2. Helen has (sat, set) down by the starter's table.   2. _____
3. She (will, shall) win the tournament if it kills her.   3. _____
4. (May, Can) she select her own golf partner?   4. _____
5. Theresa hopes the other players will (leave, let) her alone.   5. _____
6. Breaking that club (taught, learned) her a good lesson.   6. _____
7. She will need to (borrow, lend) a club from someone.   7. _____
8. Can you (bring, take) this club to her?   8. _____
9. When her name is called, she will (rise, raise) quickly.   9. _____
10. (Sit, Set) your scorecard on the starter's table.   10. _____

Your Total Score _____

If your score was 15 or less for 59-A and B, review Sections 21 and 22, pages 105-108 and pages 111-113, before continuing.

59-C: Practice Procedure. On a separate sheet of paper, write one sentence for each of the following irregular verbs: *borrow, lend, bring, take, may, can, lay, lie, rise, raise, sit, set, teach, learn, leave, let.* Be sure to use the correct meaning of each verb. Score one point for each correct sentence.

Your Total Score _____

60–A: Practice Procedure. Complete the following sentences by writing in the blank at the right the correct form of the verb in the parentheses. You will need to put some verbs in the passive voice. Score one point for each correct answer.

Answers

1. Last September we (past of fly) to Vancouver, B.C.   1. _____

2. After three days there, we (past of leave) for Alaska.   2. _____

3. Our luggage (past perfect of move) from the hotel to the ship.   3. _____

4. The bags (future perfect of put) in our stateroom before sailing time.   4. _____

5. The rain (past perfect of stop) before we sailed.   5. _____

6. The ship's whistle (future of blow) at sailing time.   6. _____

7. The gangway (past perfect of take) away earlier.   7. _____

8. Everyone (past of throw) paper streamers down to the pier.   8. _____

9. Slowly, the ship (past of start) to move into the channel.   9. _____

10. Our Alaskan adventure finally (past perfect of begin).   10. _____

60–B: Practice Procedure. Follow the procedure given for 60–A.

1. I (past perfect of think) the ship would be beautiful and it was!   1. _____

2. Before long, Marge (past of become) familiar with the various decks.   2. _____

3. I expect we (future of lose) the tugboats soon.   3. _____

4. Cecil (present perfect of give) a plan of the ship.   4. _____

5. Anne (past of get) a farewell gift of red roses.   5. _____

6. She (past perfect of know) the roses were from her son.   6. _____

7. We (future of eat) at a table for six.   7. _____

8. All passengers (present perfect of hear) the dinner chimes by now.   8. _____

9. We (future tense of show) our dining room reservations to the waiter.   9. _____

10. The ladies (past of wear) long dresses to dinner.   10. _____

Your Total Score _____

If your score was 15 or less for 60–A and B, review Section 20, pages 99-102, before continuing.

60–C: Practice Procedure. On a separate sheet of paper, write a short paragraph about any interesting subject. In the paragraph, use and identify as many forms as possible of the tenses in the chart on page 100. The lists of verbs on pages 101-102 will also help.

61-A: Practice Procedure. Complete the following sentences by writing in the blank at the right the correct form of the verb in the parentheses. Score one point for each correct answer.

Answers

1. Alaska (became, becomes) our forty-ninth state. 1. _____
2. The state's capital building (is, are) located in Juneau. 2. _____
3. Alaska is so large it (cover, covers) four time zones. 3. _____
4. Statehood (was, were) finally granted in 1959. 4. _____
5. Alaska (doesn't, don't) touch any other state in the union. 5. _____
6. In Arctic Alaska, we (saw, seen) many Eskimos. 6. _____
7. Alaskans (is, are) proud of their state. 7. _____
8. An assembly of birds and big game (is, are) in the state. 8. _____
9. Coastal Alaska (extend, extends) from the Alaska Range to the Gulf of Alaska. 9. _____
10. The coastal waters (contain, contains) many kinds of sea life. 10. _____

61-B: Practice Procedure. Follow the procedure given for 61-A.

1. Usually, the Aleutian Islands (is, are) fogbound. 1. _____
2. The Aleutians (don't, doesn't) have many tourists. 2. _____
3. Rainfall (average, averages) 150 inches a year in Ketchikan, Alaska. 3. _____
4. On the Arctic coast, rain (is, are) rare. 4. _____
5. Most of the state's highways (exist, exists) in interior and coastal Alaska. 5. _____
6. A ferry system (provide, provides) travel for passengers and vehicles. 6. _____
7. The Alaska pipeline (connect, connects) the oil fields with the port of Valdez. 7. _____
8. The pipeline (was, were) the subject of controversy. 8. _____
9. The cost of living in Alaska (is, are) high. 9. _____
10. Fishing, lumbering, and tourism (is, are) important Alaskan industries. 10. _____
11. The growing season (last, lasts) 80 days in the Yukon. 11. _____
12. Hunting licenses for nonresidents (is, are) required. 12. _____
13. Alaska's calendar of annual events (is, are) varied. 13. _____
14. The logging championships (was, were) held in Sitka in July. 14. _____
15. All of the logging teams (try, tries) to win. 15. _____

Your Total Score _____

If your score was 19 or less for 61-A and B, review Sections 15, 16, and 17, pages 81-83 and 89-91, before continuing.

62-A: Practice Procedure. In the following practice, select the one word that is the synonym for the numbered word. Write the letter that identifies the correct word in the blank provided at the right. Remember that a synonym has the same or a similar meaning. Score one point for each correct answer.

Answers

1. *expend*   (a) pay (b) perish (c) accept (d) die (e) try   1. _____

2. *participate*   (a) follow (b) evade (c) enjoy (d) pass (e) share   2. _____

3. *traction*   (a) pulling (b) slipping (c) engine (d) reducing (e) sight   3. _____

4. *staunch*   (a) loose (b) obese (c) helpful (d) failing (e) faithful   4. _____

5. *odious*   (a) attractive (b) awesome (c) aged (d) repugnant (e) serene   5. _____

6. *omit*   (a) include (b) hope (c) skip (d) give (e) enlarge   6. _____

7. *concede*   (a) pride (b) devise (c) yield (d) regard (e) hold   7. _____

8. *simplicity*   (a) decorative (b) similar (c) bulbous (d) clarity (e) large   8. _____

9. *revolt*   (a) rebel (b) withdraw (c) comply (d) reform (e) charge   9. _____

10. *deceive*   (a) trick (b) corrupt (c) dispense (d) argue (e) prove   10. _____

11. *punctilious*   (a) careful (b) stingy (c) daring (d) religious (e) tardy   11. _____

12. *rabid*   (a) mild (b) lethargic (c) mad (d) straight (e) lively   12. _____

13. *perfunctory*   (a) mechanical (b) thoughtful (c) creative (d) sly (e) greasy   13. _____

14. *alternative*   (a) elevation (b) option (c) grant (d) roomy (e) wane   14. _____

15. *motive*   (a) reason (b) action (c) whim (d) death (e) ditch   15. _____

Your Total Score _____

62-B: Practice Procedure. Below are 40 words that are frequently misspelled. Study them carefully and be prepared to write them from memory.

adequate	divide	popular	rely
already	enough	presence	rescue
although	expense	presents	sandwich
altogether	forward	president	sense
animals	insurance	principal	soldier
bungalow	material	principle	starch
cellar	necessary	professor	their
champion	orchestra	promise	there
cousin	patient	proud	total
dealt	perhaps	quiet	worry

OBJECTIVES:
1. To recognize and use the different types of adjectives and adverbs.
2. To learn and use the three degrees of comparison for adjectives.

Adjectives are words used to modify nouns or pronouns. They are the picture words which make sentences more interesting. Adjectives tell color, number, or kind.

23-A. DESCRIPTIVE ADJECTIVES

A *descriptive adjective* describes the noun or pronoun it modifies.

EXAMPLE 1

The <u>cute</u> puppy was a <u>faithful</u> pet for my <u>little</u> brother.

Analysis:
<u>cute</u>—descriptive adjective—modifies noun *puppy*
<u>faithful</u>—descriptive adjective—modifies noun *pet*

little—descriptive adjective—modifies noun *brother*

EXAMPLE 2

The <u>tall</u>, <u>blond</u>, and <u>handsome</u> boy with the <u>red</u> hat had a <u>sharp</u> car.

Analysis:
<u>tall</u>, <u>blond</u>, <u>handsome</u>—descriptive adjectives—modify noun *boy*
<u>red</u>—descriptive adjective—modifies noun *hat*
<u>sharp</u>—descriptive adjective—modifies noun *car*

23-B. PROPER ADJECTIVES

When an adjective is derived from a proper noun, it is a *proper adjective* and begins with a capital letter.

EXAMPLE 1

The <u>American</u> tourists enjoyed their trip to Ireland.

Analysis:
<u>American</u>—proper adjective—derived from proper noun *America*—tells what kind of *tourists*

EXAMPLE 2

The <u>Mexican</u> family took a bus through the <u>Italian</u> countryside.

Analysis:
<u>Mexican</u>—proper adjective—derived from proper noun *Mexico*—tells what kind of *family*
<u>Italian</u>—proper adjective—derived from proper noun *Italy*—tells what kind of *countryside*

23-C. DEFINITE AND INDEFINITE ADJECTIVES

Definite (the) and *indefinite* (a, an) *adjectives* are called *articles*. Definite means a certain person or thing, and indefinite means no one person or thing in particular. Use *a* before words that start with a consonant or with words that start with a long-sounding *u*. Use *an* before words which start with a vowel *(a, e, i, o,* and short-sounding *u)* or with words that sound as if they start with a vowel *(hour)*.

A good name is better than riches.
It is a unique painting.
An umbrella kept me dry.
The student made an error on the test.

EXAMPLE 1

The teacher needed a vacation.

Analysis:
The—definite adjective

a—indefinite adjective—no particular *vacation*

EXAMPLE 2

The magician used an assistant as a helper for the trick.

Analysis:
The—definite adjective
an—indefinite adjective—no particular *assistant*
a—indefinite adjective—no particular *helper*
the—definite adjective

23-D. POSSESSIVE ADJECTIVES

Possessive pronouns are used as adjectives when they precede and modify nouns. They are *my, his, her, its, our, their, whose,* and *your.*

EXAMPLE 1

My mother visited her cousin in the hospital.

Analysis:
My—possessive adjective—modifies noun *mother*
her—possessive adjective—modifies noun *cousin*

EXAMPLE 2

Our nephews and their nieces are related to his family.

Analysis:
Our—possessive adjective—modifies noun *nephews*
their—possessive adjective—modifies noun *nieces*
his—possessive adjective—modifies noun *family*

23-E. DEMONSTRATIVE ADJECTIVES

This, that, these, and *those* are pronouns used as adjectives. They are called *demonstrative adjectives* because they not only modify nouns, but they also specify or call attention to them. *This* and *that* are singular and describe singular nouns. *These* and *those* are plural and describe plural nouns. *This* usually refers to something near and *that* refers to something farther away.

EXAMPLE 1

This turtle was given to me by our neighbor.

Analysis:
This—demonstrative adjective—singular —modifies singular noun *turtle*

EXAMPLE 2

That book belongs to the librarian.

Analysis:
That—demonstrative adjective—singular —modifies singular noun *book*

EXAMPLE 3

These athletes are the best in the city.

Analysis:
These—demonstrative adjective—plural —modifies plural noun *athletes*

EXAMPLE 4

Those musicians played popular tunes.

Analysis:
Those—demonstrative adjective—plural —modifies plural noun *musicians*

EXAMPLE 5

These instruments belong to the band.

Analysis:
These—demonstrative adjective—plural —modifies plural noun *instruments*

Complete Application Practices 63-64, pages 123-124, at this time.

63-A: Practice Procedure. In the following sentences some adjectives are underlined. Indicate why you think they are descriptive adjectives. Score one point for each correct response.

A <u>charming</u>, <u>beautiful</u>, and <u>lofty</u> mountain in North America is <u>scenic</u> Mount Rainier.

1. _____
2. _____
3. _____
4. _____

The <u>unusual</u> and <u>outstanding</u> peaks of the <u>volcanic</u> Cascade Range cover a <u>long</u> distance.

5. _____
6. _____
7. _____
8. _____

63-B: Practice Procedure. In the following sentences some adjectives are underlined. Indicate why you think they are proper or possessive adjectives. Score one point for each correct response.

<u>Whose</u> family visited the <u>Hawaiian</u> beaches last summer?

1. _____
2. _____

The <u>Polynesian</u> people were the first settlers in <u>our</u> fiftieth state.

3. _____
4. _____

<u>My</u> <u>Oregonian</u> relatives are proud of <u>their</u> coastal shoreline.

5. _____
6. _____
7. _____

<u>His</u> teacher showed the class slides of the <u>Californian</u> coast.

8. _____
9. _____

Your Total Score _____

If your score was 12 or less for 63-A and B, review Sections 23-A, B, and D, pages 121-122, before continuing.

64–A: Practice Procedure. Complete each of the following sentences by writing in the blank provided at the right the correct adjective in the parentheses. Remember that *this* and *that* are singular and *these* and *those* are plural. Score one point for each correct response.

Answers

1. (This, These) type of athlete makes the most money.

     1. _____

2. (This, These) baseball players are easily recognized.

     2. _____

3. The teams followed the *Official Baseball Rules Book* as (that, those) rules were accepted by the teams.

     3. _____

4. (That, Those) bat in the Hall of Fame was used by Ty Cobb.

     4. _____

5. (That, Those) game we watched was between the Yankees and the Angels.

     5. _____

6. (This, These) is the man they called the "Babe."

     6. _____

7. Mike Schmidt hit several of (that, those) home runs in Three Rivers Stadium.

     7. _____

8. My father paid $10 for (that, those) seats.

     8. _____

9. Ted Williams, (that, those) former great batting champion, is in the Hall of Fame.

     9. _____

10. (This, These) type of player is respected by all the fans around the country.

     10. _____

11. The ability (that, those) pitchers had was known to all the fans.

     11. _____

64–B: Practice Procedure. Complete each of the following sentences by writing *a* or *an* in the blank provided at the right. Score one point for each correct response.

1. W. C. Fields once said, "You can't cheat (a, an) honest man."

     1. _____

2. Tahiti is (a, an) island paradise.

     2. _____

3. Have you acted in (a, an) humane way?

     3. _____

4. Cindy tried to be (a, an) hour early for her plane.

     4. _____

5. Is marble (a, an) inflexible material?

     5. _____

6. (A, An) adaptable student can get along with most people.

     6. _____

7. (A, An) humble person is often respected.

     7. _____

8. How much is (a, an) trip to Tahiti?

     8. _____

9. The museum director purchased (a, an) outstanding painting by Rubens.

     9. _____

10. Who has (a, an) uncle who buys pictures?

     10. _____

Your Total Score _____

If your score was 15 or less for 64–A and B, review Sections 23–C and E, pages 121-122, before continuing.

Degrees of Comparison

The *positive, comparative,* and *superlative* are the three degrees of comparison for adjectives. The *positive degree* is used when the person or thing modified is not being compared with another. An adjective does not change its form in the positive degree. The *comparative degree* is used when comparing two persons or things. In most cases, add *er* to an adjective to form the comparative. The *superlative degree* is used when comparing three or more persons or things. Add *est* to an adjective to form the superlative. If the adjective ends in *e,* just add *r* for the comparative and *st* for the superlative.

EXAMPLE 1

Shirley is a <u>young</u> girl.

Analysis:
    <u>young</u>—talking of only one girl—positive degree

EXAMPLE 2

She is <u>younger</u> than her cousin.

Analysis:
    <u>younger</u>—comparison between two people—comparative degree

EXAMPLE 3

Ann is the <u>youngest</u> girl in our club.

Analysis:
    <u>youngest</u>—comparison of more than two people—superlative degree

To form the comparative and superlative degrees with adjectives that end in *y,* change the *y* to *i* before adding *er* or *est.* With some one-syllable adjectives that end in a single consonant, the comparative and superlative degrees are formed by doubling the last consonant before adding *er* or *est.*

EXAMPLE 1

His costume is <u>sillier</u> than her hat.

Analysis:
    <u>sillier</u>—comparison of two things, *costume* and *hat*—comparative degree

EXAMPLE 2

Yesterday was the <u>hottest</u> day of the year.

Analysis:
    <u>hottest</u>—comparison of more than two days—superlative degree

FAST   FASTER   FASTEST   FINISH LINE

DEGREES OF COMPARISON

Most adjectives which end in *ful*, *less*, or *some* and all adjectives of more than two syllables form their degrees by adding *more* for the comparative degree (comparison between two things) and *most* for the superlative degree (comparison of more than two things).

EXAMPLE 1

Tina has a <u>more cheerful</u> voice than my sister.

Analysis:
    <u>more cheerful</u>—comparison between two people — add *more* before the adjective — comparative degree

EXAMPLE 2

Joyce is the <u>most cheerful</u> person on our street.

Analysis:
    <u>most cheerful</u>—comparison of more than two persons — add *most* before the adjective — superlative degree

Exceptions: Some adjectives are different in all three forms. Study these adjectives so that you remember them. You probably already know most of them as they are often used in speech and writing.

Positive	Comparative	Superlative
good	better	best
much	more	most
bad (ill)	worse	worst
little	less	least

EXAMPLE 1

Frank is a <u>good</u> typist.

Analysis:
    <u>good</u>—talking of only one person—positive degree

EXAMPLE 2

Janet is the <u>better</u> typist of the two.

Analysis:
    <u>better</u>—comparison between two people—comparative degree

EXAMPLE 3

Tony is the <u>best</u> typist in our class.

Analysis:
    <u>best</u>—comparison of more than two persons—superlative degree

---

TRYOUT EXERCISE

Directions: Complete each of the following sentences by writing in the blank provided at the right the correct form of the adjective in the parentheses. Check your answers with your teacher before continuing.

1. My horse is the (most pretty, prettiest) in the stable.   1. _____
2. Jane is the (more, most) bashful student in the class.   2. _____
3. Pedro is the (best, better) athlete of the two players.   3. _____
4. She is (more strong, stronger) than her brother.   4. _____
5. Greg is the (worse, worst) tennis player of the two boys.   5. _____

Complete Application Practices 65-66, pages 127-128, at this time.

65: Practice Procedure. Indicate the comparative and the superlative degrees of the following adjectives. Remember that you usually add *er* to form the comparative (comparison between two things) and *est* to form the superlative (comparison of more than two things). Watch out for the exceptions. Score one point for each correct response.

Positive	Comparative	Superlative
Examples: fresh	fresher	freshest
careful	more careful	most careful
1. loud		
2. soft		
3. much		
4. green		
5. quick		
6. beautiful		
7. old		
8. little		
9. helpless		
10. forgetful		
11. kind		
12. wonderful		
13. heavy		
14. happy		
15. tactless		
16. small		
17. good		
18. careless		
19. skillful		
20. funny		
21. handsome		
22. sad		
23. cheerful		
24. pretty		
25. bad		

Your Total Score _____

If your score was 39 or less, review Section 24, pages 125-126, before continuing.

66: Practice Procedure. Complete each of the following sentences by writing in the blank provided at the right the correct form of the adjective in the parentheses. Remember that the comparative degree is used to compare two things, and the superlative degree is used to compare more than two things. Score one point for each correct answer.

Answers

1. The Navajo Indians are the (finer, finest) rug makers among all Indian people.

1. _____

2. The (happier, happiest) hunting ground of the Indians of the Plains was between the Mississippi and the Rockies.

2. _____

3. Kit Carson, the famous scout who fought the Pueblo Indians, was the (bravest, most brave) of all the scouts.

3. _____

4. Geronimo, the (greater, greatest) Indian leader, belonged to the Apache tribe.

4. _____

5. Was he (gracefuler, more graceful) than Chief Sitting Bull?

5. _____

6. The Iroquois Indians of New York were the (stronger, strongest) of all Indian tribes.

6. _____

7. They started the game of lacrosse which is the (faster, fastest) game of them all.

7. _____

8. The Sioux Indians were (cheerfuler, more cheerful) than the Apache tribe.

8. _____

9. The Mission Indians, (nearer, nearest) tribe to California, made wonderful baskets.

9. _____

10. The Blackfeet Indians were (taller, more tall, tallest) than the Iroquois Indians.

10. _____

11. Those three tribes were the (quicker, quickest) to fight.

11. _____

12. Tecumseh was the (better, best) warrior of the Shawnee Indians.

12. _____

13. Pontiac, the celebrated leader of the Ottawa tribe, was not (heavier, more heavy) than Tecumseh.

13. _____

14. The Navajos were (finer, more fine, finest) than the Apaches in weaving.

14. _____

15. The scout was (carelesser, more careless) than the chief.

15. _____

16. Mike Barton was the (better, best) of the two guides.

16. _____

17. His sister was (worse, worst) than the first guide.

17. _____

18. Chief Sitting Bull was always the (cheerfulest, most cheerful) person on the reservation.

18. _____

19. She was the (beautifulest, most beautiful) girl of them all.

19. _____

20. They are (skillfuler, more skillful) than Jim.

20. _____

21. After his defeat, Tecumseh's attitude was (worse, worst) than the winner.

21. _____

22. The Pueblo Indians were the (calmest, most calm) of all the Indian tribes.

22. _____

23. A souvenir shop, (large, larger, largest) than a cabin, sold many trinkets.

23. _____

24. The Indian agent was the (most careful, carefulest) one of the people that I met.

24. _____

25. Some tribes were the (most peaceful, peacefulest) people in the land.

25. _____

Your Total Score _____

If your score was 19 or less, review Section 24, pages 125-126, before continuing.

Adverbs

An *adverb* is a word used to modify a verb, an adjective, or another adverb. It makes these words clearer or more specific. Adverbs answer the questions "when," "where," "how," or "to what extent."

TIME — NOW, NIGHTLY, LATER, OFTEN
PLACE — HERE, EVERYWHERE, HIGH, UP
MANNER — BEAUTIFULLY, BRILLIANTLY, BRIGHTLY, LOUDLY
DEGREE — TOO, REALLY, QUITE, VERY
ADVERBS

25-A. ADVERBS OF TIME

Adverbs of time answer the question "when." *Now, then, soon, often, seldom,* and *finally* are adverbs of time.

EXAMPLE 1

Our class <u>soon</u> will visit a press conference.

Analysis:
    soon—adverb of time—answers the question "when"—modifies the verb *will visit*

EXAMPLE 2

The mayor <u>finally</u> arrived and <u>often</u> mentioned many problems.

Analysis:
    finally—adverb of time—answers the question "when"—modifies the verb *arrived*
    often—adverb of time—answers the question "when"—modifies the verb *mentioned*

25-B. ADVERBS OF PLACE

Adverbs of place answer the question "where." The most common are *here* and *there.* Often *there* is used at the beginning of a sentence and is mistakenly identified as the subject.

When *down* and *up* are not followed by a noun, they are adverbs.

EXAMPLE 1

The editor <u>there</u> discussed the various parts of the newspaper.

Analysis:
    there—adverb of place—answers the question "where"—modifies the verb *discussed*

EXAMPLE 2

Please wait <u>here</u> for the rest of the group.

Analysis:
    here—adverb of place—answers the question "where"—modifies the verb *wait*

EXAMPLE 3

At my question the reporter looked <u>up</u>.

Analysis:
    up—adverb of place—answers the question "where"—modifies the verb *looked*

25-C. ADVERBS OF MANNER

Adverbs of manner answer the question "how." These adverbs usually end in *ly. Lovely,* *friendly, ugly,* and *lonely,* however, are adjectives, not adverbs.

129

EXAMPLE 1

We sat <u>quietly</u> during the entire presentation.

Analysis:
> quietly—adverb of manner—answers the question "how"—modifies the verb *sat*

EXAMPLE 2

The movie <u>quickly</u> and <u>carefully</u> explained the development of communication.

Analysis:
> quickly, carefully — adverbs of manner — answer the question "how" — modify the verb *explained*

25-D. ADVERBS OF DEGREE

Adverbs of degree answer the question "to what extent." The most common are *too, really, quite,* and *very.* Such adverbs often modify adjectives.

EXAMPLE

I was <u>quite</u> uncomfortable waiting in the <u>very</u> stuffy office.

Analysis:
> quite—adverb of degree—answers the question "to what extent"—modifies adjective *uncomfortable*
> very—adverb of degree—answers the question "to what extent"—modifies adjective *stuffy*

25-E. INTERROGATIVE ADVERBS

How, when, why, and *where* are *interrogative adverbs.* They introduce questions.

EXAMPLE 1

<u>When</u> did people learn to talk?

Analysis:
> When—interrogative adverb—introduces a question—modifies the verb *did learn*

EXAMPLE 2

<u>How</u> could the Indians send long-distance messages?

Analysis:
> How—interrogative adverb—introduces a question—modifies the verb *could send*

25-F. MOST FREQUENTLY USED ADVERBS

finally	indeed	nevertheless	often	sometimes	there	what
here	later	not	probably	soon	too	when
however	never	now	seldom	still	very	where

TRYOUT EXERCISE

Directions: Identify the adverbs in the following sentences by underlining them once. Check your answers with your teacher before continuing.

1. You can easily read about Thomas Edison's inventions now.
2. When can you finally give your report on Alexander Graham Bell?
3. Sherri gracefully reported there on the different satellites.
4. He quite skillfully invented the phonograph.

Complete Application Practices 67-70, pages 131-134, at this time.

67: Practice Procedure. Identify the adverbs in the following sentences by underlining them once. Can you tell why they are adverbs? Insert a *P* over adverbs of *place,* an *M* over adverbs of *manner,* a *T* over adverbs of *time,* a *D* over adverbs of *degree,* and an *I* over *interrogative* adverbs. Score one point for each correct adverb and one point for each correct identification.

Your Score

1. Mr. McGlothen frequently mentioned the black heroes in our history.   1. _____

2. I had heard about the very brave black soliders at the Battle of Bunker Hill.   2. _____

3. We certainly were impressed with the bravery of Peter Salem during the Revolutionary War.   3. _____

4. Writers were quite silent about the black patriots.   4. _____

5. When will you tell us about the black stagecoach drivers?   5. _____

6. Bill Pickett, a black cowboy, often thrilled fans with his bulldogging.   6. _____

7. You probably knew about the first black Air Force general.   7. _____

8. Yesterday we learned his name was Benjamin O. Davis.   8. _____

9. Where have the cowboys gone?   9. _____

10. Blacks indeed helped in the development of the west.   10. _____

11. The teacher will soon bring an interesting speaker to class.   11. _____

12. The teacher finally introduced Mr. Hewitt.   12. _____

13. He had slides which delightfully illustrated old-time ads.   13. _____

14. One of the best known trademarks was seen everywhere in motion-picture theaters.   14. _____

15. Is it really a popcorn advertisement?   15. _____

16. It is still seen on MGM movies.   16. _____

17. You surely knew it was Leo the lion.   17. _____

18. Sometimes the ad is better than the product.   18. _____

19. Here we see the ads for the cosmetic companies.   19. _____

20. The relentlessly pushy salesperson came to our house.   20. _____

21. Soap companies often advertise on television.   21. _____

22. Why were the Burma Shave signs enjoyed by the motorists?   22. _____

23. Potato chip ads are really clever.   23. _____

24. We found a book there on the shelf that explained the pretzel.   24. _____

25. Food ads certainly make me hungry.   25. _____

Your Total Score _____

If your score was 39 or less, review Section 25, pages 129-130, before continuing.

68: Practice Procedure. Identify the adjectives and adverbs in the following sentences. Underline the adjectives once and the adverbs twice. Score one point for each correct identification.

Your Score

1. The entire family often travels to different countries around the world.   1. _____

2. A wonderful visit to the sprawling city of Madrid was indeed a great experience.   2. _____

3. The selective tourist certainly has an exciting time in the heart of old Madrid.   3. _____

4. Why are you looking at the Icelandic trip now?   4. _____

5. Nevertheless, they did see ruined palaces and very graceful mansions on the magnificent trip.   5. _____

6. Today the happy group will buy a budget package for the trip this summer.   6. _____

7. The inexpensive price covers good hotels and sometimes the cost of a superb dinner.   7. _____

8. Too many bargains were later purchased by Jack Hunt and the two aunts.   8. _____

9. The lovely women had previously traveled extensively throughout the English countryside.   9. _____

10. When is the final payment made to the agency?   10. _____

11. Confirmed reservations probably will arrive for Mr. Hunt tomorrow.   11. _____

12. Friendly hotels do indeed offer a room with a private bath at reasonable rates.   12. _____

13. Sometimes the tour price includes all tips.   13. _____

14. Curious travelers often find exceptionally reasonable hotels in unusual places.   14. _____

15. In picturesque Amsterdam they did indeed find a delightful small hotel.   15. _____

16. When did they finally take the pleasant voyage to the historic cities along the European coast?   16. _____

17. The French family will certainly not travel extensively through the aristocratic city of Bordeaux.   17. _____

18. The hair-raising ride in the cramped taxi nevertheless presented much excitement.   18. _____

19. However, chain hotels exist in the really beautiful city of scenic Lisbon.   19. _____

20. For extra space and plushier apartments, tourists soon read the travel books carefully about the small hotels.   20. _____

Your Total Score _____

If your score was 91 or less, review Sections 23-25, pages 121-130, before continuing.

69-A: Practice Procedure. Indicate by writing in the blanks next to the adjectives and adverbs whether they are descriptive, proper, definite, indefinite, possessive, or demonstrative adjectives; whether they are adverbs of time, place, manner, or degree; or whether they are interrogative adverbs. Score one point for each correct identification.

Identification   Your Score

1. too _____ 1. _____

2. when _____ 2. _____

3. Iowan _____ 3. _____

4. his _____ 4. _____

5. why _____ 5. _____

6. the _____ 6. _____

7. Egyptian _____ 7. _____

8. this _____ 8. _____

9. an _____ 9. _____

10. carefully _____ 10. _____

11. up _____ 11. _____

12. clever _____ 12. _____

13. ugly _____ 13. _____

14. now _____ 14. _____

15. those _____ 15. _____

Your Total Score _____

If your score was 11 or less, review Sections 23-25, pages 121-130, before continuing.

69-B: Practice Procedure. Here are 40 words that are frequently misspelled. Study them carefully and be prepared to write them from memory.

allowance	personal	strict	vicinity
chose	physical	success	volume
coarse	possess	theory	weather
collar	quick	though	whether
country	raisin	through	whole
dense	rhyme	trouble	who's
favorite	rhythm	typewriter	whose
ignorant	shining	until	write
mischief	skillful	usually	written
opinion	stretch	various	yacht

70–A: Practice Procedure. In the following sentences, select one word that has the same meaning as the italized word *(synonym)*. Also, select one word that has the opposite meaning *(antonym)*. Each sentence contains a word that means the same and one that means the opposite. Write the letters of the synonym and antonym in the blanks provided. Check your dictionary. Score one point for each correct response.

	Synonym	Antonym
Example: An *expensive* radio is (a) pretty (b) costly (c) useless (d) cheap.	b	d
1. A *cordial* greeting is (a) friendly (b) exciting (c) indifferent (d) unexpected.	1. _____	_____
2. An *imminent* departure is (a) approaching (b) distant (c) sad (d) unusual.	2. _____	_____
3. A *logical* ending is (a) secluded (b) reasonable (c) unlikely (d) open.	3. _____	_____
4. A *memorable* week is (a) forgettable (b) expensive (c) noteworthy (d) merciful.	4. _____	_____
5. A *diligent* worker is (a) hard-working (b) tardy (c) careless (d) tiny.	5. _____	_____
6. A *fragile* dish is (a) flowery (b) cheap (c) strong (d) breakable.	6. _____	_____
7. A *robust* person is (a) sturdy (b) sickly (c) right (d) untruthful.	7. _____	_____
8. A *torrid* day is (a) chilly (b) hot and dry (c) topsy-turvy (d) orderly.	8. _____	_____
9. *Scandalous* behavior is (a) scientific (b) proper (c) shameful (d) sarcastic.	9. _____	_____
10. A *casual* meeting is (a) unexpected (b) planned (c) frantic (d) bitter.	10. _____	_____

Your Total Score _____

70–B: Practice Procedure. These 24 words contain an *ie* or *ei*. Write out each word twice, spelling it correctly. Refer to the spelling hints on the inside back cover of this book.

1. brief _____ _____
2. either _____ _____
3. weigh _____ _____
4. seize _____ _____
5. height _____ _____
6. shriek _____ _____
7. piece _____ _____
8. thief _____ _____
9. their _____ _____
10. rein _____ _____
11. eight _____ _____
12. grief _____ _____
13. yield _____ _____
14. alien _____ _____
15. quiet _____ _____
16. weird _____ _____
17. niece _____ _____
18. neither _____ _____
19. fiend _____ _____
20. freight _____ _____
21. siege _____ _____
22. chief _____ _____
23. feint _____ _____
24. friend _____ _____

Section 26 — Prepositions

OBJECTIVES:
1. To learn the purposes and uses of prepositions and conjunctions.
2. To understand the use of pronouns as objects of prepositions.
3. To learn the use of prepositional phrases.

Pick up your pencil. Hold it in your right hand. Now place your left hand *over* the pencil, *beneath* the pencil, *toward* the pencil, *on* the pencil, *below* the pencil. The italicized words show the relationship between your hand and the pencil. These words are called *prepositions*. A *preposition* is a word which shows a relationship between a noun or pronoun and some other part of the sentence.

EXAMPLE 1

The baby <u>with</u> the grin was very cute.

Analysis:
> <u>with</u>—preposition—shows relationship between *baby* and *grin*

EXAMPLE 2

The mother received a letter <u>from</u> her daughter.

Analysis:
> <u>from</u>—preposition—shows relationship between *letter* and *daughter*

Every preposition has a noun or pronoun as its object. If a pronoun follows a preposition, it must be in the objective case *(me, him, her, us, them)*. Be careful of compound objects when the pronoun is the second object mentioned.

EXAMPLE 1

Willie went to the show with <u>them</u>.

Analysis:
> <u>them</u>—pronoun used as object of the preposition *with*—objective case

EXAMPLE 2

The singers sang to <u>him</u> and <u>me</u>.

Analysis:
> <u>him</u>, <u>me</u>—pronouns used as compound objects of the preposition *to*—objective case

EXAMPLE 3

The dancers waltzed by Pedro and <u>us</u>.

Analysis:
> <u>us</u>—pronoun used as the second object of the preposition *by*—objective case

26-A. USES OF THE PREPOSITIONAL PHRASE

A *phrase* is a group of related words that does not contain a subject and a verb in combination. A *prepositional phrase* consists of a preposition, a noun or pronoun that is the object of the preposition, and any modifiers that fall in between. If the prepositional phrase modifies a noun or pronoun, it is an *adjective phrase*. If it modifies a verb, an adjective, or an adverb, it is an *adverbial phrase*. (A more detailed explanation of phrases is given on pages 145-147.)

EXAMPLE 1

The painter <u>with the red beard</u> won the prize.

Analysis:
> <u>with the red beard</u>—adjective phrase as it modifies the noun *painter*

EXAMPLE 2

The winner walked <u>around the room</u>.

Analysis:
<u>around the room</u>—adverbial phrase as it modifies the verb *walked*

26-B. MOST FREQUENTLY USED PREPOSITIONS

about	around	between	in	round	underneath
above	at	by	into	since	until
across	before	down	of	through	up
after	behind	during	off	till	upon
against	below	except	on	to	with
along	beneath	for	over	toward(s)	within
among	beside	from	past	under	without

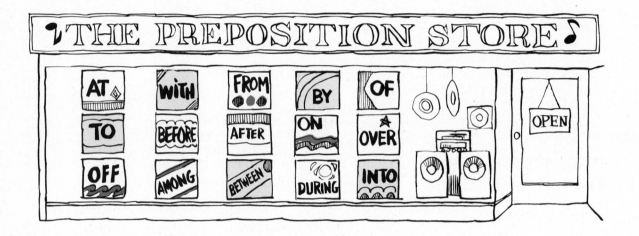

TRYOUT EXERCISE

Directions: Identify the prepositions in the following sentences by circling them once. Identify the prepositional phrases by underlining them.

1. The girl from the farm danced an Irish jig.

2. The orchestra in blue uniforms played for the parents.

3. The leader of the band looked toward our group.

Directions: Complete each of the following sentences by writing in the blank provided at the right the correct pronoun in the parentheses. Check your answers with your teacher before continuing with your assignment.

1. The teacher went to the dance with Otto and (I, me).   1. _____

2. The principal remained between Colleen and (her, she) at the door.   2. _____

3. The food was delivered by Miss Harris and (he, him).   3. _____

Complete Application Practices 71-72, pages 137-138, at this time.

136

71-A: Practice Procedure. Identify the prepositions in the following sentences by circling them. Identify the prepositional phrases by underlining them. Score one point for each preposition identified and one point for each phrase correctly identified.

Your Score

Example: The reporter wrote (about) the football players.

1. The team with the better players won the game.   1. _____
2. No one knew about their trick plays.   2. _____
3. The game was played under a clear sky.   3. _____
4. Tom and Jim did research for the football book.   4. _____
5. Other people helped in the final edition.   5. _____
6. The illustrations were designed by the author and an artist.   6. _____
7. The fans were among the noisiest this season.   7. _____
8. At the next game our friend will be the referee.   8. _____
9. The cheerleaders learned new yells during the year.   9. _____
10. The writer was indebted to many qualified coaches.   10. _____
11. The schedule was developed between the two principals.   11. _____
12. Every football play is aimed at a particular place.   12. _____
13. A quarterback with an accurate arm is worth a fortune.   13. _____
14. Everything went against the visiting team yesterday.   14. _____
15. Marcus Allen ran past the Rams' defenders very easily.   15. _____

71-B: Practice Procedure. Identify the prepositional phrases in each of the following sentences by underlining them. Identify each phrase as an adjective phrase or as an adverbial phrase by writing your answers in the blanks provided at the right. Score one point for each phrase correctly identified and one point for each correct answer as to the type of phrase.

Answers

Example: Casey Stengel of the New York Yankees was a great manager.   adjective

1. Ricky Henderson is a base runner with tremendous speed.   1. _____
2. The fans ran under the stands when it rained.   2. _____
3. Many spectators left during the game.   3. _____
4. Steve Carlton, a great pitcher for the Phillies, has many records.   4. _____
5. The youngster crawled underneath the fence.   5. _____
6. Pete Rose without great speed or size became a great player.   6. _____
7. The outfielder crashed into the fence when he caught the ball.   7. _____
8. The Yankees' team bus drove across town yesterday.   8. _____
9. The fan reached over the fence.   9. _____
10. Rod Carew originally came from Panama.   10. _____

Your Total Score _____

If your score was 39 or less for 71-A and B, review Section 26, pages 135-136, before continuing.

72: Practice Procedure. Complete each of the following sentences by writing in the blank provided at the right the correct pronoun in the parentheses. Remember that the objective case is used after prepositions. Score one point for each correct answer.

Answers

1. Mr. Polito played Verdi's operas for (they, them).   1. _____

2. The soprano sang with the choir and (he, him).   2. _____

3. Our music teacher sang some operatic songs to her son and (I, me).   3. _____

4. The orchestra played music written by the conductor and (us, we).   4. _____

5. The piano player stood between Todd and (us, we) on the stage.   5. _____

6. *Madame Butterfly* by Puccini is an opera enjoyed by my aunt and (them, they).   6. _____

7. Several of (we, us) knew that Verdi was the composer of *Aida*.   7. _____

8. The star of *La Boheme* visited with Mrs. Gilbert and (her, she).   8. _____

9. She gave two tickets to Arlene and (he, him).   9. _____

10. The music from the opera *Barber of Seville* drifted toward Betsy and (us, we).   10. _____

11. We were sorry to go without Milt and (her, she).   11. _____

12. The price of the ticket was cheaper for senior citizens and (them, they).   12. _____

13. The show started with Muriel and (her, she) at the ticket booth.   13. _____

14. Their seats were behind Frank and (I, me).   14. _____

15. The musical conductor nodded to Paula and (he, him).   15. _____

16. The musical was sponsored by (them, they).   16. _____

17. Verdi had lived for 80 years, which was news to Ms. Salazar and (her, she).   17. _____

18. We borrowed the music from our nephew and (her, she).   18. _____

19. We heard that *Falstaff* by Verdi was the last opera written by (he, him).   19. _____

20. The German opera, *Hansel and Gretel,* is familiar to my friends and (I, me).   20. _____

21. The music drew cheers from San-li and (us, we).   21. _____

22. Wagner's *Lohengrin* was scheduled to be seen by his club and (them, they).   22. _____

23. Among Lois, Len, and (I, me), $5 was spent on snacks.   23. _____

24. Aggie went past (us, we) without speaking.   24. _____

25. The conductor asked the audience to sing our national anthem with the cast and (he, him).   25. _____

Your Total Score _____

If your score was 19 or less, review Section 26, page 135, before continuing.

Conjunctions

Conjunctions join words, phrases (groups of related words), or clauses (parts of sentences that contain a subject and a verb). Conjunctions are classified as coordinating, subordinating, or correlative. (See pages 145-150 for further explanation of phrases and clauses.)

27-A. COORDINATING CONJUNCTIONS

Coordinating conjunctions join sentence parts of equal rank. Clauses of a compound sentence are connected by coordinating conjunctions. (See page 158 for the compound sentence.) Common coordinating conjunctions are *and, but, or, nor, yet.*

EXAMPLE 1

The wind <u>and</u> rain canceled the picnic.

Analysis:
> and—coordinating conjunction—joins two words to form a compound subject *wind* and *rain*

EXAMPLE 2

Hilda <u>or</u> Jack will drive the car to the beach.

Analysis:
> or—coordinating conjunction—joins two words to form a compound subject *Hilda* and *Jack*

EXAMPLE 3

We will go to the beach for scuba diving <u>or</u> for surfing.

Analysis:
> or—coordinating conjunction—connects two phrases, *for scuba diving* and *for surfing*

EXAMPLE 4

Most scuba divers are careful, <u>but</u> a few beginners don't listen to the instructions.

Analysis:
> but—coordinating conjunction—joins two clauses, *Most scuba divers are careful* with *a few beginners don't listen to the instructions*

27-B. SUBORDINATING CONJUNCTIONS

Subordinating conjunctions connect subordinate clauses to the main clause. (See page 148 for an explanation of subordinate clauses.) The most common subordinating conjunctions are:

after	for	till
although	if	unless
as	since	until
as if	so that	when
as though	than	where
because	that	wherever
before	though	while

EXAMPLE 1

You should look at many cars <u>before</u> you buy your first auto.

Analysis:
> before—subordinating conjunction—connects the subordinate clause *you buy your first auto* to the main clause *you should look at many cars*

EXAMPLE 2

<u>Because</u> my brother didn't listen to the mechanic, he bought a bad car.

Analysis:

Because—subordinating conjunction—connects the subordinate clause *my brother didn't listen to the mechanic* to the main clause *he bought a bad car*

27-C. CORRELATIVE CONJUNCTIONS

Correlative conjunctions are conjunctions used in pairs. The main ones are *either . . . or, both . . . and, neither . . . nor, not only . . . but (also), whether . . . or.*

EXAMPLE 1

<u>Neither</u> the secretary <u>nor</u> the accountant is lazy.

Analysis:

Neither, <u>nor</u>—correlative conjunctions — connects words *secretary* and *accountant*. Remember that *neither, nor* takes a singular verb when the subjects themselves are singular.

EXAMPLE 2

The applicant was <u>not only</u> a good typist <u>but also</u> a fine receptionist.

Analysis:

<u>not only, but also</u>—correlative conjunctions—connects words *a good typist* and *a fine receptionist*

EXAMPLE 3

<u>Either</u> the papers were on the desk, <u>or</u> they were in the file drawer.

Analysis:

<u>Either</u>, <u>or</u>—correlative conjunctions—connects clauses

---

TRYOUT EXERCISE

Directions: Identify the underlined words as coordinating, subordinating, or correlative conjunctions. Write your answer in the blank provided at the right. Be prepared to tell whether they connect words, phrases, or clauses. Check your answers with your teacher before continuing with your assignment.

1. President Teddy Roosevelt was <u>not only</u> a fearless president <u>but also</u> a famous Rough Rider.   1. _____

2. <u>Because</u> F. D. Roosevelt died in office, Harry Truman took over the Presidency.   2. _____

3. U. S. Grant was a great general <u>and</u> an unsuccessful president.   3. _____

4. <u>Either</u> the governor <u>or</u> the senator will run for president.   4. _____

5. My father will vote at the school <u>or</u> near the office.   5. _____

Complete Application Practices 73-76, pages 141-144, at this time.

73: Practice Procedure. Identify the conjunctions as coordinating, subordinating, or correlative. Tell whether they connect words, phrases, or clauses. Score one point for each conjunction type identified and one point for each connection explained.

Your Score

1. Was the wheel or the printing press a greater invention?
   or _____ 1. _____

2. The safety match was invented after 1843 yet prior to the invention of the safety pin.
   yet _____ 2. _____

3. Although Samuel Colt invented the revolver in 1835, Camillo Vitelli finished the pistol around 1540.
   Although _____ 3. _____

4. Neither the thresher nor the cotton gin was invented prior to 1750.
   Neither . . . nor _____ 4. _____

5. Other companies have become large corporations since Henry Ford popularized the automobile.
   since _____ 5. _____

6. Unless you heard of Cyrus McCormick, you don't know about his invention of the reaper.
   Unless _____ 6. _____

7. Both the iron-lung and the heart-lung machines help doctors in their operations.
   Both . . . and _____ 7. _____

8. When I was in high school, I took a trip to the Smithsonian Institute.
   When _____ 8. _____

9. Did the new medical drugs help in the operation or in the recovery?
   or _____ 9. _____

10. Some inventions not only solve some problems but also create other problems.
    not only . . . but also _____ 10. _____

11. Benjamin Franklin invented the lightning conductor either before 1776 or after 1776.
    either . . . or _____ 11. _____

12. Did RCA or Zenith devise the first metal glass TV picture tube?
    or _____ 12. _____

13. A patent gives the inventor the right to make and sell an invention.
    and _____ 13. _____

14. Some inventions are valuable, but other inventions are impractical.
    but _____ 14. _____

15. Unless you invent something people want, you won't be able to sell it.
    Unless _____ 15. _____

Your Total Score _____

If your score was 23 or less, review Section 27, pages 139-140, before continuing.

74: **Practice Procedure.** Construct 20 sentences using each of the following conjunctions. Tell whether the conjunctions join words, phrases, or clauses. Score one point for each correct sentence and one point for each connection explained.

Example: The inventor <u>and</u> the lawyer applied for the patent. (*and* joins words)

1. and	6. when	11. since	16. because
2. but	7. or	12. either, or	17. although
3. neither, nor	8. both, and	13. as though	18. where
4. before	9. until	14. unless	19. not only, but also
5. after	10. as	15. nor	20. while

1. _____
2. _____
3. _____
4. _____
5. _____
6. _____
7. _____
8. _____
9. _____
10. _____
11. _____
12. _____
13. _____
14. _____
15. _____
16. _____
17. _____
18. _____
19. _____
20. _____

Your Total Score _____

If your score was 31 or less, review Section 27, pages 139-140, before continuing.

75–A: Practice Procedure. Words which sound the same but are spelled differently and have different meanings are called *homonyms*. Complete each of the following sentences by writing in the blank provided at the right the correct form of the word in the parentheses. Score one point for each correct answer.

Answers

1. The mongoose (prays, preys) on snakes and rats.

1. _____

2. The (bail, bale) of hay was tossed into the stable.

2. _____

3. That (sale, sail) on the boat suddenly filled with wind.

3. _____

4. The school conducted a (pole, poll) among the students.

4. _____

5. Some doctors can't collect their money from a few (patience, patients).

5. _____

6. It's a (tail, tale) told by a new writer.

6. _____

7. The red (flour, flower) looked pretty and was fragrant.

7. _____

8. The breakfast (role, roll) was very tasty.

8. _____

9. The weather (vein, vain, vane) was the shape of a horse and its rider.

9. _____

10. The oven (grate, great) was dusty and messy.

10. _____

11. The queen's (rain, rein, reign) lasted for 20 years.

11. _____

12. The gold (ore, oar) was mined in Colorado.

12. _____

13. Fritz and Sally tied for (forth, fourth) place.

13. _____

14. What is a (fair, fare) price for that jacket?

14. _____

15. The store had some expensive (stationary, stationery) for sale.

15. _____

Your Total Score _____

75–B: Practice Procedure. Here are 40 words that are frequently misspelled. Study them carefully and be prepared to write them from memory.

abundant	carefully	fabulous	package
accumulate	character	formerly	partner
advertisement	committee	government	physician
alphabet	consider	intelligence	pleasant
annual	continue	interfere	privilege
answer	describe	jealous	quite
applause	difficult	laboratory	responsible
argument	doesn't	launch	sentence
aviation	engineer	missile	specimen
between	existence	obedient	thousand

143

76: Practice Procedure. Explain briefly the difference between the two underlined words in each of the following sentences. Use your dictionary.

1. Can a diseased person ever become a deceased person?

_____

_____

2. What do you mean when you say the capitol is in the capital city?

_____

_____

3. Are epithets ever used as epitaphs?

_____

_____

4. Our principal is a person of high principles.

_____

_____

5. Are personal matters the same as personnel matters?

_____

_____

6. Are all humans humane people?

_____

_____

7. If it only costs you $99 to fly from coast to coast, would you consider it a fair fare or a fare fair?

_____

_____

8. If a class of 30 students voted for a class president, and one girl received 14 votes, another pupil received 10 votes, and the third student received 6 votes, would the first girl have received a majority or a plurality vote? Why?

_____

_____

9. Does former mean the opposite of later or latter?

_____

_____

10. Why do you think a censor often censures certain movies?

_____

_____

Your Total Score _____

OBJECTIVES: 1. To recognize and use prepositional, infinitive, and participial phrases.
2. To recognize and use independent and dependent (subordinate) clauses.

A *phrase* is a group of related words used as a noun, an adjective, or an adverb. It does not contain a subject and a verb in combination. Most phrases consist of a preposition plus a noun or pronoun (and modifiers). (See page 136 for a list of prepositions.)

Three important types of phrases are:

1. Prepositional phrases
2. Infinitive phrases
3. Participial phrases

28-A. PREPOSITIONAL PHRASES

Prepositional phrases are used as adjectives to modify nouns or pronouns (adjective phrases) or as adverbs to modify verbs, adjectives, or other adverbs (adverbial phrases). (See page 135 for a review of prepositional phrases.)

EXAMPLE 1

She returned <u>to the library</u>.

Analysis:
> <u>to the library</u>—prepositional (adverbial) phrase — It contains a preposition *to*, plus a noun *library*, and the modifier *the*. The phrase modifies the verb *returned*.

EXAMPLE 2

Our cats always sleep <u>in the sun</u>.

Analysis:
> <u>in the sun</u>—prepositional (adverbial) phrase—It contains a preposition *in*, plus a noun *sun*, and the modifier *the*. The phrase modifies the verb *sleep*.

EXAMPLE 3

That house <u>on the hill</u> has a great view.

Analysis:
> <u>on the hill</u>—prepositional (adjective) phrase—It contains a preposition *on*, plus a noun *hill*, and the modifier *the*. The phrase modifies the noun *house*.

EXAMPLE 4

They <u>at the office</u> should know my address.

Analysis:
> <u>at the office</u> — prepositional (adjective) phrase — It contains a preposition *at*, plus a noun *office*, and the modifier *the*. The phrase modifies the pronoun *They*.

EXAMPLE 5

The hat <u>on the chair</u> <u>in my room</u> is new.

Analysis:
> <u>on the chair</u> — prepositional (adjective) phrase — It contains a preposition *on*, plus a noun *chair*, and the modifier *the*. The phrase modifies the noun *hat*.
> <u>in my room</u>—prepositional (adjective) phrase— It contains a preposition *in*, plus a noun *room*, and the modifier *my*. The phrase modifies the noun *chair*.

EXAMPLE 6

The rabbit ran <u>across the yard</u> and <u>into its hole.</u>

Analysis:

<u>across the yard</u> — prepositional (adverbial) phrase — It contains a preposition *across*, plus a noun *yard*, and the modifier *the*. The phrase modifies the verb *ran*.

<u>into its hole</u> — prepositional (adverbial) phrase — It contains a preposition *into*, plus a noun *hole*, and the modifier *its*. The phrase modifies the verb *ran*.

28-B. INFINITIVE PHRASES

The second most often used phrase is the infinitive phrase. The *infinitive phrase* consists of the preposition *to* plus a verb form. Infinitive phrases may have an object or they may be described by an adverb. *(To write the letter* is my chore—infinitive with object. I will try *to write legibly*—infinitive with adverbial modifier.) Most infinitive phrases are used as nouns either as the subject or the object of the sentence, although the phrases may also be used as adverbs or adjectives.

EXAMPLE 1

<u>To win the scholarship</u> is Enrique's ambition.

Analysis:

<u>To win the scholarship</u>—infinitive phrase containing a preposition *To* plus a verb *win* and its object *scholarship*—It is used as a noun (subject).

EXAMPLE 2

<u>To write an essay</u> is difficult for Ken.

Analysis:

<u>To write an essay</u>—infinitive phrase containing a preposition *To* plus a verb *write* and its object *essay*—It is used as a noun (subject).

EXAMPLE 3

My secretary asked <u>to leave early.</u>

Analysis:

<u>to leave early</u>—infinitive phrase containing a preposition *to* plus a verb *leave* and its adverbial modifier *early*—It is used as a noun and is the object of the verb *asked*.

EXAMPLE 4

Lois wanted <u>to lead the discussion.</u>

Analysis:

<u>to lead the discussion</u>—infinitive phrase containing a preposition *to* plus a verb *lead* and its object *discussion*—It is used as a noun and is the object of the verb *wanted*.

The following infinitive phrases are used as adverbs. They modify verbs and answer the questions "where," "why," "how," "when," or "to what extent."

EXAMPLE 1

Sharon played <u>to win the game.</u>

Analysis:

<u>to win the game</u>—infinitive phrase used as an adverb—modifies verb *played*

EXAMPLE 2

Marvin went <u>to see a movie</u> with Janice.

Analysis:

<u>to see a movie</u>—infinitive phrase used as an adverb—modifies the verb *went*

The following infinitive phrases are used as adjectives. They modify nouns.

EXAMPLE 1

His hope <u>to forgive her</u> was great.

Analysis:

<u>to forgive her</u>—infinitive phrase used as an adjective—modifies the noun *hope*

EXAMPLE 2

Toshi's plan <u>to enter college</u> succeeded.

Analysis:

<u>to enter college</u>—infinitive phrase used as an adjective—modifies the noun *plan*

EXAMPLE 3

Marlo is an actress <u>to watch.</u>

Analysis:

<u>to watch</u>—infinitive phrase used as an adjective—modifies the noun *actress*

A *participial phrase* begins with the present participle (verb form ending in *ing*—seeing, loving) or the past participle (verb form ending in *ed, t, en*—covered, kept, forgotten). (Irregular past participles may be found in the table on pages 101-102.) The participle and the rest of the phrase act as an adjective. A participial phrase does not have a subject.

EXAMPLE 1

Driven by the wind, the ship crashed on the rocks.

Analysis:

Driven by the wind—participial phrase formed by adding *en* to the verb *drive* (past participle)—modifies the noun *ship*

EXAMPLE 2

Hearing the siren, Bob drove his car to the side of the road.

Analysis:

Hearing the siren—participial phrase formed by adding *ing* to the verb *hear* (present participle)—modifies the noun *Bob*

EXAMPLE 3

Kept after school, Bill missed baseball practice.

Analysis:

Kept after school—participial phrase formed with the irregular past participle of the verb *keep*—modifies the noun *Bill*

EXAMPLE 4

Clara, seeing the oncoming headlights, swerved to the right.

Analysis:

seeing the oncoming headlights—participial phrase formed by adding *ing* to the verb *see* (present participle)—modifies the noun *Clara*

TRYOUT EXERCISE

Directions: Underline the prepositional phrases in the following sentences. In the answer column at the right indicate whether they are adjective (adj) or adverbial (adv) phrases.

1. The tree on the corner fell.   1. _____
2. Dad always sits in the black chair.   2. _____
3. That picture of our family is great!   3. _____

Directions: Underline the infinitive phrases in the following sentences. In the answer column at the right indicate whether they are used as a noun (n), an adjective (adj), or an adverb (adv).

1. Elsie worked to earn her tuition money.   1. _____
2. His desire to learn English is commendable.   2. _____
3. To graduate with honors is her goal.   3. _____

Directions: Underline the participial phrases in the following sentences. Check your answers with your teacher before continuing with your assignment.

1. The toddler, left all alone, emptied the wastebaskets.
2. Playing in the garden, the tot got very dirty.

Complete Applications 77-78, pages 151-152, at this time.

Clauses

A *clause* is a part of a sentence that contains a complete subject and a complete predicate. The two types of clauses are:

1. Independent clauses
2. Dependent (subordinate) clauses

29-A. INDEPENDENT CLAUSES

An *independent clause* expresses a complete thought and has a subject and a verb. It is the main thought of a sentence and can stand alone correctly as a simple sentence without anything attached to it.

EXAMPLE 1

The crowd roared when the score was made.

Analysis:

The crowd roared—independent clause—It is the main idea of the sentence and can be used alone as a simple sentence.

EXAMPLE 2

The band will march in the parade if it doesn't rain.

Analysis:

The band will march in the parade—independent clause—It is the main idea of the sentence and can be used alone as a simple sentence.

EXAMPLE 3

Because we arrived early, we had good seats.

Analysis:

we had good seats—independent clause—It is the main idea of the sentence and can be used alone as a simple sentence.

29-B. DEPENDENT CLAUSES

The *dependent* (or subordinate) *clause* depends upon the independent (main) clause for understanding. A dependent clause when standing alone is not a complete sentence. Just as a person needs food in order to live and a plant needs water in order to grow, a dependent clause needs an independent clause to express a complete thought.

Dependent clauses which are used as adjectives (describing nouns or pronouns) are introduced by relative pronouns *(who, whom, whose,*

that, which). (Check page 51 for a review of relative pronouns.)

EXAMPLE 1

The trip that our family took in April was to Miami.

Analysis:

that our family took in April—dependent clause introduced by the relative pronoun *that*—It modifies the noun *trip* and is an adjective clause.

148

EXAMPLE 2

The person <u>who caused it</u> left the scene of the accident.

Analysis:

<u>who caused it</u>—dependent clause introduced by the relative pronoun *who*—It modifies the noun *person* and is an adjective clause.

EXAMPLE 3

The flowers <u>which were on the table</u> were beautiful.

Analysis:

<u>which were on the table</u>—dependent clause introduced by the relative pronoun *which*—It modifies the noun *flowers* and is an adjective clause.

Dependent clauses which are used as *adverbs* are introduced by subordinating conjunctions. They modify verbs, adjectives, or other adverbs by answering the questions "how," "where," "when," "why," "to what extent," or "under what conditions." (See page 139 for a list of subordinating conjunctions.)

EXAMPLE 1

<u>When the storm hit</u>, we went in the house.

Analysis:

<u>When the storm hit</u>—dependent clause introduced by the subordinating conjunction *When*—modifies the verb *went* and is an adverbial clause

EXAMPLE 2

He taught at Collier Street School <u>until he retired</u>.

Analysis:

<u>until he retired</u>—dependent clause introduced by the subordinating conjunction *until*—modifies the verb *taught* and is an adverbial clause

EXAMPLE 3

Laura received a high mark <u>because she studied hard.</u>

Analysis:

<u>because she studied hard</u>—dependent clause introduced by the subordinating conjunction *because*—modifies the verb *received* and is an adverbial clause

EXAMPLE 4

The painting was larger <u>than she had thought.</u>

Analysis:

<u>than she had thought</u>—dependent clause introduced by the subordinating conjunction *than*—modifies the adjective *larger* and is an adverbial clause

EXAMPLE 5

<u>Before Tom arrived</u>, the guest of honor left.

Analysis:

<u>Before Tom arrived</u>—dependent clause introduced by the subordinating conjunction *Before*—modifies the verb *left* and is an adverbial clause

Dependent clauses which are used as *nouns* (subjects, objects, appositives) or predicate nouns are *noun clauses*. Most noun clauses are used either as subjects or objects of a sentence. Occasionally they are used as objects of prepositions. Look for the verb first and then determine how the clause is used.

Most noun clauses are introduced by *that, how, why, what, whatever, whoever, whether* and are followed by a group of words that are used as a single noun.

EXAMPLE 1

<u>Whoever called last night</u> was John's friend.

Analysis:

<u>Whoever called last night</u>—dependent clause used as a noun—It is the subject of the verb *was*.

EXAMPLE 2

<u>What the person said</u> is on the telephone recorder.

Analysis:

<u>What the person said</u>—dependent clause used as a noun—It is the subject of the verb *is*.

EXAMPLE 3

The doctor was asked <u>whether her patient could have visitors.</u>

Analysis:

<u>whether her patient could have visitors</u>—dependent clause used as a noun—It is the object of the verb *was asked*.

EXAMPLE 4

Denise told me <u>that she was coming to the party.</u>

Analysis:

that she was coming to the party—dependent clause used as a noun—It is the object of the verb *told.*

EXAMPLE 5

It may have been <u>that he missed the plane.</u>

Analysis:

that he missed the plane—dependent clause used as a noun—It is a predicate noun.

EXAMPLE 6

We'll sell the car to <u>whoever meets our price.</u>

Analysis:

whoever meets our price—dependent clause used as object of the preposition *to*

EXAMPLE 7

Make a contribution to <u>whatever agency you wish.</u>

Analysis:

whatever agency you wish—dependent clause used as object of the preposition *to*

TRYOUT EXERCISE

Directions: Underline the independent clauses once and the dependent clauses twice in the following sentences. In the answer column at the right, tell whether the dependent clauses are adjective (adj) or adverbial (adv).

1. If you like sweets, you will love her chocolate chip cake.   1. _____

2. The flowers that he brought were beautiful.   2. _____

Directions: Underline the noun clauses in the following sentences. In the answer column at the right tell whether they are used as subjects, objects, objects of prepositions, or predicate nouns. Check your answers with your teacher before continuing your assignment.

1. What the reporter wrote was accurate.   1. _____

2. I know that I will do better next time.   2. _____

3. Her excuse for being tardy was that she had overslept.   3. _____

4. Dave will teach tennis to whoever wants to learn.   4. _____

Complete Application Practices 79-82, pages 153-156, at this time.

77-A: Practice Procedure. Underline the prepositional phrases in the following sentences. In the answer column at the right indicate whether they are adjective (adj) or adverbial (adv) phrases. All of these sentences are popular quotations from William Shakespeare's plays. Shakespeare, the most famous of all playwrights, lived in England during the reign of Queen Elizabeth I in the latter part of the sixteenth century. Score one point for each phrase correctly underlined and one point for each phrase correctly described.

Answers

1. Brevity is the soul of wit.   1. _____

2. A rose by any other name would smell as sweet.   2. _____

3. The quality of mercy is not strained.   3. _____

4. Men of few words are the best men.   4. _____

5. Blessed are the peacemakers on earth.   5. _____

6. The better part of valor is discretion.   6. _____

7. My pride fell with my fortune.   7. _____

8. A merry heart goes through the day.   8. _____

9. Fear of death is worse than death itself.   9. _____

10. I speak in a monstrous little voice.   10. _____

77-B: Practice Procedure. Underline the participial phrases in the following sentences. Score one point for each phrase correctly underlined.

Your Score

1. Using his loudest voice, the actor recited the famous speech.   1. _____

2. Forgetting her lines, the actress tried to regain her poise.   2. _____

3. Turning the lights to blue, the stage manager made the scene appear
    like night.   3. _____

4. Taken by surprise, the audience jumped when the gun sounded.   4. _____

5. The funny actress, entering the stage backwards, caused the people
    to laugh.   5. _____

6. The woman, crying quietly, was deeply moved by the performance. 6. _____

7. Made by the famous designer, the costumes were gorgeous.   7. _____

8. The play, begun sharply at eight, ended in two hours.   8. _____

9. The audience, delighted with the performance, began to clap wildly. 9. _____

10. The roses thrown onto the stage were a sign of appreciation.   10. _____

Your Total Score _____

If your score was 23 or less for 77-A and B, review Sections 28-A and 28-C, pages 145 and 147, before continuing.

78–A: Practice Procedure. Underline the infinitive phrases in the following sentences. In the answer column, state if they are used as nouns (n), adjectives (adj), or adverbs (adv). Score one point for each phrase correctly underlined and one point for each phrase correctly described.

Answers

1. My secretary Lynn hopes to improve office efficiency.   1. _____

2. Her desire to achieve this goal is long-standing.   2. _____

3. She works hard to set a good example.   3. _____

4. Unlike Lynn, Stella doesn't want to work hard.   4. _____

5. Stella was hired to answer the telephones.   5. _____

6. Like Lynn, Pat wants to succeed.   6. _____

7. Pat's job is to take dictation.   7. _____

8. Pat's plan to improve his skills is admirable.   8. _____

9. Lynn and Pat encouraged Stella to be a better worker.   9. _____

10. They all have skills to strengthen.   10. _____

78–B: Practice Procedure. Follow the procedure for 78–A.

1. My brother wants to become a teacher.   1. _____

2. To teach English is his ambition.   2. _____

3. He studied to prepare himself.   3. _____

4. To enter teaching meant lots of hard work.   4. _____

5. His plan to earn money for college was commendable.   5. _____

6. His friend Susy hopes to enter the same college.   6. _____

7. Their enthusiasm to attend college together was expected.   7. _____

8. They worked hard to improve their grade point averages.   8. _____

9. To attain a 3.5 grade point average was their goal.   9. _____

10. Both young people want to succeed.   10. _____

Your Total Score _____

If your score was 31 or less for 78–A and B, review Section 28–B, page 146, before continuing.

78–C: Practice Procedure. Demonstrate your understanding of infinitive phrases by using them in a short paragraph. Select a topic of your own choosing and use a separate sheet of paper. Underline the phrases and be prepared to explain how each was used.

79–A: Practice Procedure. Underline the independent clauses once and the dependent clauses twice in the following sentences. In the answer column at the right, tell whether the dependent clauses are adjective (adj) or adverbial (adv) clauses. Score one point for each correctly underlined clause and one point for each correctly identified clause.

Answers

1. William F. Cody, who was also known as Buffalo Bill, became a famous entertainer.

    1. _____

2. Cody's show, which was called the Wild West, was very exciting.

    2. _____

3. Whenever Buffalo Bill rode into the arena, people cheered.

    3. _____

4. Sharpshooter Annie Oakley, who never missed her target, was a main attraction.

    4. _____

5. While some cowboys reenacted the Pony Express, others rode bucking broncos.

    5. _____

6. Cody hunted a buffalo herd in the show as Indians in war paint attacked a train.

    6. _____

7. The show, which toured the world, was a favorite of kings and commoners alike.

    7. _____

8. Cody, who wore fringed buckskin, was a superb horseman.

    8. _____

9. Until it closed in 1913, the Wild West troupe toured Europe and America.

    9. _____

10. While cowboys were popular with the audience, the Indians made the show.

    10. _____

79–B: Practice Procedure. Follow the procedure given for 79–A.

1. Cody shot at glass-ball targets while riding at full gallop.

    1. _____

2. The skills that Cody used in the show were learned as a boy in Kansas.

    2. _____

3. When Cody was in London, the Prince of Wales gave him a gold watch.

    3. _____

4. Queen Victoria, who gave him a diamond pin, was a Buffalo Bill fan.

    4. _____

5. The watch, which can be seen at the Buffalo Bill Center, contains many jewels.

    5. _____

6. Because she was a sure shot, Annie Oakley had top billing in the show.

    6. _____

7. Frank Butler, who was married to Annie Oakley, was a famous sharpshooter, too.

    7. _____

8. Before the show started, the performers paraded around the arena.

    8. _____

9. Although kings and presidents were his friends, Cody never forgot his humble beginning.

    9. _____

10. Cody, who knew their culture, hired hundreds of Indians as performers.

    10. _____

Your Total Score _____

If your score was 48 or less, review Section 29, pages 148-150, before continuing.

80-A: Practice Procedure. Underline the noun clauses in the following sentences. In the answer column at the right, tell whether they are used as subjects, objects, objects of prepositions, or predicate nouns. Score one point for each clause correctly underlined and one point for each correct identification.

Answers

1. That El Greco is a great modern artist is accepted today.   1. _____

2. Why he was not accepted during his lifetime is a long story.   2. _____

3. Then, people felt El Greco was a wild, insane painter.   3. _____

4. Today, the art world believes that he was a brilliant artist.   4. _____

5. The mystery is how his work was first overlooked.   5. _____

6. There are good reasons for why he painted in Spain.   6. _____

7. El Greco decided that only light and color were important in painting.   7. _____

8. Whoever has an El Greco painting today is fortunate.   8. _____

9. Why he distorted the figures in his paintings was revealed in his writings.   9. _____

10. El Greco believed that painters were also philosophers.   10. _____

80-B: Practice Procedure. In the spaces below, write sentences using any four of the following noun clauses as subjects, four as objects, and two as objects of prepositions. Identify each in the margin (S=subject; O=object; OP=object of preposition). Score one point for each correct sentence.

1. Whoever comes now
2. For what they accomplished
3. By what they do
4. How we play
5. Why my father likes you
6. What we say at the zoo
7. Whether it is possible
8. Whether they were right or not
9. After what we have been through
10. What one person wants to do
11. That people talk about you
12. That I should come to this

1. _____

2. _____

3. _____

4. _____

5. _____

6. _____

7. _____

8. _____

9. _____

10. _____

Your Total Score _____

If your score was 23 or less for 80-A and B, review Section 29-B, pages 149-150, before continuing.

81-A: Practice Procedure. Match each item in Column B with the item it describes in Column A. Write the identifying letter from Column B in the blank provided at the right. Score one point for each correct answer.

Column A	Column B	Answers
1. We talked *over the crowd noise.*	a. subordinating conjunctions	1. _____
2. picnics *and* ants	b. dependent clause	2. _____
3. His is the house *on the hill.*	c. prepositional phrase used as an adjective	3. _____
4. because, until, after	d. infinitive phrase used as an object	4. _____
5. on, by, for, over, with	e. correlative conjunctions	5. _____
6. The bus arrived *after we had left.*	f. prepositional phrase used as an adverb	6. _____
7. *Driving at night* bothered him.	g. independent clause	7. _____
8. Rosa asked *to use the car.*	h. infinitive phrase used as an adverb	8. _____
9. John worked *to get ahead.*	i. participial phrase	9. _____
10. neither–nor	j. prepositions	10. _____
11. a complete thought containing a subject and a verb	k. coordinating conjunction	11. _____

Your Total Score _____

If your score was 7 or less, review Sections 26-29, pages 135-140 and 145-150, before continuing.

81-B: Practice Procedure. Here are 40 words that are often misspelled. Study them carefully and be prepared to write them from memory.

ambulance	breathe	disease	leisure
appreciate	brilliant	eliminate	prompt
arithmetic	carpenter	equipped	quart
arrange	chorus	fiftieth	receive
athletes	clothes	genuine	satisfy
athletics	commit	hundred	sophomore
audience	committed	interrupt	stationary
aviator	concise	journey	stationery
bachelor	consonant	laughter	tenant
biography	disappear	legible	truly

82-A: Practice Procedure. Select the one word that is the synonym for the numbered word. Write the letter that identifies the correct word in the blank provided at the right. Remember that a synonym has the same or a similar meaning. Score one point for each correct answer.

Answers

1. *structure*   (a) building (b) conflict (c) foam (d) vein (e) harshness   1. _____

2. *indefinite*   (a) incredible (b) doubtless (c) clear (d) vague
                    (e) illogical   2. _____

3. *personal*   (a) mortal (b) enduring (c) individual (d) tame (e) annual   3. _____

4. *hindrance*   (a) aid (b) fossil (c) repulsion (d) posterior
                    (e) impediment   4. _____

5. *option*   (a) current (b) alternative (c) change (d) tall (e) love   5. _____

6. *opposition*   (a) minority (b) resistance (c) eave (d) partner
                    (e) chance   6. _____

7. *invalid*   (a) rider (b) technician (c) player (d) sufferer (e) winner   7. _____

8. *industrious*   (a) diligent (b) pampered (c) careless (d) slack
                    (e) useless   8. _____

9. *technique*   (a) dilemma (b) obstacle (c) method (d) recount
                    (e) attempt   9. _____

10. *junction*   (a) joy (b) box (c) railway (d) roadblock (e) union   10. _____

82-B: Practice Procedure. Fifteen *ie* or *ei* words have been purposely misspelled in the following paragraph. How many of them can you spot? Underline the incorrect words and spell them correctly in the answer column at the right. See the inside back cover for a review of spelling rules. Score one point for each correct answer.

Bob Morton, my best friend and nieghbor, acheived some success as a   1. _____

crime fighter last week when he siezed a thief in the course of a robbery.   2. _____

The theif tried to steal some money from the cashier in a local restaurant.   3. _____

The casheir had just recieved some change from Father McCarthy, the   4. _____

priest at St. John's Cathedral. Niether the thief nor Bob beleived that the   5. _____

encounter would end so quickly. Bob had the advantage of three inches in   6. _____

hieght and twenty pounds in weight, and this fact helped the robber yield   7. _____

to superior force. An elderly woman and her pretty, young neice tossed   8. _____

apples and oranges up toward the cieling trying to distract the robber; but   9. _____

a wierd individual, dressed as a native cheiftain, said that he was losing   10. _____

patience with their wastefulness. I don't honestly believe Bob would have   11. _____

captured this thief if he hadn't thrown peices of crushed ice at the robber, 12. _____

chilling the criminal's ardor. As a final stroke of luck for Bob, the owner of 13. _____

the restaurant gave him an anceint foreign coin as a reward and invited   14. _____

him to have a meal free of charge.   15. _____

Your Total Score _____

Classification of Sentences

Unit 9

Writing Sentences
and Paragraphs

Section 30

OBJECTIVES:
1. To recognize and use simple, compound, and complex sentences.
2. To recognize and use topic sentences.
3. To recognize and use linking words and phrases.
4. To write paragraphs applying grammar rules.

30-A. THE SIMPLE SENTENCE

We have already learned that a *simple sentence* expresses a complete thought and has a subject and a verb (page 1).

EXAMPLE 1

Gary married Cathie in April.

Analysis:
Gary—subject
married—verb

EXAMPLE 2

Tony won the golf tournament.

Analysis:
Tony—subject
won—verb

EXAMPLE 3

Denise drives trucks in New York.

Analysis:
Denise—subject
drives—verb

A simple sentence may have a *compound subject* (more than one) or a *compound verb* or both in the same sentence.

EXAMPLE 1

May and Rinji are good friends.

Analysis:
May, Rinji—compound subject
are—plural verb—agrees in number with the plural (compound) subject

EXAMPLE 2

The cat caught and killed a mouse.

Analysis:
cat—subject
caught, killed—compound verb

EXAMPLE 3

Dave and John swim and dive at the pool.

Analysis:
Dave, John—compound subject
swim, dive—compound verb

ONE INDEPENDENT   TWO INDEPENDENTS   ONE INDEPENDENT AND ONE DEPENDENT

30-B. THE COMPOUND SENTENCE

A *compound sentence* contains two or more simple sentences connected by a coordinating conjunction *(and, but, for, or, nor)*. In a compound sentence, each simple sentence is called an independent clause. Each independent clause expresses a complete thought.

EXAMPLE 1

A word processor can improve the efficiency of an office, but it is a costly piece of equipment.

Analysis:

Each of the underlined independent clauses expresses a complete thought and can stand alone as a simple sentence. Since the clauses are equal in rank, they are joined by the coordinating conjunction *but*.

EXAMPLE 2

Mother's Day is in May, and Father's Day is in June.

Analysis:

The independent clauses are joined by the coordinating conjunction *and*.

EXAMPLE 3

Milton's brother will meet him at the airport, or his sister will be there if the flight is late.

Analysis:

The independent clauses are joined by the coordinating conjunction *or*.

30-C. THE COMPLEX SENTENCE

A *complex sentence* contains an independent clause and one or more dependent clauses. An independent clause contains a subject and a verb (either or both of which may be compound) and expresses a complete thought. A dependent clause cannot stand alone and needs the independent (main) clause to make its meaning clear.

EXAMPLE 1

Melanie, who wants to become a marine biologist, won a prize at the school's science fair.

Analysis:

The underlined dependent clause does not make a complete statement and cannot stand alone. It needs the independent clause for its understanding.

EXAMPLE 2

Sunbathing, which is a popular summer pastime, can cause serious skin problems.

Analysis:

The underlined dependent clause needs the independent clause for its understanding.

EXAMPLE 3

Because the plant was left out in the hot sun too long, it almost died.

Analysis:

The underlined dependent clause needs the independent clause for its understanding.

EXAMPLE 4

Although I thought the collie was the best dog in the show, the judges gave first prize to the beagle.

Analysis:

The underlined dependent clause needs the independent clause for its understanding.

EXAMPLE 5

The storm, which caused the highest surf in fifteen years, destroyed several beach homes.

Analysis:

The underlined dependent clause needs the independent clause for its understanding.

The Paragraph

Almost every part of our lives is directed by rules. We learn to play games, drive our cars, and govern ourselves by them. Rules have necessarily been established to help us talk with each other and to express ourselves in written form. Most people pattern their speech and writing after these rules. Those who don't are often misunderstood.

The real purpose of learning grammar rules is to learn to express ourselves clearly so that other people can understand what we are trying to say or write. We have already studied most of the rules. Now we are going to apply them.

Do you remember what a sentence is? A *sentence* is a group of words expressing a complete thought. It contains at least a subject and a verb.

Do you know what a paragraph is? A *paragraph* is a group of sentences working together to explain or describe a single topic. It is usually short but must be long enough to make the topic clear. Details, reasons, or examples in paragraphs are arranged in a logical manner. The amount and kinds are left up to the writer. Each detail, however, is related to a single topic. Look at the topic and the details that support it in the following paragraph:

There is a saying that reads, "After the wreck comes the reckoning." If you were involved in an automobile accident, however minor, at any time in your life, you know that the reckoning wasn't easy. Even if there were no doctor bills or lawsuits to worry about, you probably found that there were questions to be answered, official forms to be filled out, property damage to be paid for, and perhaps days and weeks of irritating delay and inconvenience. Multiply all the details of your accident by several million, and you will realize that the task of reckoning last year's history of automobile smashups was both difficult and distressing.

In the preceding paragraph the first sentence attracts your attention and makes you want to continue reading. The listing of the various details (bills, damage, inconvenience, and so on) helps to further stimulate the reader's attention and maintain interest.

In order to write a good paragraph, the following qualities should be applied:

1. Look with an observing eye. Accurately describe the details you see.
2. Select the right words to tell what you see.
3. Develop the ability to share your experiences through the correct use of words.
4. Keep to the point.

31-A. THE TOPIC SENTENCE

A *topic sentence* expresses the central thought of the paragraph. The first sentence in a paragraph is usually the topic sentence. Sometimes it is repeated in a summary sentence to conclude the paragraph. Occasionally, for a particular effect, experienced writers prefer to place it at the end of the paragraph. But wherever it is placed, the topic sentence should catch the reader's interest so that he or she will want to continue reading.

After the topic sentence, the paragraph is developed by using other sentences to expand the topic sentence. Your ideas should be presented in a sensible, concise, and natural order. Each sentence should present additional details and keep to the point.

Linking words and phrases make it possible for sentences within a paragraph to hold together in a proper or smooth manner. That is, the reader is led through the paragraph without experiencing sudden gaps in thought. Linking words and phrases are used to tie the sentences together.

EXAMPLE 1

First call the paramedics. Then call the police.

Analysis:

> First—linking word
> Then—linking word
> Each word shows a proper time relationship between the two sentences.

EXAMPLE 2

Above the refrigerator was a storage cabinet. To the left of the refrigerator was the pantry.

Analysis:

> Above the refrigerator—linking phrase
> To the left of the refrigerator—linking phrase
> Each phrase locates the details as seen by the writer.

EXAMPLE 3

In elementary school he was a poor student. In high school he became a member of the honor society.

Analysis:

> In elementary school—linking phrase
> In high school—linking phrase
> Each phrase makes a contrast between the two sentences.

EXAMPLE 4

He arrived early. As a consequence, he was able to buy excellent tickets to the game.

Analysis:

> As a consequence—linking phrase—It states the effect of the sentence preceding it.

EXAMPLE 5

Roger is a great secretary. For instance, he takes dictation at 95 words per minute. Additionally, he is excellent on the telephone.

Analysis:

> For instance—linking phrase which gives an example
> Additionally—linking word which adds to an example or a reason

---

TRYOUT EXERCISE

Directions: Identify the following sentences as simple, compound, or complex. Write your answer in the blank provided at the right.

1. The dam's flood gates were opened, and the river level rose five feet.

1. _____

2. Because lightning hit the gym, the basketball game was cancelled.

2. _____

3. Flash floods are common in the desert.

3. _____

Directions: Construct topic sentences from the suggestions below. Check your sentences with your teacher before continuing with the assignment.

1. leaving the dance _____

_____

2. the time I laughed until I cried _____

_____

Complete Application Practices 83-90, pages 161-168, at this time.

83-A: Practice Procedure. Identify the following sentences as simple (S), compound (C), or complex (Cx). Write your answer in the blank provided at the right. Score one point for each correct answer.

Answers

1. The golfer easily sank the putt.   1. _____

2. Golf, which I like to play, has grown in popularity.   2. _____

3. Joe wants to become a good golfer, but he forgets to keep his head down when he hits the ball.   3. _____

4. Mary took golf lessons, and she improved her game.   4. _____

5. Although Rita took lessons, she still can't putt.   5. _____

6. Sarah is the new golf professional at the club.   6. _____

7. My golf clubs, which were a gift, are very expensive.   7. _____

8. The clubhouse is beautiful, but it is not very large.   8. _____

9. That player who lost his ball in the lake is really mad.   9. _____

10. Professional golfers like to play at our club.   10. _____

83-B: Practice Procedure. Follow the procedure given for 83-A.

1. Our trip, which included a visit to Washington, D.C., was exciting.   1. _____

2. More than five million tourists a year visit the Capitol.   2. _____

3. Capitol Hill, where Congress meets, is a beautiful sight.   3. _____

4. The subway train in the Capitol is fun to ride, but it doesn't go very far.   4. _____

5. Students who work as tour guides are very knowledgeable about the Capitol.   5. _____

6. There is a charge for guide service at the Capitol, but the cost is very reasonable.   6. _____

7. The Library of Congress, which is on Capitol Hill, is an impressive building.   7. _____

8. The Supreme Court is also on Capitol Hill.   8. _____

9. The Washington Monument is near the White House, and the Jefferson Memorial is at the Tidal Basin.   9. _____

10. The Smithsonian Institute houses items of our national past.   10. _____

11. Visitors may ride the Capitol subway train, but senators are given priority seating.   11. _____

12. Although you need special arrangements, it is possible for visitors to eat in the Senate Dining Room.   12. _____

13. A guided tour of the Capitol buildings is very educational.   13. _____

14. Arlington Cemetery is across the Potomac River from Washington.   14. _____

15. Many visitors go to Arlington Cemetery each year, and most of them visit the tomb of the unknown soldier.   15. _____

Your Total Score _____

If your score was 19 or less for 83-A and B, review Section 30, pages 157-158, before continuing.

84-A: Practice Procedure. Construct complete sentences by adding *independent clauses* to the dependent clauses listed below. The dependent clause may be used any place in the sentence. Try to make your sentences interesting. Write them on a separate sheet of paper. Score one point for each correct sentence.

1. whenever she talks
2. after I left
3. if they answer my letter
4. while waiting for my package
5. before leaving my office
6. as I read the article
7. when the telephone rang

8. although I was tired
9. unless you respond today
10. because he didn't send the check
11. if she answers the phone
12. when the film ended
13. although he liked the pie
14. since the letter was unanswered

84-B: Practice Procedure. Construct complete sentences by adding *dependent clauses* to the independent clauses listed below. The dependent clause may be used any place in the sentence. Try to make your sentences interesting. Write them on a separate sheet of paper. Score one point for each correct sentence.

1. she read the book yesterday
2. the plane was late
3. school starts next Monday
4. the class play was excellent
5. Raul was elected president
6. the giant wave crashed on the beach
7. the dog's name was Sandy

8. Helen is a physician
9. the dam broke
10. he demanded an answer
11. the tire was flat
12. she always liked to swim
13. Ben found the test easy
14. Eunice left in a rage

84-C: Practice Procedure. Make compound sentences from the independent clauses listed below. Match a clause from Column A with a clause from Column B using an appropriate conjunction. In the space provided, write the letter of the clause and the conjunction. Score one point for each correct match and one point for each correct conjunction.

Column A	**Column B**	Answers
1. The man coughed	A. We found a place on the sand anyway	1. _____
2. It rained hard	B. I still fell asleep	2. _____
3. Mark arrived late	C. they cancelled the picnic	3. _____
4. The play was good	D. the room was smokey	4. _____
5. The beach was crowded	E. he missed the flight	5. _____

Your Total Score _____

If your score was 29 or less for 84-A, B, and C, review Section 30, pages 157-158, before continuing.

85: Practice Procedure. The most important sentence in a paragraph is the topic sentence. It states in general terms what the paragraph is all about. Choose ten of the fifteen suggestions for paragraph topics listed below and write ten topic sentences. Score one point for each correct topic sentence.

1. television reruns _____

_____

2. an earthquake _____

_____

3. a favorite baseball player _____

_____

4. polishing the car _____

_____

5. hay fever _____

_____

6. a hamburger with onions _____

_____

7. life on a desert island _____

_____

8. travel fever _____

_____

9. a hospital stay _____

_____

10. a first airplane trip _____

_____

11. getting married _____

_____

12. waterskiing _____

_____

13. life in a large city _____

_____

14. fishing _____

_____

15. making a speech _____

_____

Your Total Score _____

If your score was 6 or less, review Section 31–A, page 159, before continuing.

86–A: Practice Procedure. Underline the linking words and linking phrases in the following paragraphs. These words make it possible for the sentences in a paragraph to relate smoothly to one another and to achieve unity in the paragraph. Score one point for each correct answer.

1. Monday started out poorly and went from bad to worse. At the outset, I overslept. When I finally woke up, it was past time to leave for work. To make it worse, I stepped on the starter of my car and nothing happened. The battery was dead. When I ran back to the house to telephone for help, I fell, cut my knee and even broke my watch in the process. The final calamity was picking up the telephone and finding it dead! As a consequence, I jumped back into bed to call it a day, and you guessed it, the bed broke. I slept in it anyway, dreaming of a better tomorrow.

2. The photograph that drew my attention was a seascape of bright blues and greens amidst frothy whites. First, I was aware of the crashing blue-green surf rolling in toward shore. Next, I was drawn to the foaming white of a giant breaker about to curl and plunge downward into a tranquil sea. At the peak of the wave was the silhouette of a single surfer, the surfboard pointed toward the sky. To the left of the surfer was another board caught in the breaker but with no sign of its owner. Finally, there was the calmness of the scene along the shore. It appeared as if the beach was simply waiting for the wave, surfer, and all to invade its world and spoil its privacy.

3. Preparing a ham omelette is really rather easy. First, crack three eggs into a mixing bowl, add three tablespoons of water or milk, and sprinkle in salt and pepper to taste. Then, cut up a small amount of ham. Next put an omelette pan over moderate heat and melt some butter or margarine. After the pan is hot, beat the eggs slightly and pour them in slowly. When the eggs are set, place the ham on one side and turn the mixture over with a spatula. Finally, remove the pan from the stove and place the omelette on a hot plate. When served, eat at once.

86–B: Practice Procedure. Try your own hand at using linking words and phrases and see how much your writing will improve. On a separate sheet of paper, write two short paragraphs selected from the topic sentences below. Title the paragraphs. Score ten points for each correct paragraph.

1. Our school's football team was number one!
2. It's easy to roller-skate.
3. The school year ended with a bang!
4. Marcia's wardrobe was exquisite.
5. I just read a wonderful book.   Your Total Score _____

If your score was 29 or less for 86–A and B, review 31–B, page 160, before continuing.

87–A: Practice Procedure. As you have learned, the topic sentence tells the reader what the paragraph is all about. It is a preview of coming attractions. The rest of the sentences provide the details promised by the topic sentence. The total paragraph should flow in an orderly way from sentence to sentence. In the paragraph below, there is no sentence order. Rearrange the sentences on a separate piece of paper until they are properly placed and the paragraph holds together. Score one point for each sentence correctly placed.

Finally, a U.S. Navy destroyer brought up the rear, her decks lined with white uniformed sailors waving and shouting to the crowds on the piers. First, the old sternwheeler, Paddlewheel Princess, sailed up the main channel with flags and patriotic bunting flying. There were three parts to the program. As the destroyer sailed along, red and blue rockets were fired off the bow. This year's Fourth of July Harbor Festival was exciting to watch from beginning to end. Next came a flotilla of about twenty sailboats of various sizes. Each boat sported multicolored sails which billowed in the stiff breeze. Without any question, the rockets were a fitting climax to a thoroughly spectacular show.

87–B: Practice Procedure. In this exercise you are given the beginning of two paragraphs. Complete one of the paragraphs in your own words. Remember to add the details in a logical order and to link the sentences so that there is smoothness from one sentence to another. Score ten points for a complete and logical paragraph.

1. I walked into the employment office knowing that I just had to get the job that had been advertised. _____

   _____

   _____

   _____

   _____

   _____

2. The film started off with a bang, and I knew from then on I was going to like it. _____

   _____

   _____

   _____

   _____

   _____

Your Total Score _____

If your score was 13 or less for 87–A and B, review Section 31, pages 159-160, before continuing.

88–A: Practice Procedure. Select one of the following topic sentences and expand it into a short paragraph of five to ten sentences. Remember to use sentences that give reasons, details, facts, similarities and differences, or examples to support the topic sentence. List your ideas on a separate sheet of paper before including them in your paragraph. Score ten points for a complete and orderly paragraph.

1. I was frightened the night I spent in my aunt's empty house.

2. As our car rounded the curve, the right front tire blew out.

3. When I found the box of candy on my desk, I was immediately suspicious.

4. My graduation present was a digital watch!

_____

_____

_____

_____

_____

_____

_____

_____

_____

_____

88–B: Practice Procedure. Follow the procedure given for Practice 88–A.

1. Selecting a career for yourself is not always easy.

2. The poem was very inspirational.

3. The doctor announced proudly, "It's twins."

4. The car sped off with the police officer in hot pursuit.

_____

_____

_____

_____

_____

_____

_____

_____

Your Total Score _____

If your score was 15 or less, review Section 31, pages 159-160, before continuing.

89-A: Practice Procedure. Match the phrases in Column B with the words they describe in Column A. Be especially careful, as some of them are similar. Place the letter that identifies your answer in the blank provided at the right. Score one point for each correct answer.

Column A	Column B	Answers
1. paragraph	a. expresses the central thought of a paragraph	1. _____
2. topic sentence	b. linking words	2. _____
3. compound sentence	c. contains an independent clause and one or more dependent clauses	3. _____
4. That boy and girl are members of the team.	d. contains a compound subject	4. _____
5. as a result, for instance	e. contains a dependent clause	5. _____
6. The secretary who took the dictation is absent.	f. a group of words (with subject and verb) that expresses a complete thought	6. _____
7. The owner of the sailboat scraped and painted it.	g. a group of sentences dealing with a single topic	7. _____
8. next, first, finally	h. contains two or more independent clauses connected by a coordinating conjunction	8. _____
9. simple sentence	i. linking phrases	9. _____
10. complex sentence	j. contains a compound verb	10. _____

Your Total Score _____

If your score was 7 or less, review Unit 9, pages 157-160, before continuing.

89-B: Practice Procedure. Here are 40 words that are frequently misspelled. Study them carefully and be prepared to write them from memory.

accidently	certainly	elementary	height	muscle
achieve	circular	enthusiasm	imaginary	neither
agreeable	conscience	executive	judgment	occur
analyze	convenient	exercise	knowledge	occurred
appropriate	corridor	experience	language	partial
awkward	definite	faucet	library	personnel
calendar	descriptive	frequently	machinery	siege
candidate	division	generally	minimum	strength

167

90–A: Practice Procedure. Select the one word that is the *antonym* for the numbered word. Write the letter that identifies the numbered word in the blank space provided at the right. Remember that an antonym means the opposite of the given word. Score one point for each correct answer.

Answers

1. *apparent*   (a) visible (b) obscure (c) glaring (d) obvious   1. _____

2. *cautious*   (a) careless (b) wary (c) vigilant (d) dignified   2. _____

3. *concise*   (a) short (b) exact (c) lucid (d) rambling   3. _____

4. *elegant*   (a) coarse (b) refined (c) elaborate (d) beautified   4. _____

5. *expanded*   (a) shrunk (b) bloated (c) scraggy (d) puffy   5. _____

6. *explicit*   (a) plain-spoken (b) informed (c) veiled (d) visible   6. _____

7. *frigid*   (a) heated (b) bleak (c) hungry (d) cold   7. _____

8. *gullible*   (a) stupid (b) skeptical (c) superstitious (d) fanatical   8. _____

9. *inevitable*   (a) unerring (b) uncertain (c) infallible (d) reliable   9. _____

10. *insolent*   (a) overbearing (b) polite (c) abject (d) lofty   10. _____

90–B: Practice Procedure. Select the one word that is the *synonym* for the numbered word. Write the letter that identifies the word in the blank space provided at the right. Remember that a synonym means nearly the same as the given word. Score one point for each correct answer.

1. *acid*   (a) sugary (b) tart (c) loud (d) muffled   1. _____

2. *bias*   (a) prejudice (b) review (c) discovery (d) fact   2. _____

3. *creditable*   (a) sinful (b) frail (c) praiseworthy (d) thoughtless   3. _____

4. *curious*   (a) indifferent (b) bored (c) absent (d) inquisitive   4. _____

5. *durable*   (a) mortal (b) frugal (c) short-lived (d) lasting   5. _____

6. *fluctuate*   (a) determine (b) confirm (c) depart (d) waver   6. _____

7. *frail*   (a) brittle (b) seedy (c) weak (d) vigorous   7. _____

8. *humble*   (a) lofty (b) stiff (c) vain (d) modest   8. _____

9. *juvenile*   (a) waning (b) criminal (c) belated (d) youthful   9. _____

10. *perpetual*   (a) infrequent (b) scarce (c) erratic (d) constant   10. _____

11. *potent*   (a) powerful (b) harmless (c) premature (d) relaxed   11. _____

12. *subsequent*   (a) before (b) following (c) actual (d) present   12. _____

13. *terse*   (a) fixed (b) tense (c) condensed (d) nominal   13. _____

14. *ultimate*   (a) farthest (b) nearest (c) first (d) midway   14. _____

15. *vapor*   (a) gelatin (b) fog (c) marble (d) clay   15. _____

Your Total Score _____

Section 32

OBJECTIVES: 1. To recognize and use punctuation marks.
2. To know when to use capital letters.

Punctuation in writing indicates pauses, gestures, and desired changes of expression. Punctuation keeps words from running together so the meaning is clear.

Notice how ridiculous this information sounds without punctuation, capitalization, or paragraph division.

Most people have difficulty with the usage of two too and to and and but both conjunctions are usually easy to use correctly but even those who should know sometimes confuse two too and to two which follows one and comes before three is of course a number too often confused with to usually is an adverb modifying an adjective such as too large too sometimes means also in addition to likewise besides etc in which case it is still an adverb to like in of and at is a preposition although to is also used with the verb form to form an infinitive such as to run everywhere you go you will find those who do not understand the usage of two too and to never never permit yourself to confuse the three

Did you understand it? Your own writing can be just as confusing if you do not punctuate properly.

Now read the same information separated into paragraphs, capitalized properly, and punctuated correctly.

Most people have difficulty with the usage of "two," "too," and "to." "And" and "but," both conjunctions, are usually easy to use correctly; but even those who should know sometimes confuse "two," "too," and "to."

"Two," which follows "one" and comes before "three," is, of course, a number. "Too," often confused with "to," usually is an adverb modifying an adjective, such as "too large." "Too" sometimes means "also," "in addition to," "likewise," "besides," etc., in which case it is still an adverb. "To," like "in," "of," and "at," is a preposition, although "to" is also used with the verb form to form an infinitive, such as "to run."

Everywhere you go you will find those who do not understand the usage of "two," "too," and "to." Never, never permit yourself to confuse the three.

PUNCTUATION

**STATEMENT
OF FACT**

EXCLAMATION

QUESTION

32-A. THE PERIOD .

Periods as End Punctuation

The *period* in punctuation serves the same purpose as the stop sign on a highway. It brings you to a halt. *The period marks the end of a* *declarative sentence* (a statement of fact) *or an* *imperative sentence* (a command). Every sentence that is a statement should end with a period.

EXAMPLES

The twins like to play baseball. (declarative sentence)

Often, their parents watch them play. (declarative sentence)

Strike him out. (imperative sentence)

Watch for the runner to try and steal second base. (imperative sentence)

Periods Within a Sentence

Use a period after most abbreviations and an initial. Remember, however, that the use of periods and capitalization in some abbreviations can vary. Several styles are acceptable as in *a.m.*, *A.M.*, *am*, and *AM*. Try to be consistent in your usage.

EXAMPLES

Oct. (October)

N.Y. (New York)

a.m. (ante meridiem or before noon)

p.m. (post meridiem or after noon)

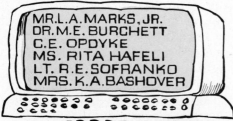

EXAMPLE

<u>Mr.</u> <u>E.</u> <u>B.</u> Martin and <u>Ms.</u> <u>D.</u> <u>A.</u> Bell will marry in Newark, <u>N.J.</u>

Analysis:

<u>Mr.</u>—abbreviation for Mister
<u>E. B.</u>—first and middle initials
<u>Ms.</u>—abbreviation for Miss or Mistress
<u>D. A.</u>—first and middle initials
<u>N.J.</u>—abbreviation for New Jersey

Chart of Popular Abbreviations

ad	advertisement
a.m.	ante meridiem (before noon)
amt.	amount
anon.	anonymous
ans.	answer
atty.	attorney
Ave.	Avenue
B.A.	Bachelor of Arts
Blvd.	Boulevard
Capt.	Captain
cm	centimeter
COD	cash on delivery
dept.	department
doz	dozen
Dr.	Doctor
e.g.	for example
etc.	et cetera (and so forth)
ft	foot
g	gram
in	inch
int.	interest
IQ	Intelligence Quotient
kg	kilogram
l	liter
lit.	literal, literally
Lt.	Lieutenant
m	meter
M.D.	Doctor of Medicine
memo	memorandum
mg	milligram
mm	millimeter
Mr.	Mister
Mrs.	Mistress
Ms.	Miss or Mistress
no.	number
oz	ounce
pd.	paid
p.m.	post meridiem (after noon)
qt	quart
recd.	received
Rev.	Reverend
sec.	secretary
Sr.	senior
St.	saint
St.	Street
USA	United States of America
viz.	namely
vol.	volume

32-B. THE QUESTION MARK ?

A question mark is also used as a full stop in punctuation. *A question mark is used after an interrogative sentence.* These sentences ask direct questions.

EXAMPLES

What is your name? Where do you live? Do you have a driver's license?

32-C. THE EXCLAMATION POINT !

An exclamation point is used after words, phrases, or sentences to express sudden emotion or feeling (joy, fear, pain, happiness, anger) *and forceful commands.* Use exclamation points sparingly in your own writing, because they are like a voice raised in a burst of feeling. Reserve them to express truly strong feeling.

EXAMPLES

We won!

Jump!

Save my baby!

Don't touch me!

My sunburn really hurts!

TRYOUT EXERCISE

Directions: Fill in the necessary period (.), question mark (?), and exclamation point (!) in the following sentences.

1. She really hit that ball hard

2. Who is up next

3. This is the last inning

Directions: In the first column, write the proper abbreviation for each word given. In the second column, write the proper word for each abbreviation given. Check your answers with your teacher before continuing with your assignment.

1. meter _____
2. quart _____
3. secretary _____

1. Ave. _____
2. ft _____
3. pd. _____

Complete Application Practices 91-92, pages 175-176, at this time.

32-D. THE COMMA ,

Commas are used as signposts or signals in writing. They are similar to a traffic sign on the highway. When you want to make a turn while you are driving a car, you signal and then turn. In writing, if you want to change your thoughts, insert some other ideas, or identify parts, you use the comma. Often, the sound of the spoken sentence with a pause and change in voice pitch will serve as a guide in the placement of commas in writing.

Commas clarify the meaning of your sentences. They show you where one word or group of words ends and the next word or group of words begins.

KATY, MATTHEW, JASON, AND EILEEN ENJOY EXERCISING.

COMMAS SEPARATE WORDS IN A SERIES

A comma separates words and numbers in a series. Notice how these sentences read without the comma, and then see how they sound with a comma.

EXAMPLE 1

wrong: Tess Mark and I went swimming.

right: Tess, Mark, and I went swimming.

EXAMPLE 2

wrong: The flowers were yellow blue and orange.

right: The flowers were yellow, blue, and orange.

Note: It is also correct to omit the comma after a word in a series when it is followed by *and.*

EXAMPLE 3

wrong: George placed his passport airline tickets and hotel reservations on the counter.

right: George placed his passport, airline tickets, and hotel reservations on the counter.

EXAMPLE 4

wrong: The ages of the children were 2 4 and 8.

right: The ages of the children were 2, 4, and 8.

EXAMPLE 5

wrong: On our trip we visited Mexico Costa Rica and Panama.

right: On our trip we visited Mexico, Costa Rica, and Panama.

A comma may be used to set off an appositive. An *appositive* is a word or group of words that functions as a noun. An appositive explains the noun or pronoun that it follows.

EXAMPLE 1

Lupe, <u>my assistant</u>, is very ambitious.

Analysis:

<u>my assistant</u>—appositive—explains who Lupe is

EXAMPLE 2

Mr. Webber, <u>our English teacher</u>, is personable.

Analysis:

<u>our English teacher</u>—appositive—explains who Mr. Webber is

If the comma is not used in setting off the appositive, the meaning is changed. Notice how the commas change the meaning of these sentences.

EXAMPLE 1

Maria, our visitor from Mexico is beautiful.

Analysis:

You are addressing Maria and describing your visitor from Mexico.

EXAMPLE 2

Maria, our visitor from Mexico, is beautiful.

Analysis:
You are describing Maria who actually is your visitor from Mexico.

Use a comma after a dependent clause at the beginning of a sentence. The comma sets off the independent (main) clause. The slight pause indicated by the comma prevents reading words together. If the comma is omitted or misplaced, the meaning of the sentence is changed.

EXAMPLES

wrong: When the storm hit it did so with a fury.

right: When the storm hit, it did so with a fury.

wrong: After the tiger had eaten the trainer left the zoo.

right: After the tiger had eaten, the trainer left the zoo.

A quotation (direct speech) is set off by commas from the rest of the sentence. (See pages 184-185 for more information on punctuation with quotation marks.)

EXAMPLES

The mother exclaimed, "Don't spill that milk!"

Stuart asked, "Will you go to the movies with me tonight?"

"The test will be on Friday," the teacher announced.

The comma is used to set off the second and all following items in dates and addresses.

EXAMPLES

His last concert in the United States was on June 25, 1984, in Chicago, Illinois.

Send your check for $12 to 19245 Ventura Boulevard, Encino, California.

The first major league night game was played in Cincinnati, Ohio, on May 24, 1935.

Use the comma to set off most parenthetical expressions (unrelated words in a sentence). These expressions interrupt the thought of the sentence. In speaking, you would pause before and after using the expression.

EXAMPLES

Winston, you know, is in college now.

Joji, to be honest with you, is a dud.

Wilma, I bet, will be late again.

Note: When commas are used to set off words or phrases, two of them are needed unless the phrase is at the beginning or the end of the sentence.

Such words as of course, indeed, for instance, moreover, and no doubt are set off by commas from the rest of the sentence.

EXAMPLES

Linda, of course, is her mother's pride and joy.

He is, no doubt, an A student.

The ballot, for instance, is in both English and Spanish.

USE A **COMMA** AFTER A DEPENDENT CLAUSE STANDING FIRST IN A SENTENCE

Introductory words are separated from the rest of the sentence by a comma. A comma is also placed after addressing a person by name. If the person's name is used in the middle of the sentence, two commas are used to set it off.

EXAMPLES

No, she can't have dinner with you tonight.

Mrs. Goldberg, ask your question now.

Please, Bart, answer the telephone.

Okay, I'll be in class tomorrow.

A comma is used before a coordinating conjunction in a compound sentence (and, but, for, or, nor).

EXAMPLES

The painting was finished by 10 a.m., and the carpet layers arrived at noon.

Tyrone wanted to go swimming, but the surf was too rough when he arrived.

He was always late with his assignments, for he was a lazy student.

She ate breakfast on the run, or she didn't eat breakfast at all.

Note: The comma may be omitted before coordinating conjunctions if the two clauses are short or have the same subjects. For instance: The telephone rang and she got up to answer it. He failed the test and he didn't care.

Common Comma Usage

1. To separate words and numbers in a series.
2. To set off an appositive.
3. After a dependent clause at the beginning of a sentence.
4. To set off quotations.
5. With addresses and dates.
6. To set off parenthetical expressions (unrelated words).
7. To set off such words as *of course, indeed, for instance, moreover, no doubt.*
8. After introductory words that are separated from the rest of the sentence.
9. Before a coordinating conjunction in a compound sentence.

TRYOUT EXERCISE

Directions: Insert the necessary commas in the following sentences. Check your answers with your teacher before continuing with your assignment.

1. I bought a shirt a pair of pants and a sweater.
2. Because she left the house early I overslept.
3. John to tell the truth was a good student.
4. Cathie their daughter-in-law is from Australia.
5. Debbie was born on March 12 1969 in Houston Texas.

Complete Application Practices 93-98, pages 177-182, at this time.

91-A: Practice Procedure. Fill in the necessary periods, question marks, and exclamation points in the following sentences. Remember that a period is placed at the end of a sentence that states a fact or gives a command and after some abbreviations and initials. A question mark is placed after a sentence which asks a direct question. An exclamation point is placed after words or sentences that express sudden feeling or emphasis. Score one point for each correct response.

Your Score

1. Ours is a nation of laws   1. _____
2. Why do we have laws   2. _____
3. Protect our freedoms   3. _____
4. Laws reflect a nation's values   4. _____
5. When do laws change   5. _____
6. Laws change when values change   6. _____
7. Obey the law, or else   7. _____
8. No law is perfect   8. _____
9. Can a law be repealed   9. _____
10. Down with unfair laws   10. _____

91-B: Practice Procedure. Follow the procedure given for 91-A.

1. Who makes our laws   1. _____
2. Common law came to the United States from England   2. _____
3. Is the common law system used in Australia   3. _____
4. Remember, the law is the law   4. _____
5. Most rules are based on common sense   5. _____
6. Roman law was the first great legal system   6. _____
7. Emperor Justinian organized Roman law into a code   7. _____
8. Did Napoleon create the French Civil Code   8. _____
9. Write a new code of law   9. _____
10. Who developed the civil law system   10. _____

Your Total Score _____

If your score was 15 or less for 91-A and B, review 32-A, B, and C, pages 169-171, before continuing.

91-C: Practice Procedure. Using a topic of your own choosing, write a short paragraph demonstrating your ability to properly use the period, the question mark, and the exclamation point as end punctuation. Use a separate sheet of paper.

92: Practice Procedure. In the first answer column, write the proper abbreviation for each word given. In the second answer column, write the proper word or words for each abbreviation given. If necessary, use your dictionary. Score one point for each correct answer.

Answers

Answers

1. Bachelor of Arts _____   26. pd. _____

2. California _____   27. ad _____

3. April _____   28. YMCA _____

4. Wednesday _____   29. N.Y. (NY) _____

5. quart _____   30. W.Va. (WV) _____

6. Boulevard _____   31. in _____

7. Sunday _____   32. Ariz. (AZ) _____

8. Street _____   33. dept. _____

9. liter _____   34. recd. _____

10. ounce _____   35. vol. _____

11. Florida _____   36. Pvt. _____

12. answer _____   37. Ms. _____

13. dozen _____   38. Col. _____

14. anonymous _____   39. etc. _____

15. meter _____   40. mm _____

16. amount _____   41. a.m. _____

17. Washington _____   42. R.S.V.P. _____

18. assistant _____   43. M.D. _____

19. Reverend _____   44. COD _____

20. after noon _____   45. Minn. (MN) _____

21. foot _____   46. p.m. _____

22. Mister _____   47. P.S. _____

23. Captain _____   48. Fri. _____

24. Lieutenant _____   49. yd _____

25. memorandum _____   50. Tues. _____

Your Total Score _____

If your score was 39 or less, review 32-A, page 170, before continuing.

93–A: Practice Procedure. Fill in the necessary periods, question marks, and exclamation points in the following sentences. Score one point for each correct answer.

Your Score

1. Where is the Great Barrier Reef Marine Park   1. _____
2. You're correct   It's in Australia   2. _____
3. Wow   That park is really enormous   3. _____
4. It's as large as England and Scotland combined   4. _____
5. The park contains over 400 species of coral   5. _____
6. Visitors can watch reef life from a glass-bottom boat   6. _____
7. You can also snorkel and scuba dive   7. _____
8. Can you walk on the reefs at low tide   8. _____
9. Why do we want to protect undersea life   9. _____
10. Many people enjoy the park each year   10. _____

93–B: Practice Procedure. Follow the procedure given for 93–A.

1. Some park attractions are not beneath the sea   1. _____
2. Wow   Are there really over three million seabirds   2. _____
3. Yes   There are even some shearwaters and terns   3. _____
4. Are there turtles, too   4. _____
5. The park has the largest number of loggerhead turtles in the Pacific 5. _____
6. Watch out   That's a snapping turtle   6. _____
7. Each female turtle deposits from 60 to 200 eggs above the high-tide line   It's almost unbelievable   7. _____
8. Do pollutants endanger the park   8. _____
9. Silt from mainland rivers has polluted some reef areas   9. _____
10. Wow   Australia must be proud of its unusual park   10. _____

93–C: Practice Procedure. Write and punctuate correctly three sentences for each type of end punctuation—the period, question mark, and exclamation point. Use a separate sheet of paper. Score one point for each correct sentence.

Your Total Score _____

If your score was 27 or less for 93–A, B, and C, review 32–A, B, and C, pages 169-171, before continuing.

94–A: Practice Procedure. Fill in the necessary commas in the following sentences. Score one point for each comma correctly placed.

Your Score

1. Eileen my secretary is a good dependable and devoted employee.   1. _____

2. She types takes dictation and supervises the office.   2. _____

3. Chris her assistant types answers the telephone and files.   3. _____

4. Martin a part-time worker helps on Monday Tuesday and Friday.   4. _____

5. Our office the fifth floor location overlooks the park the post office and the city hall.   5. _____

6. Jamco our parent company sells rock sand and gravel.   6. _____

7. Our retail store on Main Street is painted red white and blue.   7. _____

8. Jack Linda and Erica work in the retail store.   8. _____

9. Erica our newest employee is tall blue-eyed and blond.   9. _____

10. J. B. Seymour our company president is a former actor singer and dancer.   10. _____

94–B: Practice Procedure. Follow the procedure given for 94–A.

1. Bill Mr. Seymour's youngest son drives a company truck.   1. _____

2. *Work hard* our company's motto is on our stationery.   2. _____

3. The company owns ten trucks two vans and a motorcycle.   3. _____

4. Another son Derek is a lawyer.   4. _____

5. Derek the lawyer advises his father on legal investment and tax matters.   5. _____

6. Rose Manufacturing a new company in town is challenging our business.   6. _____

7. Mr. Rose and Marilyn Leon and Tricia are from Chicago.   7. _____

8. Wilson Moreno and Mori a public relations firm will help us regain our business.   8. _____

9. We will advertise on radio on TV and in the newspaper.   9. _____

10. Our advertisement will appear in the newspaper on March 15 16 and 17.   10. _____

Your Total Score _____

If your score was 45 or less for 94–A and B, review 32–D, pages 171-172, before continuing.

94–C: Practice Procedure. Write a short paragraph on a separate sheet of paper to demonstrate your understanding of the use of the comma in a series and with appositives.

Name _____ Date _____

Teacher _____ Score _____

95–A: Practice Procedure. In the following sentences, insert a comma in its proper place after dependent clauses at the beginning of a sentence and with quotations. Score one point for each comma correctly placed.

Your Score

1. As we started on our world trip our friends shouted "Bon Voyage!"   1. _____
2. Before the plane left we had a party at the airport.   2. _____
3. Our daughter asked "You didn't forget your passports, did you?"   3. _____
4. "We didn't forget the passports this time" I replied.   4. _____
5. One friend remarked "You are really two lucky people!"   5. _____
6. When the luggage went on the plane we began to get excited.   6. _____
7. After the flight announcement was made people moved toward the flight gate.   7. _____
8. "Flight 94 for Mexico City leaves in ten minutes" announced the attendant.   8. _____
9. The flight attendant asked "Where are your tickets?"   9. _____
10. As we took our seats a flight attendant greeted us with "Welcome aboard!"   10. _____

95–B: Practice Procedure. Follow the procedure given for 95–A.

1. As soon as we were seated a flight attendant said "Fasten your seat belts for takeoff."   1. _____
2. "Your seat should be in an upright position" said the attendant.   2. _____
3. When the plane moved forward the lights dimmed.   3. _____
4. While the plane waited to take off an attendant asked "Would you like some gum?"   4. _____
5. At the end of the runway a long line of planes waited to take off.   5. _____
6. The pilot announced "We are fifth in line to take off."   6. _____
7. When the lights of the plane in front of us disappeared we knew we were next.   7. _____
8. As the plane rushed down the runway I crossed my fingers for luck.   8. _____
9. My friend by the window exclaimed "The city lights are dazzling!"   9. _____
10. I replied "The lights remind me of a giant jewel box!"   10. _____

Your Total Score _____

If your score was 18 or less for 95–A and B, review 32–D, page 173, before continuing.

96–A: Practice Procedure. In the following sentences, insert a comma where needed around addresses, dates, and unrelated expressions. Score one point for each comma correctly placed.

Your Score

1. It wasn't until August 5 1775 you know that a ship entered San Francisco Bay.

   1. _____

2. Francis Drake it's true did land near the bay on June 17 1579.

   2. _____

3. The bay area Indians of course had lived there long before the Spanish came.

   3. _____

4. Father Serra you know established a series of California missions.

   4. _____

5. Mission Dolores for example was the San Francisco mission.

   5. _____

6. The distance from Mexico no doubt was why the Mexicans almost forgot about San Francisco.

   6. _____

7. On July 9 1846 moreover the United States flag was raised in San Francisco.

   7. _____

8. Yerba Buena of course was San Francisco's original name.

   8. _____

9. Because of the gold rush no doubt San Francisco's population grew to over 56,000 people.

   9. _____

10. Indeed the discovery of silver caused another jump in population.

   10. _____

96–B: Practice Procedure. Follow the procedure given for 96–A.

1. Of course on April 18 1906 an earthquake and a fire almost destroyed San Francisco.

   1. _____

2. The city nevertheless recovered and today is a growing metropolis.

   2. _____

3. As you may know the city is built on many hills.

   3. _____

4. It is indeed a mixture of many ethnic backgrounds.

   4. _____

5. The city moreover is proud of its ethnic distinctions.

   5. _____

6. San Francisco California is famous you know for its fine restaurants.

   6. _____

7. Many excellent seafood restaurants for example are located at Fisherman's Wharf.

   7. _____

8. Moreover a former chocolate factory is now a restaurant row.

   8. _____

9. Indeed restored Victorian houses are found in most parts of the city.

   9. _____

10. For example a Queen Anne type house can be seen at 1800 Pacific Avenue Pacific Heights.

   10. _____

Your Total Score _____

If your score was 32 or less for 96–A and B, review 32–D, page 173, before continuing.

97-A: Practice Procedure. Fill in the necessary commas, periods, question marks, and exclamation points in the following sentences. This is a special practice for the use of commas before coordinating conjunctions in compound sentences and for introductory words. Score one point for each punctuation mark correctly placed.

Your Score

1. Hooray We're going to the beach and we'll have a great time   1. _____

2. Do you like the beach at Venice or do you prefer the one at Santa Monica   2. _____

3. I like the beach in Maui but I prefer the surf at Makaha Beach   3. _____

4. Have you ever surfed at Huntington Beach California   4. _____

5. I'd like to learn to surf but my last teacher gave up on me   5. _____

6. Surely Tim you can learn to surf if you really try   6. _____

7. Okay I'm game to try if you are   7. _____

8. Martha Tim Jan and Michael piled into their van and they drove to the beach   8. _____

9. Of course it was crowded when they got to the beach   9. _____

10. I'll let you out here and you find a good place on the beach   10. _____

97-B: Practice Procedure. Follow the procedure given for 97-A.

1. Great The waves are just right and there aren't too many people surfing   1. _____

2. Most of the people it seems weren't in the water   2. _____

3. Jan would you put the lunch under the umbrella   3. _____

4. Yes I'll help Michael with the surfboards Martha   4. _____

5. Martha where did he park the van   5. _____

6. Well they all looked for the van but it was nowhere to be seen   6. _____

7. Without a word Michael appeared with three friends helping him carry the surfboards   7. _____

8. The van it seems was parked five blocks away   8. _____

9. Wow You guys came along just at the right time   9. _____

10. Yes we're going to use the boards first   10. _____

Your Total Score _____

If your score was 39 or less for 97-A and B, review Sections 32-A, B, C, and D, pages 169-174, before continuing.

98-A: Practice Procedure. Insert the necessary commas in the following sentences. This is a review for all comma usage. Score one point for each comma correctly placed.

Your Score

1. When we were in Alaska we saw the cities of Ketchikan Juneau and Sitka.

   1. _____

2. Our ship the Island Queen was large and comfortable.

   2. _____

3. For example our stateroom on the ship was air conditioned.

   3. _____

4. Our friends especially liked the ship and they had sailed on it before.

   4. _____

5. Of course Linda Colin's sister was an official with the steamship line.

   5. _____

6. After the ship sailed I bumped into Dr. Marian Herrick an old friend.

   6. _____

7. Dr. Herrick Colin Pat Helen and I shared a table in the dining room.

   7. _____

8. The last time I had seen Dr. Herrick was on June 30 1984 when she retired.

   8. _____

9. Dan her husband was unable to take the trip with Dr. Herrick.

   9. _____

10. His business responsibilities I understand kept Dan from taking the trip.

    10. _____

98-B: Practice Procedure. Follow the procedure given for 98-A.

1. Leon our waiter asked "What would you like to eat this morning?"

   1. _____

2. I replied "Bring me some coffee please and then I'll decide."

   2. _____

3. Colin ordered orange juice hot cereal scrambled eggs bacon and wheat toast.

   3. _____

4. Pat his wife said "Colin you must be starved!"

   4. _____

5. Pat Marian and Helen ordered just juice coffee and toast.

   5. _____

6. I of course had the same as Colin.

   6. _____

7. After we finished eating Colin and I went out on deck.

   7. _____

8. To tell the truth we had overeaten and we needed the fresh air to revive us.

   8. _____

9. Colin said "Never again!"

   9. _____

10. When lunchtime came however both of us had forgotten our vow.

    10. _____

Your Total Score _____

If your score was 35 or less for 98-A and B, review Section 32-D, pages 171-174, before continuing.

98-C: Practice Procedure. On a separate sheet of paper, demonstrate your understanding of the use of commas in an interesting, well-written paragraph. Tell about a trip you have taken or hope to take, a film you have seen, or a book you have read.

32-E. THE SEMICOLON ;

The semicolon is used to separate independent clauses of a compound sentence when they are not joined by a coordinating conjunction. It is used as a slow down signal, stronger than a comma, but not a complete stop. A semicolon looks like a comma with a period over it (;). You can remove a semicolon and put a period in its place, and you will have two complete sentences instead of one.

EXAMPLES

The dress shop was open at the mall; the shoe store was closed.

It rained in the morning; it cleared up in the afternoon.

The semicolon is used between independent clauses of a compound sentence when they are joined by a conjunctive adverb (moreover, however, consequently, nevertheless, therefore, besides, then).

EXAMPLES

The story was suspenseful up to the final chapter; however, at that point it just fell apart.

We planned to spend three days in Atlanta; therefore, we decided to call our friends, the Roberts, who live there.

The day dawned bright and cheery; consequently, we planned a picnic in the park.

32-F. THE COLON :

A colon (one period above another period) is used before an example, a series of words, or a list. The colon often follows terms like *as follows, thus, in the following manner,* or *for example.*

EXAMPLES

She attended four schools: 107th Street Elementary, Byrd Junior High School, Sumpter High School, and Harvard University.

You should do the exercise in the following manner: lie flat on the floor, breathe deeply for a count of ten, bring your right leg down to your chest in three counts, then bring your left leg down to your chest in three counts.

A colon can be used after the salutation in a letter.

EXAMPLES

Dear Dr. Hale:

Dear Mr. and Mrs. Finnegan:

Use the colon between the hour and minutes in writing the time.

EXAMPLES

The meet will begin at 11:00 a.m.

Our work hours are from 8:00 a.m. to 5:00 p.m.

32-G. THE DASH —

The dash marks a sudden change in the sentence. It is used when a sentence is interrupted abruptly and an entirely different sentence or thought is added.

EXAMPLES

My friend Midge—you remember she was a real beauty—is a model now.

Arriving at the airport—it was like a zoo—was a traumatic experience for her.

Then he reached his hand through the open door—but I'm not going to tell you more of the story.

The dash may be used in place of the comma where emphasis is desired.

EXAMPLES

There it was in his glove compartment—a gun.

Beauty—it's only skin deep.

At that moment he announced the winner—my film.

32-H. THE PARENTHESES ( )

Parentheses are used to set off additions or expressions which are not necessary to the sentence. Unlike the dash, parentheses tend to de-emphasize what they set off. Parentheses are also used to enclose figures within a sentence.

EXAMPLES

Libby planted her garden with several kinds of summer vegetables (squash, beans, tomatoes, and carrots).

Mrs. Talbot enjoyed doing handwork (knitting, crocheting, and tatting) while she watched television.

New Year's Day (January 1) is a national holiday.

Traveling only by surface transportation (automobile, bus, bicycle, and motorcycle), Tom made the trip in only eight hours.

32-I. THE APOSTROPHE '

The apostrophe shows ownership or possession. (See pages 35-36 for additional examples.)

EXAMPLES

The student's notebook was lost.

The students' books were lost.

The apostrophe is also used to show omission of a letter. These words are *contractions.*

EXAMPLE 1

It's in the garage behind the paint cans.

Analysis:

It's—It is—The apostrophe takes the place of the *i* in the word *is.*

EXAMPLE 2

Her parents weren't on the plane that crashed.

Analysis:

weren't—were not—The apostrophe takes the place of the *o* in the word *not.*

EXAMPLE 3

They're not home yet.

Analysis:

They're—They are—The apostrophe takes the place of the *a* in *are.*

32-J. THE QUOTATION MARKS " "

Quotation marks are used to enclose the exact words of a person (direct quotation).

EXAMPLES

Cicero wrote, "There is no place more delightful than one's own fireside."

"I never forget a face, but in your case I'll make an exception."
GROUCHO MARX

USE **QUOTATION MARKS** TO ENCLOSE EXACT WORDS

"Drink your milk before you leave the table," the child's father cautioned.

In a stern voice, the police officer commanded, "Pull over!"

A mistake is often made when the quotation is broken by the identification of the person making the quote. Close the first part of the quotation and start again when the direct quote is continued. Place commas before and after the part of the sentence not enclosed with the quotation marks.

If the identifying expression ends the sentence and the quotation continues, put a period after the expression. Begin the rest of the quotation with a quotation mark and a capital letter.

EXAMPLES

"Open your books to page 72," said the teacher, "and begin reading at the bottom of the page."

"Your head is in the way," complained the small child. "I can't see the parade."

Use quotation marks to set off the titles of chapters within a book, magazine articles, and reports. Titles of books, magazines, plays, poems, and other whole publications should be underlined when written in longhand and italicized when printed.

EXAMPLES

"Dining Out" is a regular article in his newsletter.

The Washington Post is a famous newspaper in our nation's capital.

Use quotation marks to enclose unusual words or expressions.

EXAMPLE

By failing that test he is "up the river without a paddle."

Follow these simple rules when placing quotation marks with other marks of punctuation.

1. Place periods and commas *inside* quotation marks. (I answered, "I am not needed." "You must go," he insisted.)
2. Place semicolons and colons *outside* quotation marks. (He always called it "my camp on the river"; actually, it was an estate with a view of the river.)
3. Place question marks or exclamation points inside the quotation marks if they punctuate the quotation only. (She asked, "Are we too late?")
4. Place question marks or exclamation points outside the quotation marks if they punctuate the entire sentence. (Why did she say, "We are too late"?)

Do not use quotation marks in an indirect quote. The statement must be the direct and exact words of a person for quotation marks to be used.

EXAMPLE 1

They said that they would be late for dinner.

Analysis:
No quotation marks are needed because this is an indirect quote.

EXAMPLE 2

He replied that the race hadn't started yet so there was no need to hurry.

Analysis:
No quotation marks are needed because this is an indirect quote.

Two questions are always asked about numbers: (1) When do you write the number in words? (2) When do you use figures instead of a number in words? Keep in mind the following rules about numbers.

Definite numbers above ten should be in figures.

EXAMPLES

The bus held 56 passengers.

Our teacher ordered 33 books for the class.

He was 26 years old when he got married.

Only 11 members of the team were present.

Indefinite numbers should be written in words.

EXAMPLE 1

Over eighty people were invited to the party.

Analysis:
eighty—written out because *Over* is indefinite

EXAMPLE 2

Their youngest child must be nearly twenty by now.

Analysis:
twenty—written out because *nearly* is indefinite

EXAMPLE 3

Almost fifty people had gathered at the scene of the accident.

Analysis:
fifty—written out because *Almost* is indefinite

Numbers at the beginning of a sentence should be written in words. These are just like capitalizing the first letter of a sentence.

EXAMPLES

Twenty people answered the ad.

Thirty different kinds of birds were in the aviary.

Ten train cars jumped the track.

When writing a percentage, use figures with the word percent. The symbol % is used only in statistical copy. When you write out the word *percent,* use it as one word. This practice is preferred to that of writing *percent* as two words.

EXAMPLES

The state sales tax is now 6½ percent.

The interest rate for new cars is 14 percent.

A common problem is not knowing when to use *st, th,* or *d* in a date. Remember, *if the figure* (or date) *follows the month, you do not use st, th, or d.*

EXAMPLES

December 7, 1941   November 11, 1918

If, however, the date comes before the month, use st, th, or d.

EXAMPLES

7th of December, 1941
11th of November, 1918

TRYOUT EXERCISE

Directions: Fill in the necessary punctuation in the following sentences. Check your answers with your teacher before continuing with your assignment.

1. Remember said the coach we are out to win the championship!
2. She prefers poultry chicken, turkey, duck to the following seafood, beef, and pork.
3. A sense of humor   its a persons greatest attribute.

Complete Application Practices 99-100, pages 187-188, at this time.

Name _____ Date _____

Teacher _____ Score _____

99–A: Practice Procedure. Complete each of the following sentences by writing in the blank provided at the right the correct form of the word in the parentheses. Score one point for each correct response.

Answers

1. The festival was to have begun on the (5, 5th) of September.   1. _____

2. Because of a rainstorm, it didn't begin until September (6, 6th).   2. _____

3. (18, Eighteen) high school bands were entered.   3. _____

4. Nearly (20, twenty) pianists had signed up to perform.   4. _____

5. Of those pianists who signed up, only (17, seventeen) actually played. 5. _____

6. Approximately (10, ten) persons asked to play the piano and a second instrument as well.   6. _____

7. (4, Four) of the pianists also played the banjo.   7. _____

8. The price of the tickets was (10, ten) percent greater than last year. 8. _____

9. The high school bands that performed represented (11, eleven) states. 9. _____

10. The festival lasted (5, five) days.   10. _____

Your Total Score _____

If your score was 7 or less, review Section 32–K, page 186, before continuing.

99–B: Practice Procedure. In the space provided, write the contraction for each underlined expression. A contraction has an apostrophe for an omitted letter or letters. Score one point for each correct answer.

1. I shall go.   1. _____

2. They are not here.   2. _____

3. That was not the case.   3. _____

4. He will play.   4. _____

5. Dylan is not at home.   5. _____

6. She is eating.   6. _____

7. I am reading.   7. _____

8. It does not matter.   8. _____

9. They cannot win.   9. _____

10. She will enroll.   10. _____

11. We will run.   11. _____

12. They do not sing.   12. _____

13. I am a student.   13. _____

14. We are going.   14. _____

15. It is late.   15. _____

Your Total Score _____

If your score was 11 or less, review Section 32–I, page 184, before continuing.

100–A: Practice Procedure. Insert all necessary punctuation marks in the following sentences. This is a complete review of punctuation. Score one point for each mark correctly placed.

Your Score

1. The Bradley family is planning for a family reunion on July 4 1992

    1. _____

2. It is scheduled to take place at Webber Park in Buffalo New York from 900 am to 800 pm

    2. _____

3. Dr J B Bradley the familys oldest living member and Sue Bowdan J B s sister will be there

    3. _____

4. Wow Theyre pretty old people

    4. _____

5. Yes replied my mother but Im sure theyll be there

    5. _____

6. Do you suppose that Donna my cousin from Atlanta Georgia and Cecil my cousin from Vancouver B C will come I asked

    6. _____

7. Ill bet that Tamara Toby Spence and Melvin Bradley from London England wont be there

    7. _____

8. They I suppose live too far away

    8. _____

9. If you dont mind Ill write a special letter and encourage them to come Dad said

    9. _____

10. Dad theyll really like that I suppose my sister replied

    10. _____

100–B: Practice Procedure. Follow the procedure for 100–A.

1. The letter was sent to London England but it was misdirected to Dublin Ireland instead

    1. _____

2. James the Bradley familys long-lost nephew received the letter

    2. _____

3. Thinking the letter was for him James read it and shouted to Peggy his wife Theres to be a Bradley family reunion in America

    3. _____

4. Oh cant we go Peggy responded

    4. _____

5. James said that they could go but then he discovered the letter was for his uncle in London England

    5. _____

6. Tomorrow said James Ill call Uncle Melvin

    6. _____

7. Uncle Melvin theres to be a family reunion in America on July 4 1992 announced James

    7. _____

8. Uncle Melvin said that a family reunion was a great idea

    8. _____

9. They wrote a joint letter to America and said Well all be there

    9. _____

10. Say can you guess where the Bradleys of Dublin and London will be on July 4 1992

    10. _____

Your Total Score _____

If your score was 94 or less for 100–A and B, review Section 32, pages 169-186, before continuing.

100–C: Practice Procedure. Choose a topic and write a paragraph or sentences on a separate sheet of paper to demonstrate your understanding of these types of punctuation: end punctuation, commas in a series and with appositives, commas with dependent clauses and quotations, quotation marks, and contractions.

Section 33 Capital Letters

Capitalize the first word of every sentence. The first letter of a direct quotation or a sentence within a quotation is capitalized.

EXAMPLES

The river overflowed its banks.

Everyone ran for high ground!

Next Jamie yelled, "We can't hear you!"

Always use capital "I" for the pronoun "I" any place in the sentence.

EXAMPLES

Liza and I are in the same class.

Must I stay?

Capitalize the days of the week, months of the year, and holidays.

EXAMPLES

Thanksgiving is the fourth Thursday of November.

He bowls every Tuesday night.

Is Labor Day the first Monday in September?

Many football bowl games are played on New Year's Day.

Capitalize proper nouns, abbreviations of proper nouns, and proper adjectives. (See pages 25-26 for a review of proper nouns and page 121 for a review of proper adjectives.)

EXAMPLES

We drove east on U.S. Highway 66.

John Paul Jones was a famous American naval hero.

We took the Island Princess, a British ship, to Alaska.

Mexico City is the capital of Mexico.

Lela is bilingual; she speaks both English and Spanish.

Our dog is a Labrador retriever.

Aunt Mabel and Uncle Joe once lived in Downey, California.

Capitalize important events and documents.

EXAMPLES

Norm refereed the Super Bowl three times!

Magna Carta is an important part of the history of freedom.

CAPITALIZE PROPER NOUNS

The Congressional Medal of Honor is the nation's highest military medal.

Capitalize the principal words in the titles of complete literary and artistic works. Such titles include books, magazines, newspapers, movies, plays, songs, paintings, sculptures, and poems. These titles are usually underlined or italicized.

EXAMPLES

Reader's Digest has long been a favorite magazine.

Robinson Crusoe, a novel about a castaway, was written by Daniel Defoe.

Every evening my mother reads The Detroit News.

We saw a production of Night of the Iguana last night.

In summary, a capital letter is used in the following situations:

1. To begin every sentence.
2. For the pronoun *I* any place in a sentence.
3. For the days of the week, the months of the year, and holidays.
4. For proper nouns and proper adjectives.
5. For important events and documents.
6. For the principal words in the titles of literary and artistic works.

TRYOUT EXERCISE	**Directions:** In the following sentences, add the necessary capital letters by circling each small letter that should be capitalized. Check your answers with your teacher before continuing with your assignment.

1. on thanksgiving we will visit our grandparents in dallas, texas.
2. my parents' wedding anniversary is january 1, new year's day.
3. on friday i plan to see alfred hitchcock's movie titled rear window.

Complete Application Practices 101-106, pages 191-196, at this time.

101-A: Practice Procedure. In the following sentences, add the necessary capital letters by circling each small letter that should be capitalized. Score one point for each correct response.

Your Score

1. rita, gabriel, and eunice traveled to baja california to see the gray whales.   1. _____

2. there they met mister juan sanchez.   2. _____

3. mister, or señor, sanchez works as a guide for garcia tour company.   3. _____

4. he takes visitors to the san ignacio lagoon.   4. _____

5. gray whales abound in the lagoon.   5. _____

6. baja california is in mexico, and it is not the u.s. state of california.   6. _____

7. eunice and her friends visited the lagoon in february.   7. _____

8. they saw many gray whales in the pacific ocean.   8. _____

9. from november to april the whales migrate through the lagoon.   9. _____

10. the mexican government protects the whales.   10. _____

101-B: Practice Procedure. Follow the procedure given for 101-A.

1. *taming the colorado* is a fascinating book.   1. _____

2. it was written by ingrid cheffers.   2. _____

3. at one time mrs. cheffers was the special assistant to the president of sante fe railroad.   3. _____

4. she received an emergency message at her office in yuma, arizona, about a problem with the colorado river.   4. _____

5. the colorado had overflowed its banks at gila, arizona.   5. _____

6. the date was december 5, 1906.   6. _____

7. the river normally flowed into the gulf of california, but sometimes it tried to run into the salton sea.   7. _____

8. the agriculturally rich imperial valley was in danger.   8. _____

9. president theodore roosevelt asked e. h. harriman to save the imperial valley from destruction.   9. _____

10. mrs. cheffers initiated operation big dump and 2,850 carloads of rock, gravel, and clay solved the colorado problem.   10. _____

Your Total Score _____

If your score was 62 or less for 101-A and B, review Section 33, pages 189-190, before continuing.

102: **Practice Procedure.** Fill in all the necessary punctuation and capitalization in the following story. Indicate capital letters by circling each small letter that should be capitalized. Score one point for each correctly capitalized word and one point for each punctuation mark correctly placed.

Your Score

while we sat in our rambling tan and yellow cabin among the trees at   **1.** _____

416 spencer falls lane at big bear lake we watched the gloomy rain fall all   **2.** _____

morning long finally the storm passed and the dark grey clouds passed   **3.** _____

over the sun shone brightly on the wet grass yes the day soon was as   **4.** _____

pleasant as any other august day of course we knew that it was frequently   **5.** _____

the case with a warm summer rain this time however the rain had swelled   **6.** _____

the river and washed away our small wooden bridge elaine my youngest   **7.** _____

sister sat beside the washed-out bridge she was unhappy because of its   **8.** _____

loss it was then that a shiny blue convertible drove up beside her the four   **9.** _____

of us our names are william martina ella and david watched as the car   **10.** _____

approached it was around 315 p m august 15 1984   **11.** _____

the driver a grouchy stranger hollered out the window in an angry way   **12.** _____

how deep is this river kid   **13.** _____

my young sister wrinkled her brow but she replied not too deep   **14.** _____

can i make it if i drive through it right here the man asked speak up   **15.** _____

stupid i dont have all day the stranger demanded   **16.** _____

i think so replied my sister in fact im positive about it   **17.** _____

the driver shifted into gear and started into the swift stream midway   **18.** _____

across the car began to settle into the mud the furious wet and be-   **19.** _____

draggled driver sloshed through the swirling water toward my sister soft   **20.** _____

mud clung to his jacket and pants the fellow was purple with rage by the   **21.** _____

time he reached my sister   **22.** _____

you jerk why did you tell me i could drive through the water he yelled its   **23.** _____

over five feet deep in that spot   **24.** _____

with an innocent expression my young sister looked toward the sunken   **25.** _____

car then in a small voice she said slowly i cant understand it the water is   **26.** _____

only up to here on the ducks swimming out there   **27.** _____

Your Total Score _____

If your score was 97 or less, review Sections 32 and 33, pages 169-190, before continuing.

103-A: Practice Procedure. Fill in all necessary punctuation and capitalization in the following sentences. Indicate capital letters by circling each small letter that should be capitalized. Score one point for each punctuation mark correctly placed and one point for each correctly capitalized word. Your Score

1. the airport announcer said flight 1010 for washington dc norfolk and miami is ready for boarding   1. _____

2. the miller family of new york city prepared to board the plane   2. _____

3. tim sally and leona miller and jonathon and helen their parents were anxious to leave   3. _____

4. jonathon the father was taking the family to visit relatives in florida   4. _____

5. sally carried a copy of *seventeen* magazine to read on the flight   5. _____

6. she i believe likes *seventeen* better than *harper's bazaar*   6. _____

7. leona and tim both like *people weekly* magazine and *time* magazine   7. _____

8. tim read an article in *time* entitled play and avoid stress   8. _____

9. he told leona read it and it will help you   9. _____

10. youre going to read that stuff questioned sally of her brother and sister   10. _____

103-B: Practice Procedure. Follow the procedure for 103-A.

1. departure of the millers plane was changed from 1000 a m to 100 p m   1. _____

2. the delay of course was a disappointment and it meant they would arrive at miami international airport three hours late   2. _____

3. after the delay was announced mr miller said to his family lets take a walk around kennedy airport   3. _____

4. sally the youngest miller daughter said you all go and ill stay here and read   4. _____

5. tim announced that he was hungry and then he said lets eat instead   5. _____

6. mr and mrs miller leona and tim walked to the airport restaurant the skyroom   6. _____

7. as his parents expected tim ordered a double hamburger fries and a chocolate malt   7. _____

8. tim do you think that will hold you until we have lunch on the plane asked mr miller   8. _____

9. well said tim i think so but i sure wouldnt want to starve in the meantime   9. _____

10. just then sally arrived at the table and said hurry the plane is ready to take off   10. _____

Your Total Score _____

If your score was 138 or less for 103-A and B, review Sections 32 and 33, pages 169-190, before continuing.

104-A: **Practice Procedure.** Fill in all necessary punctuation and capitalization in the following sentences. Indicate capital letters by circling the small letter that should be capitalized. Score one point for each correct response.

Your Score

1. say do you know who discovered the new world asked mr baxter the teacher

1. _____

2. yes louis replied i think it was columbus

2. _____

3. louis continued by saying columbus was from genoa italy but he sailed for spain

3. _____

4. mr baxter then asked who knows the names of the spanish ships columbus sailed

4. _____

5. tina waved her arm and shouted i do

5. _____

6. mr baxter said all right tina tell us the names of the ships

6. _____

7. after she stood up straight and tall tina said that the ships were the nina the pinta and the santa maria

7. _____

8. which ship was the flagship asked the teacher and how much did it weigh

8. _____

9. before he raised his hand carlos shouted out it was the santa maria and it weighed 100 tons

9. _____

10. youre right replied mr baxter but youre wrong in not raising your hand first

10. _____

104-B: **Practice Procedure.** Follow the procedure given for 104-A.

1. have you seen the doges palace in venice italy i asked diane

1. _____

2. ive seen it in photographs but ive never visited the palace in person she replied

2. _____

3. st marks cathedral is located on st marks square in venice

3. _____

4. isnt the water rising there and wont that ruin those buildings i asked miss tucker our teacher

4. _____

5. it sure is interrupted barry and youd better go soon if youre thinking of going there

5. _____

6. id rather visit paris france alfreda remarked

6. _____

7. i would for id like to visit versailles a palace just outside of paris commented rosalie

7. _____

8. is that where the famous hall of mirrors is located selena asked

8. _____

9. yes rosalie replied thats where the treaty ending world war I was signed

9. _____

10. traveling must be fun and someday im going to visit france england scotland italy germany switzerland and spain selena remarked

10. _____

Your Total Score _____

If your score was 168 or less for 104-A and B, review Sections 32 and 33, pages 169-190, before continuing.

105: Practice Procedure. Match each item in Column B with the item it describes in Column A. Write the identifying letter from Column B in the blank provided at the right. Items in Column B are used more than once. Score one point for each correct answer.

Column A	Column B	Answers
1. used to separate words in a series	**a.** period	1. _____
2. used to set off unrelated words in a sentence	**b.** question mark	2. _____
3. used between hours and minutes	**c.** exclamation point	3. _____
4. denotes ownership or possession	**d.** comma	4. _____
5. used after an abbreviation or initial	**e.** colon	5. _____
6. used at the end of a declarative sentence	**f.** dash	6. _____
7. used to start every sentence	**g.** quotation marks	7. _____
8. used for important events and documents	**h.** capital letter	8. _____
9. used before a series or list introduced by "as follows"	**i.** semicolon	9. _____
10. used to separate independent clauses of a compound sentence not joined by a coordinating conjunction	**j.** apostrophe	10. _____
11. used after introductory words which are separated from the rest of the sentence		11. _____
12. used for proper nouns and adjectives		12. _____
13. used to set off titles of chapters within a book		13. _____
14. used to show the omission of a letter		14. _____
15. used for separation in dates and addresses		15. _____
16. used to set off an appositive		16. _____
17. used to indicate sudden change in a sentence (the sentence is suddenly broken off)		17. _____
18. used for the principal words in a song title		18. _____
19. used before a coordinating conjunction in a compound sentence		19. _____
20. used after words expressing sudden feeling		20. _____
21. used after the salutation in a business letter		21. _____
22. used after an interrogative sentence		22. _____
23. used for holidays		23. _____
24. used at the end of an imperative sentence when the command is forceful		24. _____
25. used to enclose exact words of a person		25. _____

Your Total Score _____

If your score was 19 or less, review Sections 32 and 33, pages 169-190, before continuing.

106–A: Practice Procedure. Select the one word that is the antonym for the numbered word. Write the letter of the word that correctly identifies the italicized word in the blank provided at the right. Remember that an antonym means the opposite.

Answers

1. *petty* (a) exciting (b) important (c) inferior (d) small (e) precious

1. _____

2. *despair* (a) anger (b) fear (c) fatalism (d) hope (e) skepticism

2. _____

3. *euphoria* (a) well-being (b) health (c) elation (d) depression (e) sanity

3. _____

4. *tumult* (a) event (b) registration (c) bubble (d) turmoil (e) order

4. _____

5. *diminish* (a) confuse (b) earn (c) review (d) augment (e) retire

5. _____

6. *luxurious* (a) squalid (b) beautiful (c) soapy (d) furry (e) special

6. _____

7. *famine* (a) starvation (b) levity (c) abundance (d) draught (e) turmoil

7. _____

8. *commence* (a) end (b) begin (c) speak (d) succeed (e) near

8. _____

9. *jubilant* (a) pleasing (b) irksome (c) sad (d) happy (e) inspiring

9. _____

10. *cautious* (a) careful (b) sterile (c) wistful (d) affective (e) reckless

10. _____

11. *hallowed* (a) sacred (b) devoted (c) tasteful (d) sinful (e) plausible

11. _____

12. *sarcastic* (a) sassy (b) repulsive (c) sour (d) burning (e) polite

12. _____

13. *harmonious* (a) musical (b) discordant (c) happy (d) lively (e) congenial

13. _____

14. *humidity* (a) dampness (b) dryness (c) dew (d) rain (e) snow

14. _____

15. *contagious* (a) rude (b) opposite (c) immune (d) disease (e) snow

15. _____

Your Total Score _____

106–B: Practice Procedure. The following 40 words are frequently misspelled. Study them carefully and be prepared to write them from memory.

accompany	periodical	realize	singular
biscuit	persistent	representative	society
column	precede	satisfaction	stenographer
constitution	preference	scarcely	studying
dependent	procession	schedule	succeed
disappoint	pronounce	secretary	temporary
guarantee	protein	seize	tendency
luncheon	quality	sensible	thirteen
miserable	quietly	sequel	tragedy
naturally	realistic	serious	tying

Section 34

Word Blunders

Unit 11
Word Choice

OBJECTIVES: 1. To recognize misused words in everyday speech and writing.
2. To learn the proper usage of commonly misused words.

Have you ever been misunderstood or embarrassed by mispronouncing a word or by using the wrong word to convey your thought?

The simple mistakes we make in speaking and writing may be called *word blunders*. How many of these word blunders do you avoid?

34-A. WHO'S AND WHOSE

Who's is the contraction for *who is*. Remember that a contraction has an aspostrophe (') for an omitted letter or letters.

Whose shows ownership or possession. It is used as a possessive adjective and modifies a noun. *Whose* is the possessive case of *who*.

EXAMPLE 1

Who's the best typist in class?

Analysis:
> Who's—contraction for *who is*—Who is the best typist in class?

EXAMPLE 2

That doctor who's operating now is talented.

Analysis:
> who's—contraction for *who is*—That doctor *who is* operating now is talented.

EXAMPLE 1

Whose automobile is that?

Analysis:
> Whose—possessive adjective—modifies the noun *automobile*

EXAMPLE 2

The artist whose cartoon was funniest won the prize.

Analysis:
> whose—possessive adjective—modifies the noun *cartoon*

34-B. IT'S AND ITS

It's is the contraction for *it is*. The apostrophe takes the place of the letter *i* which is omitted. The contraction *it's* acts as the subject and the verb of a clause or sentence.

EXAMPLE 1

It's a wonderful vacation resort.

Analysis:
> It's—contraction for *it is*—It is a wonderful vacation resort.

EXAMPLE 2

It's the best gift I have ever received.

Analysis:
> It's—contraction for *it is*—It is the best gift I have ever received.

Its shows ownership or possession. It is used as a possessive adjective and is followed by a noun. *Its* is the possessive case of *it*.

EXAMPLE 1

Its view was beautiful.

Analysis:
> Its—possessive adjective—modifies the noun *view*

EXAMPLE 2

Its tail was long and bushy.

Analysis:
Its—possessive adjective—modifies the noun *tail*

34-C. THEIR, THERE, AND THEY'RE

There is an adverb. It is never used to show ownership. Be careful in your choice of the verb form with *there*. *There* is never used as a subject and therefore does not determine the singular or plural form of the verb. The subject is usually the noun or pronoun which follows the verb form. If that noun or pronoun is singular, the verb form should be singular; if it is plural, the verb form should be plural.

EXAMPLE 1

There is our new office manager.

Analysis:
There—adverb—modifies the verb *is*. The singular verb form *is* agrees with the singular subject *manager*.

EXAMPLE 2

There were 130 passengers on the airplane.

Analysis:
There—adverb—modifies the verb *were.* The plural verb form *were* agrees with the plural subject *passengers*.

EXAMPLE 3

I flew there for a relaxing vacation.

Analysis:
there—adverb—modifies the verb *flew*

Their denotes ownership or possession. It is used as a possessive adjective and modifies a noun. *Their* is the possessive case of *they*.

EXAMPLE 1

The dogs and their pups barked all day.

Analysis:
their—possessive adjective—modifies the noun *pups*

EXAMPLE 2

We went with their friends to Yellowstone National Park.

Analysis:
their—possessive adjective—modifies the noun *friends*

They're is the contraction for *they are.* Remember that a contraction has an apostrophe (') for an omitted letter or letters.

EXAMPLE

They're the best musicians in school.

Analysis:
They're—contraction for *they are. They are* the best musicians in school.

TRYOUT EXERCISE	Directions: Complete each of the following sentences by writing in the blank provided at the right the correct form of the word in the parentheses. Check your answers with your teacher before continuing with your assignment.

1. (It's, Its) a grand day for a picnic.   1. _____

2. (Who's, Whose) typewriter is that?   2. _____

3. (They're, Their) willing to take the trip.   3. _____

4. (Their, There) is a strange smell in the kitchen.   4. _____

5. (It's, Its) growl was scary.   5. _____

6. (Who's, Whose) the most considerate teacher?   6. _____

7. (Their, There) books were left on the football field.   7. _____

Complete Application Practices 107-108, pages 199-200, at this time.

107: Practice Procedure. Complete each of the following sentences by writing in the blank provided the correct form of the word in the parentheses. Remember that *who's* and *it's* are contractions; *whose* and *its* show possession or ownership. Score one point for each correct response.

Answers

1. (It's, Its) a wise talker who knows how to listen.   1. _____

2. (Who's, Whose) considered to be the best known proverb writer?   2. _____

3. The story and (it's, its) characters were interesting.   3. _____

4. (Who's, Whose) sorry now?   4. _____

5. (It's, Its) a wise student that knows his or her weaknesses.   5. _____

6. Our flag and (it's, its) colors fly wherever there are Americans.   6. _____

7. Abraham Lincoln, (who's, whose) fame has grown with the years, said, "With malice toward none, with charity for all."   7. _____

8. (Who's, Whose) the man who said, "Where liberty dwells, there is my country"?   8. _____

9. (Who's, Whose) saying was, "Give me liberty or give me death"?   9. _____

10. (It's, Its) a statement that Patrick Henry made in 1775.   10. _____

11. The fable with (it's, its) proverb "One falsehood spoils a hundred truths" makes sense.   11. _____

12. (Who's, Whose) teacher quotes Shakespeare and Franklin?   12. _____

13. (It's, Its) a mistake not to be able to be silent.   13. _____

14. (Who's, Whose) place in history is assured?   14. _____

15. (Who's, Whose) responsible for that idea?   15. _____

16. (It's, Its) difficult to sweep other people off their feet if you can't be swept off your own.   16. _____

17. (It's, Its) tragedies are finished by a death.   17. _____

18. Mark Twain (who's, whose) stories were humorous once said, "It is difficult to tell a humorous story."   18. _____

19. (Who's, Whose) the playwright that is considered the greatest of them all?   19. _____

20. (It's, Its) an old proverb that states, "You can't drive straight on a twisted lane."   20. _____

21. (Who's, Whose) the man who said, "I only regret that I have but one life to give for my country"?   21. _____

22. (It's, Its) truth cannot be denied.   22. _____

23. The society and (it's, its) editors did a tremendous job in restoring old documents.   23. _____

24. If you are there before (it's, its) over, you are on time.   24. _____

25. Benjamin Franklin, (who's, whose) place in history is secure, once said, "Without justice, courage is weak."   25. _____

If your score was 19 or less, review page 197 before continuing.   Your Total Score _____

108: **Practice Procedure.** Complete each of the following sentences by writing in the blank provided at the right the correct form of *there, their,* or *they're.* Remember that *there* is an adverb, *their* shows ownership, and *they're* is a contraction for *they are.* Score one point for each correct response.   Answers

1. When Virginia and Michael Fargione graduated from high school, (their, there, they're) parents took them on a trip.

1. _____

2. (Their, There, They're) tour took them to many different European museums and palaces.

2. _____

3. The twins enjoyed traveling (their, there, they're) with the family.

3. _____

4. (Their, There, They're) parents visited relatives in Italy and France.

4. _____

5. (Their, There, They're) originally from Rome and Paris.

5. _____

6. (Their, There, They're) are many beautiful palaces and museums in Europe.

6. _____

7. What gave them (their, there, they're) biggest thrill was the Palace of Versailles outside of Paris.

7. _____

8. (Their, There, They're) was a special treat for them when they toured Versailles.

8. _____

9. (Their, There, They're) they took a balloon trip over the famous palace grounds.

9. _____

10. (Their, There, They're) still telling friends about the beautiful panoramic view of Versailles.

10. _____

11. (Their, There, They're) next stop was at the Louvre in Paris.

11. _____

12. Some of the invaluable and rare treasures (their, there, they're) include the Mona Lisa and the statue of Venus de Milo.

12. _____

13. Is (their, there, they're) an admission fee to enter the museum?

13. _____

14. In the Cluny Museum, opposite the Sorbonne, (their, there, they're) are storehouses of art from the Middle Ages.

14. _____

15. (Their, There, They're) going to visit the museum in the United States next summer.

15. _____

16. They read that (their, there, they're) is a valuable collection of modern art in the Hirshhorn Museum in Washington, D.C.

16. _____

17. The Metropolitan Museum of Art and The Brooklyn Museum are famous for (their, there, they're) primitive art.

17. _____

18. (Their, There, They're) vacation last summer included a visit to the Prado in Madrid.

18. _____

19. (Their, There, They're) they saw paintings by many famous Spanish artists.

19. _____

20. (Their, There, They're) still planning to visit the Museum of Bullfighting the next time.

20. _____

If your score was 15 or less, review page 198 before continuing.   Your Total Score _____

34-D. GOOD AND WELL

Good is an adjective meaning skillful, admirable, or having the right qualities. It describes a noun and answers the question "what kind of."

EXAMPLE 1

Bruce Springsteen is a good singer.

Analysis:
> good—adjective—describes noun *singer* — answers question "what kind of"

EXAMPLE 2

This concert is good.

Analysis:
> good—predicate adjective—describes noun *concert*

Well is an adverb telling how something is done. It usually modifies a verb and answers the question "how."

EXAMPLE 1

Pam Brown rides a horse well.

Analysis:
> well—adverb—modifies the verb *rides* — answers the question "how"

EXAMPLE 2

My sister and her husband dance well together.

Analysis:
> well—adverb—modifies the verb *dance* — answers the question "how"

34-E. IN AND INTO

In is a preposition and means within a place. The person or thing is already there.

EXAMPLE 1

The students sat in the auditorium.

Analysis:
> in—preposition—The students are already in the auditorium.

EXAMPLE 2

The players were in the dressing room.

Analysis:
> in—preposition—The players are already in the dressing room.

Into is also a preposition, but it means the moving or going from outside to inside.

EXAMPLE 1

The performers are going into the theater.

Analysis:
> into—preposition—shows movement from outside to inside the theater

EXAMPLE 2

The lifeguard ran into the water.

Analysis:
> into—preposition—shows movement from outside to inside the water

34-F. ALMOST AND MOST

Almost is an adverb meaning nearly.

EXAMPLE 1

We almost missed the plane.

Analysis:
  almost—adverb—means nearly

EXAMPLE 2

Yesterday I almost wrecked my car.

Analysis:
  almost—adverb—means nearly

Most is an adjective or adverb meaning the greatest in number or quality.

EXAMPLE 1

Scott is the most perfect boy in the neighborhood.

Analysis:
  most—adverb—means the best or greatest

EXAMPLE 2

Mr. Kelleher has the most foreign cars in our town.

Analysis:
  most—adjective—greatest in number

34-G. BESIDE AND BESIDES

Beside means to be next to or at the side of something.

EXAMPLE 1

The waitress placed the silverware beside the plate.

Analysis:
  beside—next to or at the side of

EXAMPLE 2

My uncle sits beside the phone and waits for his friend to call.

Analysis:
  beside—next to or at the side of

Besides means in addition to or extra.

EXAMPLE 1

Besides the mosquitoes, there were other disagreeable things at the picnic.

Analysis:
  Besides—in addition to

EXAMPLE 2

My mother received roses besides a potted plant and some gardening tools.

Analysis:
  besides—in addition to

34-H. SURE AND SURELY

Sure is an adjective meaning to be certain or positive.

EXAMPLE 1

I am sure of my facts.

Analysis:
  sure—adjective—means certain or positive

EXAMPLE 2

The way he drives he's sure to get hurt.

Analysis:
  sure—adjective—means certain or positive

Surely is an adverb meaning certainly. If you can replace *surely* with *certainly,* you know *surely* is correct.

EXAMPLE 1

Lois is surely a successful lawyer.

Analysis:
  surely—adverb—means certainly

EXAMPLE 2

Hugh is surely the finest athlete in school.

Analysis:
  surely—adverb—means certainly

Real is an adjective meaning genuine. It describes a noun.

EXAMPLE 1

It was <u>real</u> gold.

Analysis:
> <u>real</u>—adjective—describes noun *gold*—means genuine

EXAMPLE 2

The <u>real</u> pearl necklace was stolen.

Analysis:
> <u>real</u>—adjective—describes noun *necklace* — means genuine

Very is an adverb meaning extremely. It usually modifies an adjective.

EXAMPLE 1

The artist is a <u>very</u> successful portrait painter.

Analysis:
> <u>very</u>—adverb—modifies the adjective *successful*—means extremely

EXAMPLE 2

Ansel Adams is one of our <u>very</u> best photographers.

Analysis:
> <u>very</u>—adverb—modifies the adjective *best* — means extremely

To is a preposition followed by a noun or pronoun in the objective case. (See pages 135 and 145 for a review of prepositional phrases.) Another use of *to* is with the infinitive phrase (*to* plus a verb form). (See page 146 for an explanation of infinitive phrases.)

EXAMPLE 1

Ms. Lowell read her poetry <u>to</u> our writing class.

Analysis:
> <u>to</u>—preposition

EXAMPLE 2

We brought the dessert <u>to</u> the picnic.

Analysis:
> <u>to</u>—preposition

EXAMPLE 3

Pierre forgot <u>to</u> bring the sandwiches and potato salad.

Analysis:
> <u>to</u>—beginning of infinitive phrase—*to* plus the verb form *bring* and its object

Too is an adverb. It means *also* and *besides*. In addition it can mean *very* and *excessively*.

EXAMPLE 1

We went to the movie <u>too</u>.

Analysis:
> <u>too</u>—adverb—modifies the verb *went*—means also

EXAMPLE 2

Mrs. Witcher thinks her son is <u>too</u> good for words.

Analysis:
> <u>too</u>—adverb—modifies the adjective *good* — means excessively

Two is a number and is usually an adjective.

EXAMPLE 1

The <u>two</u> horses were tied for first place.

Analysis:
> <u>two</u>—adjective—number

EXAMPLE 2

They needed <u>two</u> volunteers for the fire department.

Analysis:
> <u>two</u>—adjective—number

Then is an adverb meaning at that time. It answers the question "when" of the verb.

EXAMPLE 1

The bookstore <u>then</u> bought four copies.

Analysis:
> then—adverb—answers the question "when" of the verb *bought*

EXAMPLE 2

The writer <u>then</u> autographed the book.

Analysis:
> then—adverb—means at that time—answers the question "when" of the verb *autographed*

Than is a conjunction which makes or shows a comparison of two or more things.

EXAMPLE 1

She is smarter <u>than</u> her brother.

Analysis:
> than—conjunction showing a comparison of two people, *She* and *brother*

EXAMPLE 2

Our toy poodle barks louder <u>than</u> the police dog next door.

Analysis:
> than—conjunction showing a comparison between *toy poodle* and *police dog*

Different from is always used in comparing different things. Never use *different than*.

EXAMPLE 1

The last year in high school is <u>different from</u> the first year at college.

Analysis:
> different from—used in comparing different things—never *different than*

EXAMPLE 2

The pressures of the Olympic Games are <u>different from</u> the college games.

Analysis:
> different from—used in comparing different things—never *different than*

Between is used when referring to two people or things.

EXAMPLE 1

Karen sat <u>between</u> Dennis and Russ.

Analysis:
> between—referring to two people, *Dennis* and *Russ*

EXAMPLE 2

The workers dug a deep hole <u>between</u> my house and the street.

Analysis:
> between—referring to two things, *house* and *street*

BETWEEN (TWO ONLY)

AMONG (MORE THAN TWO)

Among is used when referring to more than two people or things.

EXAMPLE 1

Among my fondest memories are a picnic, a swim, and a summer evening.

Analysis:
Among—referring to more than two things

EXAMPLE 2

There was great enthusiasm among the cheerleaders, fans, and players.

Analysis:
among—referring to more than two people

Whenever you use either *between* or *among*, the pronoun which follows is always in the objective case (*me, him, her, us, them*). (See pages 42-44 for a review of the case forms of pronouns.)

EXAMPLE 1

The officer stood between him and me.

Analysis:
him, me—objects of the preposition *between*—objective case

EXAMPLE 2

He ran quickly among them to stop the fight.

Analysis:
them—object of the preposition *among* — objective case

34-M. LIKE AND AS

Like is a preposition followed by a noun or pronoun in the objective case.

EXAMPLE 1

Debbie talks like him.

Analysis:
like—preposition—has object *him*

EXAMPLE 2

He acts just like me.

Analysis:
like—preposition—has object *me*

EXAMPLE 3

Her complexion is like peaches and cream.

Analysis:
like—preposition—has objects *peaches* and *cream*

As is a conjunction and introduces a clause.

EXAMPLE 1

As he ran, he looked back.

Analysis:
As—conjunction—introduces the clause *As he ran*

EXAMPLE 2

As the lunch bell rang, she finished her lunch.

Analysis:
As—conjunction—introduces the clause *As the lunch bell rang*

EXAMPLE 3

The driver honked his horn as he drove by her house.

Analysis:
as—conjunction—introduces the clause *as he drove by her house*

34-N. AS—AS, SO—AS

As—as is used in comparing equal things.

EXAMPLE 1

A rose smells as sweet as any flower.

Analysis:
as, as—compares equal things

EXAMPLE 2

Lions <u>as</u> well <u>as</u> tigers are popular animals in the zoo.

Analysis:
   <u>as</u>, <u>as</u>—compares equal things

So—as is used in making a negative comparison.

EXAMPLE 1

Our car is not <u>so</u> expensive <u>as</u> our neighbor's.

Analysis:
   <u>so</u>, <u>as</u>—negative comparison between cars

EXAMPLE 2

My father claims movies now are not <u>so</u> exciting <u>as</u> they were years ago.

Analysis:
   <u>so</u>, <u>as</u>—negative comparison between movies

TRYOUT EXERCISE	**Directions:** Complete each of the following sentences by writing in the blank provided at the right the correct form of the word in the parentheses. Check your answers with your teacher before continuing with your assignment.

1. (Between, Among) the three students, Noriko had the nicest smile.

   1. _____

2. Nick and Francis certainly can read (good, well).

   2. _____

3. They parked their bikes (beside, besides) the Rolls Royce and the Mercedes.

   3. _____

4. My mother and father are (to, too, two) wonderful people.

   4. _____

5. Strawberries are (different from, different than) boysenberries in color and size.

   5. _____

6. Between the boss and (I, me) there was a good understanding.

   6. _____

Complete Application Practices 109-110, pages 207-208, at this time.

109: Practice Procedure. Complete each of the following sentences by writing in the blank provided at the right the correct word in the parentheses. Score one point for each correct response.   Answers

1. Who (beside, besides) Abraham Lincoln was assassinated while President of the United States?

1. _____

2. Their deaths were (real, very) sad tragedies.

2. _____

3. General Eisenhower became, (as, like) Grant did, President of the United States.

3. _____

4. What was the difference (between, among) the two great Civil War generals, Lee and Grant?

4. _____

5. "(To, Too, Two) the victor belongs the spoils" is a true statement.

5. _____

6. The Civil War battles were different (from, than) the wars today.

6. _____

7. Wars (than, then) did not have airplanes.

7. _____

8. Sherman's army marched (in, into) Atlanta from the north.

8. _____

9. Some historians say that military leaders now are not (as, so) good as years ago.

9. _____

10. Robert E. Lee was a (real, very) Southern gentleman.

10. _____

11. U. S. Grant and George Washington will live (between, among) the best military leaders of all time.

11. _____

12. George Washington's strategy was better (than, then) that of any other Revolutionary War general.

12. _____

13. (It's, Its) very reassuring to have a strong national defense system.

13. _____

14. Frequently, (their, there) are people whose views differ on the space program.

14. _____

15. (To, Too, Two) of the most famous U.S. space explorers were Neil Armstrong and Edwin Aldrin, Jr.

15. _____

16. (Their, There) first manned landing on the moon was a historic event.

16. _____

17. (Who's, Whose) the first American that flew in space?

17. _____

18. In 1965, Edward White was the first American (than, then) to take a "space walk."

18. _____

19. The Americans and Russians (sure, surely) know more about space programs than other countries.

19. _____

20. (Who's, Whose) spaceship was named *Columbia?*

20. _____

21. Michael Collins sat (beside, besides) Neil Armstrong and Edwin Aldrin, Jr. on the first spaceship to the moon.

21. _____

22. All astronauts fly spaceships (good, well).

22. _____

23. We can recognize a spaceship by (it's, its) insignia.

23. _____

24. Our astronauts fly (as, so) well as any others in the world.

24. _____

25. His space uniform looks (as, like) mine.

25. _____

If your score was 19 or less, review Section 34, pages 197-206.   Your Total Score _____

110: Practice Procedure. Construct sentences using the following pairs of words. You may use each pair in the same sentence or make up a separate sentence for each word. Score one point for the correct use of each word.

1. who's _____

    whose _____

2. in _____

    into _____

3. beside _____

    besides _____

4. it's _____

    its _____

5. between _____

    among _____

6. their _____

    there _____

7. good _____

    well _____

8. as—as _____

    so—as _____

9. sure _____

    surely _____

10. theirs _____

    there's _____

11. to _____

    too _____

12. real _____

    very _____

13. than _____

    then _____

14. almost _____

    most _____

15. like _____

    as _____

Your Total Score _____

If your score was 23 or less, review Section 34, pages 197-206, before continuing.

Section 35

Speech Duds

SAY:

SPEAK!

DON'T SAY:

SHHH!

Say:	Don't Say:
almost everybody	most everybody
an hour	a hour
anyway	anyways
anywhere	anywheres
aren't you	ain't you
back of	in back of
better	more better
brought	brung
burst	busted
can hardly	can't hardly
different from	different than
drowned	drownded
feel bad	feel badly
grew up	growed up
have a	have got a
have gone	have went
he doesn't	he don't
he says	he sez
inside the	inside of the
kind of	kind of a
long way	long ways
might have	might of
not nearly	nowhere near
off the	off of the
ought not	hadn't ought
ought to have gone	ought to of gone

Say:	Don't Say:
plan to go	plan on going
prohibit from	prohibit to
seldom	seldom ever
should have	should of
sort of	sort of a
this (book, pencil)	this here (book, pencil)
this kind	these kind
those (books)	them (books)
thrown	throwed
try to	try and
very good	awfully good
was scarcely	wasn't scarcely
were you	was you
where	where at
wished on	wisht on
with regard to	with regards to

TRYOUT EXERCISE

Directions: Complete each of the following sentences by writing in the blank provided at the right the correct word or words in the parentheses. Check your answers with your teacher before continuing with your assignment.

1. (Try and, Try to) pick up some travel brochures on Mexico and Canada.

1. _____

2. It would be a treat to visit either place as we (seldom ever, seldom) leave our city.

2. _____

3. What (kind of, kind of a) trip has your family planned?

3. _____

4. Summer vacation is (not nearly, nowhere near) so far away as I thought.

4. _____

5. (In back of, Back of) the counter are inviting pictures of Toronto and Mexico City.

5. _____

6. We (can hardly, can't hardly) wait for the plane tickets to arrive.

6. _____

Complete Application Practices 111-118, pages 211-218, at this time.

111: Practice Procedure. Complete each of the following sentences by writing in the blank provided at the right the correct word or words in the parentheses. Check the list of "Speech Duds" on the previous pages to make your choice. Score one point for each correct answer.

Answers

1. We (can hardly, can't hardly) wait for the lecture on Mexico and Canada.

1. _____

2. Mr. Diaz spoke for (a hour, an hour) in the morning.

2. _____

3. Later Mr. Knowlton, from the Canadian Tourist Bureau, (brought, brung) his slides to the room.

3. _____

4. (Ain't you, Aren't you) glad you arrived early for a seat?

4. _____

5. Lisa (should have, should of) attended the lecture because she is going to visit Mexico City.

5. _____

6. We still (feel bad, feel badly) about having to babysit.

6. _____

7. (Anywhere, Anywheres) you travel is interesting.

7. _____

8. Miss Silva and her father (wisht, wished) they had gone on the tour.

8. _____

9. When you arrive in Mazatlan, please (try and, try to) buy one of their paintings.

9. _____

10. Look for some pretty pottery which is (inside the, inside of the) specialty shops.

10. _____

11. (Back of, In back of) the courtyard is a picture of a handsome matador.

11. _____

12. Acapulco is a (long way, long ways) from Maine.

12. _____

13. The Navarro family (have gone, have went) to Mexico City many times.

13. _____

14. What (kind of, kind of a) government does Mexico have?

14. _____

15. (This kind, These kind) of poster will look good in my room.

15. _____

16. (Anyway, Anyways), my aunt was lucky to find a Mexican doll.

16. _____

17. Mr. Dodez gave me (this, this here) book on bullfighting.

17. _____

18. My father was (thrown, throwed) off a burro he tried to ride in Veracruz.

18. _____

19. Mexican baskets are different (from, than) those of other countries.

19. _____

20. (He don't, He doesn't) pretend to speak Spanish.

20. _____

21. What (sort of, sort of a) plane did you fly to Quebec?

21. _____

22. (Where, Where at) did you go when you toured Victoria and Vancouver, B.C.?

22. _____

23. Bermuda was (not nearly, nowhere near) so pretty as Victoria, B.C.

23. _____

24. Some of us (seldom, seldom ever) get the chance to travel to foreign countries.

24. _____

25. They (ought to have gone, ought to of gone) with their parents to scenic Canada.

25. _____

If your score was 19 or less, review Section 35, pages 209-210.

Your Total Score _____

112: **Practice Procedure.** Complete each of the following sentences by writing in the blank provided at the right the correct word or words in the parentheses. Score one point for each correct answer.

Answers

1. Cheryl had a (awfully good, very good) chance to work for Star Picture Company.

   1. _____

2. (Back of, In back of) the studio was a large cafeteria.

   2. _____

3. (Was, Were) you ever in a motion picture studio?

   3. _____

4. What (kind of, kind of a) career does she plan to follow?

   4. _____

5. Mrs. Connelly (says, sez) she will do some writing.

   5. _____

6. Unfortunately, Cheryl fell (off the, off of the) first movie set she visited.

   6. _____

7. People (ought not, hadn't ought) to have laughed when it happened.

   7. _____

8. Some movie stars treated her (better, more better) than others.

   8. _____

9. Her friends think it is a (sort of a, sort of) treat to work in pleasant surroundings.

   9. _____

10. She (don't, doesn't) mind the hours of the job.

    10. _____

11. I (might have, might of) gotten the job if I knew how to write.

    11. _____

12. The workers (have an, have got an) excellent medical and dental insurance plan.

    12. _____

13. If it is possible, (try and, try to) take writing courses in high school and college.

    13. _____

14. In my school there (was scarcely, wasn't scarcely) a writing course offered to the students.

    14. _____

15. (Where, Where at) do you go to school?

    15. _____

16. The Perez twins (plan to go, plan on going) to a special writer's workshop.

    16. _____

17. (Almost everybody, Most everybody) hopes to get a job that is enjoyable and rewarding.

    17. _____

18. My brothers (have, have got) a dream about writing the great American novel.

    18. _____

19. A person who doesn't finish his/her training or schooling (seldom, seldom ever) gets a good job immediately.

    19. _____

20. (Them, Those) courses in the studios for young actors sound exciting.

    20. _____

21. My grandfather (grew up, growed up) in Hollywood.

    21. _____

22. (This, This here) story about my favorite actress was true.

    22. _____

Your Total Score _____

If your score was 16 or less, review Section 35, pages 209-210, before continuing.

113-A: Practice Procedure. Add *able* to the words listed below and write their correct spelling in the blank provided. If the word ends in *e,* drop the *e* before adding *able.* If, however, the word ends in *ce* or *ge* (change), keep the *e* (changeable). Score one point for each correct spelling.

1. advise _____
2. believe _____
3. change _____
4. debate _____
5. embrace _____
6. endure _____
7. enforce _____
8. excite _____
9. excuse _____
10. live _____

11. love _____
12. manage _____
13. move _____
14. notice _____
15. remove _____
16. sale _____
17. service _____
18. trace _____
19. unchange _____
20. use _____

113-B: Practice Procedure. Listed below are eight pairs of homonyms (words which sound alike but have different meanings). In the blank provided, define each word. Score one point for each correct definition.

1. bridal _____
   bridle _____
2. coarse _____
   course _____
3. creak _____
   creek _____
4. gilt _____
   guilt _____
5. pain _____
   pane _____
6. pause _____
   paws _____
7. soar _____
   sore _____
8. ware _____
   wear _____

Your Total Score _____

114: Practice Procedure. Here are 100 words that are frequently misspelled. Study them carefully and be prepared to write them from memory.

accommodate	descend	marvelous	recollect
acknowledge	desirable	messenger	recommend
aggravate	desperate	mischievous	reliable
allegiance	determined	mortgage	relieve
amateur	dialogue	mosquito	respectfully
analysis	distinguish	mysterious	respectively
apparent	document	nuisance	ridiculous
appointment	eligible	occasion	separate
approximately	embarrass	opportunity	sergeant
assignment	emphasize	organized	significant
attendance	enthusiastically	parliament	soldier
auditorium	essential	particular	straightened
benefited	eventually	peculiar	substitute
chimney	exaggerate	permissible	surgeon
circumstance	extraordinary	politician	syllable
comparison	grammar	possession	sympathetic
competition	gymnasium	preparation	tongue
congratulate	hesitate	proceed	tremendous
congressional	immediate	prominent	unconscious
consequently	initiative	properly	unnecessary
correspondence	interpret	prosperous	valuable
courteous	irresistible	publicity	vegetable
deceive	license	receipt	view
decision	lieutenant	recipe	villain
delicious	loneliness	recognize	weird

115: Practice Procedure. Complete each of the following sentences by writing at the right the correct word or words in the parentheses. This is a review quiz on all of the preceding units. Score one point for each correct answer.

Answers

1. What (kind of, kind of a) bargain did he get at the antique show?   1. _____

2. Joel knows a good bargain (anywhere, anywheres).   2. _____

3. The auctioneer motioned to Rose and (they, them) to sit down.   3. _____

4. (Who, Whom) has ever looked for antiques?   4. _____

5. It is often better (than, then) going to a movie.   5. _____

6. The price for the Paul Revere Silver Bowl (sure, surely) surprised me.   6. _____

7. (What, Which) is the more expensive of the two items—the gun or the old sword?   7. _____

8. Mr. Thom, (who, whom), in my opinion, is a great judge of antiques, left for Europe.   8. _____

9. (Who, Whom) did he take with him on his trip?   9. _____

10. His friend, (who, whom) he knew for 20 years, went with him.   10. _____

11. My family (seldom, seldom ever) attends antique shows.   11. _____

12. Neither my sister nor my aunt spent (her, their) money at the show.   12. _____

13. We would like to hear your story (to, too, two).   13. _____

14. One of the dealers was at the auction, but (he, they) didn't bid on any of the items.   14. _____

15. The expert showed Justin and (I, me) the expensive painting.   15. _____

16. They and (I, me) left early for the trip home.   16. _____

17. My father bought an old lamp for (he and she, him and her).   17. _____

18. Each of the auctioneers has (his, their) own favorite collection.   18. _____

19. (Who's, Whose) collection of Chinese porcelain did they buy?   19. _____

20. Ms. Cook stayed (inside the, inside of the) store all day.   20. _____

21. The Heritage Collection has paintings (which, what) are priceless.   21. _____

22. Anyone (who, which, whom) is experienced enough can make some good purchases.   22. _____

23. With (who, whom) did you travel?   23. _____

24. Our trip was considered a success by my brother and (she, her).   24. _____

25. A committee of them and (we, us) gave the report to the class.   25. _____

Your Total Score _____

215

116: Practice Procedure. Complete each of the following sentences by writing in the blank provided at the right the correct word or words in the parentheses. This is a review quiz of material in all the preceding units. Score one point for each correct response.

Answers

1. Ms. Dobson and (he, him) like their job at the auctioneers.   1. _____

2. Tina is not as experienced as (I, me).   2. _____

3. The paper had (an awfully good, a very good) article on old coins.   3. _____

4. Miss Lauder and her sister will enjoy the show if (she, they) read about the different items for sale.   4. _____

5. We traveled (a long way, a long ways) to buy that Persian rug.   5. _____

6. (Back of, In back of) the old store is a lovely view.   6. _____

7. (It's, Its) an unusually good buy for $100.   7. _____

8. With (whoever, whomever) you go, be selective in your purchases.   8. _____

9. Ms. Strock knows quite (good, well) the value of the different items.   9. _____

10. (Try and, Try to) understand the differences between silver and pewter.   10. _____

11. Those old stamps are different (from, than) any I ever saw.   11. _____

12. (Their, There) furniture store has many valuable desks.   12. _____

13. (Him, His) going to Europe was a surprise to me.   13. _____

14. (He and I, He and me) enjoyed the trip very much.   14. _____

15. Have you ever seen a (happier, more happy) person than Jim?   15. _____

16. Mr. Robinson is one of the (most careful, carefulest) buyers of glassware.   16. _____

17. (This, These) pictures of the Hope Diamond are terrific.   17. _____

18. (Was, Were) you able to see them?   18. _____

19. (A, An) unknown salesperson sold the most articles today.   19. _____

20. My brother is the (better, best) appraiser of jewelry of the two men.   20. _____

21. The sales slip from Miss Ortiz and (she, her) came in the mail.   21. _____

22. (Between, Among) Jan and John there was an understanding.   22. _____

23. A philatelist is a person (who, whom) collects stamps.   23. _____

24. Was it (she, her) who found the rare book in the cellar?   24. _____

25. Our principal, (who, whom) lived in China, spoke about Oriental rugs.   25. _____

Your Total Score _____

117: **Practice Procedure.** Complete each of the following sentences by writing in the blank provided at the right the correct word in the parentheses. This is a short review quiz on material in the preceding units. Score one point for each correct response.

Answers

1. How many of you (has, have) a hobby?   1. _____

2. It (doesn't, don't) matter what your hobby is.   2. _____

3. Everybody (is, are) able to afford a hobby.   3. _____

4. A little relaxation and travel (keep, keeps) us happy.   4. _____

5. It's a great feeling to be able to (sit, set) in a chair and read.   5. _____

6. (Bring, Take) a newspaper article to me on travel.   6. _____

7. (Will, Shall) you take me to a lecture on England tomorrow?   7. _____

8. Would you (borrow, lend) me your book on London?   8. _____

9. There (is, are) a few ideas on how to travel inexpensively in this booklet.   9. _____

10. Years ago my brother (collects, collected) baseball cards.   10. _____

11. Many of my friends (trade, trades) stamps.   11. _____

12. Have you ever (saw, seen) a stamp show?   12. _____

13. (Do, Does) anyone in class subscribe to a coin magazine?   13. _____

14. Old pennies and Kennedy half-dollars (was, were) my special interest.   14. _____

15. All of us (has, have) our own special collection.   15. _____

16. Several of us (know, knows) the value of that old coin.   16. _____

17. Frequently my family (drive, drives) me to the museum.   17. _____

18. Two of my friends (save, saves) insects and exotic plants.   18. _____

19. Monica (should, would) like to see your apiary.   19. _____

20. (Can, May) you tell him what an apiary is?   20. _____

21. I (tell, told) him that this morning.   21. _____

22. (Leave, Let) us hear it again.   22. _____

23. He was willing to (borrow, lend) me one of his nonpoisonous snakes.   23. _____

24. Let me (raise, rise) the window before we continue.   24. _____

25. (Was, Were) you the only one to touch the snake?   25. _____

Your Total Score _____

118: Practice Procedure. Complete each of the following sentences by writing in the blank provided at the right the correct word or words in the parentheses. This is a review quiz on material in the preceding units. Score one point for each correct answer.

Answers

1. *Mutiny on the Bounty* (was, were) an interesting book and movie.   1. _____

2. The captain's crew (was, were) given many floggings.   2. _____

3. He (don't, doesn't) care too much for that type of movie.   3. _____

4. My younger brother (become, becomes) old enough today to drive the car.   4. _____

5. None of my sisters (want, wants) to drive the car.   5. _____

6. You (drove, drive) when you get to be sixteen.   6. _____

7. Our driving teacher (learned, taught) us how to pass the test.   7. _____

8. Antonio (pretends, pretended) to be sixteen when he was only fifteen years old.   8. _____

9. The car (will, shall) break down before another 100 miles.   9. _____

10. My father (has, have) a car agency and mechanic shop.   10. _____

11. Bring your car here and (let, leave) me drive it.   11. _____

12. We (borrowed, loaned) the car from our uncle.   12. _____

13. Fred, please don't (lie, lay) on your desk now.   13. _____

14. Rolls Royce cars (has, have) always been very expensive.   14. _____

15. The car salesperson (see, sees) many potential buyers every day.   15. _____

16. Fred, have you (fall, fell, fallen) asleep?   16. _____

17. Where (was, were) we?   17. _____

18. One of the local dealers occasionally (give, gives) the customers a good trade-in.   18. _____

19. Last week my mother (buys, bought) a car from Midway Motors.   19. _____

20. Not everyone (get, gets) a good buy on a car.   20. _____

21. Last week we (will drive, drove, drives) 100 miles to attend a speed race.   21. _____

22. The driver and mechanic (ride, rides) together for all their races.   22. _____

23. (Bring, Take) me the results of the Indianapolis 500 race.   23. _____

24. You have to (learn, teach) me what to check on a car.   24. _____

25. (Has, Have) anyone in this class or the next one ever driven in a stock car race?   25. _____

Your Total Score _____

APPLICATION PRACTICE SCORE SUMMARY

Unit 1   The Sentence

Page	Application Practice	Drill	Points Possible	Student Score
3	1	Subject and Verb Recognition	50	
4	2	Subject and Verb Recognition	60	
5	3	Complete or Incomplete Sentences	8	
6	4	Types of Sentences	25	
7	5	Kinds of Sentences	20	
8	6	Sentences	25	
11	7	Nouns, Verbs, and Pronouns	102	
12	8	Nouns, Verbs, and Pronouns	118	
15	9	Verbs, Adjectives, and Adverbs	85	
16	10	Parts of Speech	38	
19	11	Parts of Speech Drill	44	
	11–A		22	
	11–B		10	
	11–C		12	
20	12	Parts of Speech Review	173	
	12-A		130	
	12-B		43	
21	13	Parts of Speech Review	123	
22	14	Matching Definitions and Spelling	10	
23	15	Matching Definitions and Alphabetizing	45	
24	16	Matching Definitions and Alphabetizing	23	

Unit 2   Nouns

Page	Application Practice	Drill	Points Possible	Student Score
29	17	Noun Identification	100	
30	18	Noun Identification	96	
33	19	Noun Plurals	50	
34	20	The Difficult Noun Plurals	50	
37	21	Singular and Plural Possession	50	
38	22	Singular and Plural Possession	25	
39	23	Matching Definitions and Spelling	10	
40	24	Synonyms	20	

Unit 3   Pronouns

Page	Application Practice	Drill	Points Possible	Student Score
47	25	Pronoun Practice for Person, Number, and Case	25	
48	26	Case Identification	23	
	26–A		10	
	26–B		13	
49	27	Indefinite Pronouns	23	
50	28	Case Forms of Personal Pronouns	25	
57	29	Relative, Demonstrative, Possessive, and Interrogative Pronouns	22	

Page	Application Practice	Drill	Points Possible	Student Score
58	30	Interrogative Pronouns and Pronoun Review	20	
59	31	Who–Whom Practice	25	
60	32	Case Review	25	
61	33	Drill on Pronouns	22	
62	34	Drill on Pronouns	22	
63	35	Final Drill on Pronouns	22	
64	36	Drill on Nouns and Pronouns	55	
65	37	Matching Exercises and Synonyms	25	
66	38	Antonyms and Spelling	15	

Unit 4   Verbs

Page	Application Practice	Drill	Points Possible	Student Score
71	39	Find the Verb	50	
	39–A-B		40	
	39–C		10	
72	40	Helping Verbs	55	
	40–A-B		40	
	40–C		15	
73	41	Predicate Nouns, Pronouns, and Adjectives	50	
74	42	Extra Practice on Verbs	75	
79	43	Verb and Subject Agreement	25	
80	44	Verb and Subject Agreement	25	
	44–A-B		20	
	44–C		5	
85	45	Noun, Verb, and Pronoun Review	25	
86	46	Noun, Verb, and Pronoun Review	25	
87	47	Word Building and Spelling	10	
88	48	Definitions	25	

Unit 5   The Time of Verbs

Page	Application Practice	Drill	Points Possible	Student Score
93	49	Present Tense	20	
	49–A		10	
	49–B		10	
94	50	Past and Future Tense	25	
	50–A-B		20	
	50–C		5	
97	51	Perfect Tense	19	
98	52	Tense Review	21	
103	53	Irregular Verbs	25	
104	54	Verb Review	25	
109	55	Lie–Lay Practice	25	
110	56	Sit–Set Practice	25	
115	57	Shall–Will and Should–Would Practice	30	
	57–A-B		20	
	57–C		10	
116	58	May–Can Practice	30	
	58–A-B		20	
	58–C		10	

Page	Application Practice	Drill	Points Possible	Student Score
166	88	Paragraph Construction	20	
167	89	Matching and Spelling	10	
168	90	Antonyms and Synonyms	25	

Unit 10   Punctuation and Capitalization

Page	Application Practice	Drill	Points Possible	Student Score
175	91	End Punctuation	20	
176	92	Abbreviation Practice	50	
177	93	End Punctuation Review	36	
178	94	Comma Usage—Series and Appositives	58	
179	95	Comma Usage—Dependent Clauses and Quotations	24	
180	96	Comma Usage—Addresses, Dates, and Unrelated Expressions	42	
181	97	Stop and Go Practice	50	
182	98	Complete Comma Review	46	
187	99	Review of Contractions and Numbers	25	
	99–A		10	
	99–B		15	
188	100	Punctuation Review	120	
191	101	Capitalization	79	
192	102	Punctuation and Capitalization	123	
193	103	Punctuation and Capitalization Review	174	
194	104	Punctuation and Capitalization Review	212	
195	105	Punctuation Matching Practice	25	
196	106	Antonyms and Spelling	15	

Unit 11   Word Choice

Page	Application Practice	Drill	Points Possible	Student Score
199	107	It's, Its—Who's, Whose	25	
200	108	Their, There, They're Practice	20	
207	109	Commonly Misused Words	25	
208	110	Misused Words Practice	30	
211	111	Speech Duds	25	
212	112	Speech Duds	22	
213	113	Spelling Practice	36	
214	114	Spelling		

Review

Page	Application Practice	Drill	Points Possible	Student Score
215	115	Final Review 1	25	
216	116	Final Review 2	25	
217	117	Final Review 3	25	
218	118	Final Review 4	25	

INDEX

superlative degree, 125-126
sure and *surely,* 202